Tourism Social Science Series
Volume 15

The Study of Tourism: Foundations from Psychology

Tourism Social Science Series

Series Editor: **Jafar Jafari**

University of Algarve, Portugal
University of Wisconsin-Stout, USA
Tel (715) 232-2339; Fax (715) 232-3200; Email jafari@uwstout.edu

Associate Editor (this volume): Bob McKercher
Hong Kong Polytechnic University, China

The books in this Tourism Social Science Series (TSSSeries) are intended to systematically and cumulatively contribute to the formation, embodiment, and advancement of knowledge in the field of tourism.

The TSSSeries' multidisciplinary framework and treatment of tourism includes application of theoretical, methodological, and substantive contributions from such fields as anthropology, business administration, ecology, economics, geography, history, hospitality, leisure, planning, political science, psychology, recreation, religion, sociology, transportation, etc., but it significantly favors state-of-the-art presentations, works featuring new directions, and especially the cross-fertilization of perspectives beyond each of these singular fields. While the development and production of this book series is fashioned after the successful model of *Annals of Tourism Research*, the TSSSeries further aspires to assure each theme a comprehensiveness possible only in book-length academic treatment. Each volume in the series is intended to deal with a particular aspect of this increasingly important subject, thus to play a definitive role in the enlarging and strengthening of the foundation of knowledge in the field of tourism, and consequently to expand the frontiers of knowledge into the new research and scholarship horizons ahead.

Published TSSSeries Titles:

Tourism Social Science Series
Volume 15

The Study of Tourism: Foundations from Psychology

PHILIP L. PEARCE
James Cook University, Australia

United Kingdom • North America • Japan
India • Malaysia • China

Emerald Group Publishing Limited
Howard House, Wagon Lane, Bingley BD16 1WA, UK

First edition 2011

British Library Cataloguing in Publication Data
A catalogue record for this book is available from the British Library

ISBN: 978-1-84950-742-4
ISSN: 1571-5043 (Series)

Contents

SECTION 3: REFLECTIONS AND DIRECTIONS

List of Contributors

John C. Crotts	Department of Hospitality and Tourism Management, School of Business, College of Charleston, USA
John D. Hunt	College of Natural Resources, University of Idaho, USA
Seppo E. Iso-Ahola	Kinesiology Department, School of Public Health, University of Maryland, USA
Josef A. Mazanec	Institute for Tourism and Leisure Studies, Vienna University of Economics and Business, Austria
Joseph T. O'Leary	Warner College of Natural Resources, Colorado State University, USA
Philip L. Pearce	School of Business, James Cook University, Australia
Abraham Pizam	Rosen College of Hospitality Management, University of Central Florida, USA
Stanley C. Plog	Best Trip Choices, Inc., USA
Chris Ryan	Waikato Management School, University of Waikato, New Zealand
Ton van Egmond	Center for Sustainable Tourism and Transport, NHTV Breda University of Applied Sciences, the Netherlands

Preface

Several individuals deserve public acknowledgment for their roles in bringing this volume to fruition. Bob McKercher, from Hong Kong Polytechnic University, provided some rapid and timely comments on draft chapters when asked to do so. This was much appreciated particularly when we were confronted with tight time lines at the end of this project. Some of his observations have certainly improved these pages. Jafar Jafari, working from his seasonal base in Portugal, has played a strong role as overall editor in attending to the stylistic issues of this book series. His thorough work in shaping the appearance of the chapters is a notable contribution to the volume and assists in making this particular book fit with the parallel volumes concerned with the economics- and geography-based beginnings of tourism scholarship. A direct debt should also be paid to Dennison Nash. It was his first effort in delivering a worthwhile monograph on the pioneering anthropologists and sociologists in tourism, which has made it easier to produce subsequent volumes in this same spirit. He had no model with which to work and I thank him for providing us with the prototype. More locally, at James Cook University, my postgraduate student Lu Huan (Ella) was most helpful in working with me to assemble references and manage drafts. At least we had some humorous moments in attending to the elements of the task.

Perhaps though, the biggest thank you should go to the authors. The final participants were willing to write in a way that was uniquely challenging and I feel they managed to complete the task with considerable skill. The efforts are not all alike and I believe that adds to the interest of this kind of descriptive autobiographical work. As editor of the volume and charged with instructions to conform to some extent to the book series mandate, I have at times sliced and reformatted aspects of their stories. I trust that the authors view the final products as acceptable and see their work as massaged rather than mauled by my efforts.

There is conformity in this volume to American spelling and while I acknowledge the need to be consistent on this issue for any quality publisher, the task has meant an ongoing fight with both my own Australian/British English spelling proclivities and the nuances of several spell-checking programs. For example, the term behavior is used extensively but cannot be used when the original article or book was presented as a study in tourist behaviour. Both for the contributing authors and the readers, if these and related subtleties in expression prove annoying, then I hope some tolerance of the global reach of English can be compensation. As expressed in later pages of this volume, it is scholarly contributions in English, in whichever spelling format the work appeared, which binds these authors together. It may be possible in later works to assess parallel contributions from scholars who are literate and productive in other languages. I hope readers can enjoy getting to know a little more about the careers and the lives of this set of tourism research pioneers.

Philip L. Pearce
James Cook University, Australia

SECTION 1

PREPARATION AND PROSPECTS

Chapter 1

Preparation and Prospects

Philip L. Pearce
James Cook University, Australia

THE APPROACH AND ITS MOTIVES

This volume provides personal accounts of the careers of 10 select scholars who have made important contributions to the study of tourism. In particular, the individuals providing the autobiographies have contributed especially to the study of tourist behavior and experience. Their work implicitly or explicitly approaches tourism study from the perspective of psychology, social psychology, applied sociology, or derivatives from those traditions in marketing and recreation. Curiously, perhaps, few of the scholars would be described at this point in their career as a psychologist, social psychologist, or microsociologist. They are more likely to be called marketing researchers, tourism researchers, consumer behavior analysts, or recreation specialists.

The publication of an academic monograph with the special intent of showcasing the careers of some senior tourism scholars has mixed motives. A first motive for this enterprise lies in humanizing the "names" that are on so many papers and publications. For many younger scholars and graduate students, an understanding of their senior colleagues can be somewhat difficult; not only are there generational contrasts but there has often been a hesitation within scholarly communities to disclose the mix of personal and professional forces leading individuals to their present position. For active scholars and for those who are beginning their careers in tourism and

The Study of Tourism: Foundations from Psychology
Tourism Social Science Series, Volume 15, 3–22
ISSN: 1571-5043/doi:10.1108/S1571-5043(2011)0000015004

recreation studies, as well as those analyzing entertainment and events, the autobiographies provided here can be particularly insightful. They are written in a familiar and conversational style—a topic that we deal with presently—and this format offers a succinct educational overview of the beginnings of tourist studies and tourism analysis as well as the construction of careers and achievements. The lessons and instructional value of these autobiographies will be drawn together at the end of this volume rather than at this juncture, but a mindful way of approaching these accounts is to value them both for the ideas they contain and the pivotal career issues they embody.

A second motive and one that introduces a slightly more somber tone can also be identified. As the prolific psychologist Philip Zimbardo reminds us, we are rather inclined to ignore our own mortality and the finite nature of our work and life (Zimbardo and Boyd 2008). Expressed politely, the authors contributing to this volume are older and senior figures likely to have already written more than they are going to write in the future. I do not wish to deny the prospect that many of the scholars might add further insights into the tourism they study, but it is a simple reality that the autobiographies are prepared in the later stages of our contributors' careers.

In addition to humanizing the scholars and noting the genesis of ideas and careers in a timely fashion, a third motive informs the production of this book. The additional purpose explores the interplay of institutional and individual forces in the development of a study area. In common with other efforts to understand the evolution of tourism scholarship (Nash 2007:18), an array of interesting questions can be raised and developed further by the information contained in these personalized academic histories. Some of these questions address the way academic disciplines or study areas develop in response to community and institutional pressures for funding. These considerations include, in most countries, the importance of attracting adequate student numbers to support courses and hence academic staff and researchers. It is of course central to such discussion to define exactly how fields of study are labeled and presented as well as to consider their acceptance within and outside the university environment. Some of the scholarly contributions in the following section highlight quite clearly how rising (and falling) numbers of students can massage the shape of an academic research career.

Associated disciplinary or fields of study questions address concerns as to whether or not the area of research effort and learning labeled as tourism has found only a temporary resting place or does indeed occupy an enduring place in the academic sunshine. The following career autobiographies weave personal histories around these notions of department and discipline growth and change, the impacts of student interest in courses, and the factor of university acceptance of styles of research. Some of the auto-biographies provide insights into the development and management of consulting services to the tourism and related sectors. More than most accounts, this volume showcases the personal responses to the challenge of deciding on and building a tourism research career particularly where that career is specifically about studying the behaviors and experiences of those who travel.

The Value of Past Reflections

There is, though, perhaps an even more fundamental question to prepare readers for this monograph. Does the past really matter? A contemplation of the importance of the past may be familiar to many scholars in a guise that specifically relates to their experience within their institutional framework. It is not uncommon for new heads of department and deans to proffer such lines as "I am drawing a line in the sand" or "the past is another country to which we will not return." There exist stronger and weaker forms of this rampant managerialism within universities, but the approach does challenge the premise of this monograph that there is something to be gained by looking at past eras and reviewing the histories of individual scholars. The kind of dismissive managerial thinking outlined raises the issue that if earlier days are deemed of little importance by many academic managers, why should we be concerned with histories in this monograph? Further, some psychologists have argued that what we do now is very much about prevailing forces rather than past antecedents. Seligman (2008), a leader in establishing the positive psychology framework, suggests that for individual well-being and as an explanation of the present behavior, the contemplation and consideration of past events is overrated. Such a view diverges from traditional clinical, personality and developmental studies that have emphasized both the formative periods in individual development and stressed the strong power of key early events and incidents in shaping adult life.

Additionally, the value of understanding the lives and ideas of the scholarly contributions of the authors in this work is challenged further by the communication technologies of the 21st century. A rather puzzled student recently asked this author "how did you study at university without the internet?" It is a question that might be accompanied by such queries as what is a manual typewriter, what is a card reader, and did you really learn statistics using hand calculators and mental arithmetic? Of course for the contributing authors to this monograph, their formative papers were constructed under just these conditions and with these tools. Few older researchers probably remember with any fondness the painstaking process of manually retyping whole manuscripts or correcting errors with products variously labeled "White Out" or "Tippex," but at least some of us are grateful for the understanding of statistical analysis generated when one does them by hand. Undoubtedly, too, some researchers will recall instances of serendipitous scholarly discovery in libraries in those days when researchers regularly strolled among book stacks in computer-free libraries.

It is the contention of this introduction and this book that the past does matter. It matters more because of the broad patterns and threads of continuity and career appraisal that we can glean from these memories rather than the objective past itself. More than most other kinds of employment, research workers track themes that can have long genetic histories both of their own making and coproduced with others. The continuities may be imperfect, but understanding why researchers make the choices they do and conduct the programs of studies that often characterize successful contributions to study fields is not easily appreciated with a focus purely on present circumstances.

The Challenges for Authors

It will become clear to readers from several of the autobiographies that constructing these records of career development and life influences was not an easy or simple task for many scholars. It is well established that our memory banks are rather fallible storage entities and the construction and reconstruction of our memories of ourselves and our activities is an ongoing process (Braun et al 2002; Wiseman 2007). What does this mean for the career histories to be presented in the following sections? As several authors confess in their chapters, they cannot remember some of the details of what they did, in what order or, at times, why they did things. What matters instead is how they frame that memory in terms of a contemporary communication. The contributing authors have written for the generations of scholars following them and the sincerity of this effort can be traced in the sense of purposeful advice and career commentary that some of the researchers seek to provide. The value of the autobiographies might then be seen to exist a little less in what transpired some decades ago but how authors now interpret those events and the implications they draw from those incidents for others. Quite some time ago, the distinguished Harvard psychology historian Edmund Boring (1950) referred to this process as presentism—effectively how one's sense of now reshapes the memory of the past.

The Required Task

The style of composing such renditions of one's career was a point noted briefly before and one worthy of some further consideration. It is instructive to identify at this point exactly what was asked of the contributors. The following extract from the initial communication conveys the core elements of the task:

Communication to potential authors from Philip Pearce, April 30, 2009:

> I have been invited by the Editor of the *Tourism Social Science Series* to edit and put forward a book proposal. Currently, the book series is pursuing a linked set of volumes exploring the beginnings and foundations of studies in tourism or relevant to tourism. The first published volume in the series is: Dennison Nash (editor) 2007 *The Study of Tourism Anthropological and Sociological Beginnings.*
>
> The intention of the book series editorial team is to have separate volumes which explore in turn the contributions of geography, economics and applied psychology/marketing. They have asked me to contact key figures in the psychology/ marketing fields to ascertain who might be interested in contributing. I have identified a number of people, including of course yourself, from lists of productive scholars, members of associations and scholarly societies, and overall prominence in the area of tourism, leisure, and recreation study.
>
> The distinctive feature of the series, of which Nash's edited volume is the prototype, is an attempt to reveal the emergence of work on the applied psychology/marketing studies in

tourism. The contribution to be made by the invited scholars is a personal history as follows:

Points to cover:

1. Your early academic and social background.
2. Your social (include intellectual) context at the time you became interested in studying tourism:
   a. Subjects with which you were preoccupied.
   b. Events of significance.
   c. Significant others.
3. Getting involved:
   a. Pros and cons and processes involved.
4. Your first works in the field and their implications.
5. Contextual pros and cons at that time.
6. Where you are now in your study of tourism, and in retrospect, how have you "progressed" in your study of the subject?
7. If not previously answered, where do you stand now in terms of major intellectual currents, particularly as they pertain to the study of tourism?

Note: Though your personal histories undoubtedly will differ in length, think of about 25 double-spaced typewritten pages on the average.

The invitation contains and was indeed interpreted as containing several kinds of challenges. Not only was the form of writing required more personal and self-disclosing than traditional academic fare, but the request implicitly asks for judgments about and syntheses of research directions. This component of the request demands at least a modicum of accurate reflection or record keeping. The request also seeks to elicit an intellectual history rather than a deeply personal account, but the intersection of these personal and professional fields can often be considerable.

A modest insight into the challenges involved is provided in part by extrapolating from an earlier pre-Internet study of my own concerned with telling travel stories (Pearce 1991). In that study, I constructed sets of 10 travel stories, half of which were negative and half positive, and the implicit motivations underpinning the stories were linked to the five levels of Maslow's motivational framework expressed in a tourism context.

Using a sample of tourists and travel agents, I discovered that positive stories could be told to everyone whereas negative stories, where the motives were not fulfilled or thwarted, had a more complex patterning of potential listeners. While it was fine to tell dramatic and negative stories of physical challenges, food poisoning, and lost luggage, there was a clear reticence to convey widely those stories involving failed achievement, damage to one's self image, and some relationship struggles. The implications for the present work are arguably quite direct. These accounts of professional life as autobiographies and personal histories are not confessional pieces, so there is an understandable reticence to reveal deep anxieties, personal weaknesses, and areas of former or continuing incompetence. As a counterpoint to these issues, there is the challenging task of managing modesty.

As is somewhat obvious from the initial request, the authors have been chosen because they have been productive and acclaimed scholars in the study field of tourist behavior and markets. There is, therefore, an underlying oxymoron in the request—write about your famous career modestly. As the volume editor, I decided to remove many of the authors' self-effacing remarks at the start of their autobiographies. Undoubtedly, these remarks were sincere, but for readers to encounter repeated success deflecting appraisals would arguably make for tedious reading. I have, however, let stand the colorful remarks of our first author, John Hunt, whose comments can represent all colleagues on this issue.

The Personalities of Scholars

It is useful to gauge the further difficulty of the autobiographical request by referring to some work documenting the personality profiles of scholars and academics. This work was undertaken within the discipline of psychology itself. Rushton et al (1983:93), using the findings from a battery of personality tests, report that the creative researcher can be described as "ambitious, enduring, seeking definiteness, dominant, showing leadership, aggressive, independent, non-meek, and non-supportive." This analysis suggests that the problems for our contributors may be largely about managing their self-assertiveness and potential arrogance. It can be confidently suggested that we are not dealing with academics fitting a stereotype of being retiring, shy figures working away quietly in remote locations.

Smart et al (2000) confirm some of the characteristics noted by Rushton et al in their detailed monograph reporting the matches between six personality types of academics and educators and types of academic environments. They assert that the investigative type of academic researcher has a forceful rather than a retiring style of personality and, while not necessarily extroverts, such research leaders acquire the skills of being confident presenters and communicators. The work of Smart et al is based on Holland's theory of the fit between people and environments, and it could be suggested that the confident, investigative personality style is a particularly good fit for the applied and public roles often demanded of tourism-interested researchers in their communities. It will be for readers themselves to assess whether humility is well served in the autobiographies, and if at times it is not, then perhaps the difficulty of the task can be referred to as evidence softening any adverse images created.

Audience Characteristics

In preparing readers for the specific autobiographies in this monograph, the preceding attention has been focused on the authors and their role. It is now time to redirect our gaze to the nature of the audiences and, even more importantly, the study areas and the topics that define the intellectual history with which we are concerned. In considering the theme of audiences, a potentially useful expression and distinction that some colleagues of mine and I have been using is Generation T (Pearce et al 2011). What is Generation T and who belongs to this newly designated group? The answer lies not in an individual's birth date or early years, but instead identifies the educational routes that have prepared readers to attend to this book. The defining feature of Generation T membership is an education focused on tourism, tourists, and related topics. This kind of education is multidisciplinary and tends to explore contemporary issues with less concern for the patterns of thought that have been built over time.

Generation T membership is growing and many individuals educated in this way now work in universities across the globe and undoubtedly contribute well to the analysis and teaching of tourism and allied fields. The Generation T label is not appropriate if individuals have studied a single discipline as a major focus of undergraduate or first-degree education. None of the contributing authors in this book are a part of Generation T; indeed, a fully tourism-focused degree program and education was not possible in most countries at the time when our scholars were finding their academic feet.

There are disadvantages in belonging to Generation T. The challenge for those with a hybrid social science and business education—perhaps the most common mix for Generation T personnel—can be a modest basis on which to interrogate new patterns of thought, most especially when these concepts and ideas derive from a long established discipline such as psychology. From a more positive perspective, Generation T scholars may have a considerable breadth of interest in the tourism field and find multiple touch points of interest for their own research pursuits in focused discussion such as that provided in these autobiographical contributions. The essence of this Generation T designation arguably fits well with the purposes of this book and the educational opportunities it attempts to serve. For all readers with a Generation T education as well as those who arrive at these pages with a background in a field outside of psychology but with an interest in studying the human dimensions of tourism—geographers, sociologists, and anthropologists would all seem to be potential traveling companions for this expedition—it is important to reach beyond the simplest stereotypes of psychology to build an understanding of the tourism and psychology nexus.

Representing Psychology—Earliest Days

How then might we succinctly represent psychology as the base and oldest discipline that has been the building block for studies in consumer behavior, market segmentation, tourist experience appraisals, social and cultural exchanges among interacting parties, and more generally the world of the tourist, tourist or leisure visitor? This is indeed a daunting task. Most undergraduate tourism textbooks that "introduce" the subject of psychology contain 600–900 pages (Martin et al 2007). The chapters on clinical topics and detailed analysis of brain function tend to occupy 25% of these kinds of texts, but issues of more direct relevance to many in tourism such as motivation, individual differences, social behavior, cultural contact, cognition, memory, and decision-making still support a healthy forestry industry. In another context, I have tracked the historical figures in the evolution of psychology and their relevance to a concern with happiness and well-being (Pearce et al 2011). At least some of these historical scholarly contributions can be cited here as they provide the backdrop to the world in which our contributors received their own education in psychology and small group behavior.

Wilhelm Wundt (1832–1920) is a formative figure in the history of the discipline. He was the person responsible for the first planned psychology laboratory (in Leipzig in 1879) and is particularly remembered for his approach to the topic of sensation that he studied empirically. He also provided a detailed account of popular folk psychologies. Wundt shares the stage of founding fathers with William James (1842–1910), America's foremost pioneering psychologist from Harvard. James' interests in memory and consciousness and his attention to the experience of people resonate with some very contemporary 21st century concerns. Francis Galton (1822–1911), the British polymath, who was a cousin of Charles Darwin (1809–1882), is a figure whose inventiveness and assessment of people's abilities remain a creative force even a century after his death. One comment about Wundt, reputedly from William James, reminds us that academic commentary on other peoples' work is not a recent invention. James was known to have complained that Wundt was so prolific that even when his ideas were criticized he would be energized and write another book reexamining that topic (Boring 1950:346). This is echoed by the kind of remarks one still hears in elitist circles: "No thought unpublished" is one I personally remember from my days at Oxford. It was not meant kindly.

Representing Psychology—20th Century Growth

In the first half of the 20th century, dominant figures shaping the development of psychology included Sigmund Freud (1856–1939), from Vienna, with his emphasis on unconscious forces and his revolutionary views on personality development. Freud's ideas were challenged by Carl Jung (1875–1961), Alfred Adler (1870–1937), and numerous other figures with an interest in individuals with problems. Nevertheless, the psychoanalytic approach, as Freud's system of ideas became known, successfully found its way into public discussion and even to this day remains a part of the image of the discipline. This is particularly the case for those with little exposure to its details. As Wiseman (2007) pointedly observes, many of Freud's ideas such as Freudian slips are problematic because "even though Freud claimed to be a scientist many of his ideas are completely untesticle" (2007:188).

In the United States, John Watson (1878–1958) and Kurt Lewin (1890–1947) provided contrasting approaches with the former emphasizing only the assessment and consideration of visible behaviors and the latter building models of the internal forces shaping motivation and social life.

Lewin is at times a forgotten figure in the history of ideas about human behavior, but many contemporary approaches that stress the multiple forces immediately acting on a person (such as those found in structural equation modeling formulations and attitude research) are very much in accord with Lewin's approach. Watson's work was the source of the movement that became known as behaviorism, while Lewin's ideas, together with the notion of needs developed by Henry Murray (1893–1988), were central to the development of social motivation studies.

William McDougall (1871–1938) presented the first consistent account and text on social psychology in 1908, thus offering a link that would later see some conjunction of interests with microsociological concerns as evidenced in the work of Erving Goffman (1922–1982). This social psychology field would flourish in the 1930s as attitudes became a dominant interest area with multiple applications for assessing views of people in the military, for investigating prejudice, and for appraising public reactions to television and politics. Key figures in these developments in studying attitudes were Gordon Allport (1897–1967) at Harvard and, after World War II, Hilde Himmelweit (1918–1980) at the London School of Economics. For tourism researchers, this social psychology component in the history of psychology underpins much of the development of marketing and consumer studies. These emphases shifted some of the work of psychologists beyond the strong individual emphasis of the German researchers and clinicians.

These formative figures in the history of psychology and the currents of thought they engendered in others were notably located in three centers of the world: first Germany, then the United States, and somewhat more belatedly, Britain. The quick synopsis of the contributions of these early figures in psychology has brought us to the mid-20th century. It is a time when the most senior contributors of this volume began their psychology education. In the ensuing decades of the 1960s and the 1970s, all the researchers whose autobiographies are presented in this volume commenced their academic study and it is important to understand the emphases in psychology in these decades that would nourish their development.

Representing Psychology—The Influential Years

World War II had many effects on the development of psychology. While pockets of study persisted in Europe after the war concluded, there was a tendency for scholars to confine their writing to those in the same language group, whereas earlier there had been a steady traffic of people and ideas across the Atlantic and English Channel. The persistence of this pattern of language-specific publication and influence is noted and traced in some of the career histories in this monograph. German psychology lost its prominence, not least because key figures emigrated due to Nazi persecution or personal distaste with the Nazi influence and legacy. American and British psychologists had been involved in the allied war effort with notable contributions on selecting people for positions, code-breaking, the analysis of propaganda, soldiers' welfare, and postwar counseling (Furnham 2008). B. F. Skinner (1904–1990), who was based at Harvard, became the pivotal figure of influence in the behaviorists group, and these ideas attracted followers globally. The emphasis of this approach with its insistent attention on considering only observable behavior was very much about learning and patterns of activity. The approach did, however, legitimize observation as an allied research tool to that of experimentation. Studies of learning dominated the behaviorist thinking and the acquisition of new routines was understood through reinforcement principles derived principally from studies of white rats. Behavior modification, built on these reinforcement principles, became an important topic inside and outside the laboratory and powered the growth of the professional psychologists who were more interested in the application of ideas rather than their development. While the dominance of behaviorists has been superseded in contemporary psychology, its influence is not entirely lost and, as will be discussed subsequently, there are heirs to the approach in certain kinds of tourist behavior work.

Some key figures opposed the dictates of behaviorism. Edward Tolman (1886–1959) developed an expansive form of behaviorism and speculated that his maze running rats did indeed develop a memory, in effect a cognitive map of where they were going (Tolman 1948). This was a view in contrast to the prevailing thought that there were simply sequences of learned reflexes guiding action. Tolman's initial reactionary thoughts had some parallels with the ideas of Jean Piaget (1896–1980) whose detailed empirical observation of his own children's behavior led him to propose innate cognitive structures shaping intellectual growth. Noam Chomsky (1928–), later famous as a political commentator, agreed with Piaget in the sense that his own studies of language argued that humans possessed deep innate brain structures that provided our species with a unique readiness to learn languages. In Chomsky's considered view, simple iterative stimulus–response links were inadequate explanations for language acquisition.

Sir Frederick Bartlett (1886–1969) and later Donald Broadbent (1926–1993), both from Cambridge in the United Kingdom, followed their World War II work on signal detection and attention with studies of memory and information processing. They also began writing about concepts that stressed the mental structures and organizing schema of the mind. These varied approaches were brought together in the 1967 publication edited by Ulric Neisser and entitled *Cognitive Psychology*. Thinking, the mind and its skills were back on the psychologists' agenda. Many powerful figures were drawn into the cognitive psychology conversation and studies of thinking by Jerome Bruner, from Harvard and then Oxford, as well as decision-making by Irvin Janis from Yale became further topics of interest. The Nobel Prize winning efforts of first Simon on information processing and systems, and later again Tversky and Kahnemann on the biases in human judgment, are all a part of this strong cognitive tradition.

Social psychologists were never quite as fully ensnared in the behaviorists' web as were their colleagues studying individual behavior. Even when the former dominated psychology departments and thousands of undergraduates observed the behavior of scores of laboratory-bred Wistar white rats, social psychology researchers were happily sitting in other corridors of the department assessing the very mentalistic concept of attitudes. The fact that they were not always respected or afforded high status by behaviorists was one of the outcomes of ingroup-outgroup differentiation which is common everywhere (de Botton 2004). It was usually these social psychology figures who attracted the students who had any kind of interest in leisure, tourism, or recreation behavior.

The growth in cognitive psychology and the persistence of social psychology in the 1960s and 1970s were both important foundation areas for leisure and tourism interests. As many of the scholars making these contributions are still active researchers, their life span will not be recorded from this juncture. Several key approaches have been spawned from the grudging acceptance or at least tolerance of the social and cognitive directions within the discipline. One powerful influence has been the specification of a tightly argued model of attitudes. The work that was originally conceived by Fishbein and Ajzen in the 1970s and developed further by Ajzen is known as the theory of reasoned application, which then transmuted into the theory of planned behavior. The importance of the theory of planned behavior can be described through noting its valuable role in integrating the long tradition of attitude research and measurement already mentioned in the work of the earliest psychologists. The ability to assess attitudes within a conceptual scheme that gives weight to behavioral intentions, the value of others' opinions, and one's own perceived competency to control the behavior—all key elements of the theory of planned behavior—has been and remain fundamental in considering attitudes toward tourism services, leisure behavior, consumption of hospitality products, and natural environment behaviors. Quite recently, it has been employed for studies noting attitudes toward sustainable behaviors (Bowen and Clarke 2009).

In addition to the emphasis on attitudes, those psychologists (and often they were social psychologists) with a more applied orientation began to connect their empirical research styles to problems of their age. Peter Warr in England developed some of the foundation studies on psychology at work and prefigured numerous interests in attitude assessment related to management. Michael Argyle at Oxford influenced many doctoral students through his work on nonverbal behavior, social skills, then relationships, and finally happiness. There was a laboratory and experimental orientation in Argyle's early social skills work and a continuing rigorous use of evidence in the other topics he considered. A similar comment can be made about Henri Tajfel who was concerned with studying group membership. Members of his Bristol Group became some of the first psychology researchers to emphasize identity and provide a link to the politics of ethnicity.

The North American social psychologists too addressed contemporary topics with Solomon Asch working on conformity, Stanley Milgram conducting a set of famous experiments on obedience, Philip Zimbardo simulating and studying prison behavior, and John Darley and Bibb Latane experimenting with public responsiveness and helping. For a fuller historical review of these developments, the volume by Evans *The Making of Social Psychology* (1980) provides an interview-based review of scholarly contributions, which is somewhat similar in spirit to the present volume. It does not deal with the topic of tourism. There is a widespread use of control groups and experimental groups in these social psychology foundation studies. There is often the elimination of alternative explanations through controlling contexts and conditions. Multiple statistical procedures are used to substantiate the significance of the observed contrasts. The broad conversation might have been about topics of public interest but the in-house conversations were centered on clever research designs, sample selection, statistical assumptions, and probability values.

A focus on mental processes and applied topics in the 1960s and 1970s also paved the way for a reconsideration of one of William James' interests, the study of emotion and affect. The take-up of this topic in tourism has been slow but arguably somewhat faster in the field of marketing.

How visitors and tourists react emotionally to new circumstances and how we can measure and monitor their moods are topics growing in importance as the facets of the experience economy are better appreciated (Schmitt 2003). The differences between the terms "emotion" and "affect" require some elaboration for Generation T scholars and others less familiar with the subtleties of psychology diction. Emotion is widely regarded as the more specific of the two terms and is usually linked with a reaction to a defined object, event, or experience (Fredrickson 2001). An emotional reaction then is one of short duration that includes a clearly identifiable physiological response such as the elevation of heart rate or pupil dilation. Emotions also include relatively uncontrolled but widely recognized facial expressions, as well as a linked set of subjective feelings and thoughts. Well-known emotions include fear, anger, and surprise.

The related term "affect" is seen as a more generalized summary of those feelings that are consciously accessible. One's affective state is effectively a general ongoing subjective experience, and mood is typically associated with the term "affect." An individual's prevailing style on a day-to-day basis has a lot to do with his or her affective state or enduring mood, whereas the reaction to meeting an old friend or being robbed is the province of emotion. Behaviorists had almost removed emotion and affect from the realm of scientific study and its reintroduction in the latter years of the 20th century has been important in the evolution of the concept of positive psychology (a development with which we will be concerned in later discussion).

Other writings in the discipline of psychology in the 1960s and 1970s have relevance for the world in which our autobiographers were receiving their undergraduate and higher education. A group of scholars sometimes known as the humanists or the third force share some approaches to the tasks of repairing and developing human potential (behaviorists and cognitive psychologists may be seen as occupying the other two "force" positions). The two most prominent figures in this third force were Carl Rogers and Abraham Maslow. Basing some of his work on the lives of the very successful people rather than damaged individuals, Maslow presented a hierarchical model of human motivation emphasizing human striving toward a pinnacle of deep personal well-being. The work has become very well known in undergraduate textbooks on management and introductory psychology, but this popularization omits much of the subtlety of Maslow's assessments. Murray's work on needs is a strong predecessor of Maslow's approach and it is the latter's attempt to organize earlier lists of needs into a pattern that is memorable. Maslow's hierarchy of needs does not, as many think, involve a staged deterministic model of personal growth, but rather presents possible patterns of motivational forces (Rowan 1998). The preeminence of any pattern and a concentration on one set of motives is influenced by a Lewin-like consideration of the person's life space and situational context. The borrowings from Maslow in the tourism and general management literature are important in motivation studies. The work of Csikszentmihayli on the topic of flow, although more a product of the last two decades than the 1960s and 1970s, also derives from the humanistic tradition and will feature again at other points in this monograph (Csikszentmihalyi 1975, 1990).

Environmental psychology also appears as a topic of study in the 1970s (Bell et al 1978). It was conceived as a separate field of study from the interests of geographers. For the environmental psychologist, people and their perceptions and behaviors are of central interest in any setting rather than following the geographers' explorations of way space shapes experience. This group of psychologists expanded the applications to people's behavior in built and natural settings and included some interest in the topic of tourism. The notion that there are happy places, or at least places seen as highly desirable for migration and often leisure, represents one thread in the evaluation work of environmental psychology. The leisure and tourism interest was strengthened when Mehrabian and Russell (1974) discussed their assessment tools and measures to examine the emotional character of places. Like their social psychology neighbors, there is no abandonment of highly empirical and often positivist works in this approach.

In the formative years of psychology, the human behaviors of interest were those of a kind of generalized citizen, often implicitly an individual from middle-class America. The cross-cultural psychologists had a different focus and from the 1970s stressed the variability in human behavior and thought across countries (Bochner 1982). Anthropologists and sociologists have had much to say on cultural variability at the international scale and it has not always been easy for the psychologists' contributions to be audible. Toward the end of the 20th century, international and ethnic differences in psychology are no longer of minor interest to the world of research. Richard Nisbett, a prominent cognitive psychologist, for example, has articulated strong perspectives on this topic in his book on the geography of thought (Nisbett 2003). He suggests that the original psychological pursuit of universal ways in which the mind works now needs to be reframed. In this view, the legacy of cultural evolution and local experience must be incorporated into understanding cognitive functioning. There have been voices expressing these kinds of views for 30–40 years, and it is noteworthy that some of the autobiographies in the following section commence their accounts with a clear interest in assessing and considering cultural and group variability.

There have been and continue to be important developments in all components of psychology as the last century concludes and the new millennium develops. Some of this work weaves its way into the research interests and approaches of the tourism researchers and is noted in their career histories. Notable examples include the evolution of crime and community studies, refined market profiling approaches, the application of concepts such as mindfulness, and the emergence of studies of happiness and well-being. These developments are, however, later inputs into marketing, tourist, and recreation behavior studies. The particular way in which the researchers continue to find sources of ideas in their careers during the middle and later stages of their work will be considered at the end of this volume. Our immediate attention is now drawn to the start-up phases of specific tourist behavior work, its fledging status in the 1970s, and its evolution through the 1980s.

The Appearance of Tourism Psychology Studies

There is no single starting point for psychological studies in tourism. Instead, there is at first a trickle of early publications in allied areas. In the formative period of developing ideas about tourism, there was the interesting phenomenon of nonpsychologists writing about psychology topics. Cosgrove and Jackson (1972), both geographers, included a range of remarks about social interaction and tourist activities in their work *The Geography of Recreation and Leisure*. George Young, a politician and economist, included ideas about motivation in his *Tourism—Blessing or Blight?* (Young 1973). Neulinger's 1974 *Psychology of Leisure* was a little more in line with mainstream psychology approaches, but did not explore tourism and tourist behavior. Psychologists in traditional departments appeared not to notice this incursion into areas where they had built up several decades of subtle analysis. Once initiated, this trend for nonpsychologists to write about inherently social psychology or mainstream psychology topics became quite well established. The tendency appeared to drift toward contrasting poles: tourists were either commended or condemned. Examples of these contrasts are to be found in the work of Waters (1966) who enthusiastically promoted the positive contributions of tourists to cross-cultural exchange, while Turner and Ash (1975) depicted tourists as *The Golden Hordes* and Rosenow and Pulsipher (1978), building on a

Clint Eastwood theme, used a mixed approach: *The Good, the Bad and the Ugly.*

Starting points though depend a little on where one chooses to look. In the museum and attraction world, there was some rich early work observing visitors. It was work done by psychologists and was consistent with the exacting measurement and observation approach pioneered by Galton and not all that different from the style of the behaviorists. Robinson (1928) provided a set of studies entitled "The behavior of the museum visitor." Melton (1933, 1936, 1972) conducted similar work in museums and art galleries in Philadelphia and developed the phrase "museum fatigue," a concept later to be explained by mindfulness (Langer 1989).

Looking in a slightly different direction, it can also be suggested that studies in national parks and particularly studies concerned with providing educational services to visitors also had some traction with researchers during the 1960s and 1970s. Tilden (1977) and Sharpe (1976) wrote monographs about interpretation while others explored the value of visitor centers and the problems of crowding (Schreyer and Roggenbuck 1978; Zube et al 1978). Ideas about taking leisure seriously and designing spaces for different kinds of visitors became rallying points for US leisure and recreation researchers who were in effect concerned with domestic tourists and the management of their experiences (Stankey and Wood 1982; Stebbins 1982).

A small article in the popular publication *Psychology Today* (Rubenstein 1980) reporting a survey of tourist motivation may have raised some awareness that a few psychologists were beginning to explore the world of travel and tourist behavior. By the time the 1980s arrived, tourism had its own journals, and *Annals of Tourism Research* and the *Journal of Travel Research* were both nearly a decade old. Select studies of psychological approaches to tourist experience and behavior began to be published, although occasional articles also appeared in social and applied psychology journals. Some of Crompton's work on pleasure motivation was to be a source of influence, while the approach labeled psychographic segmentation appealed to new generations of marketers (Crompton 1979; Schewe and Calantone 1978). Much of the previous writing in the journals had been by sociologists, geographers, economists, and anthropologists, and as Stringer and Pearce (1984) reported in a special issue of *Annals of Tourism Research*, the psychology-specific research effort was still surprisingly "fragmentary ... no more than a casual encounter between tourism and social psychology rather than the product of a serious relationship" (1984:13). There were of course select and important contributions often made by some of the authors of this volume. Additionally, a powerful line of work in economic psychology and linked more closely to economic assessments of tourism was also developed in the mid-1980s (van Raaij 1986). But to continue to recount developments from this time would spoil the autobiographies. They present these times and subsequent periods in more detail and with more insight than can be offered by a single editor.

Introducing the Authors

It remains a further pleasure, not a task, to introduce the authors. The ordering of the contributions follows the timing of their first substantial publication. There are 10 contributors drawn from five countries. Six contributors have built most of their careers in the United States, although not all of them were born there. John Hunt and Stanley Plog are the first two autobiographers and their fundamental work has been cited by textbook writers and students of tourism over many years. Interestingly, their careers have not always been conducted in universities and the insights they provide about commercial research consulting as well as publishing offer much for all readers. Abraham Pizam, Joseph O'Leary, Seppo Iso-Ahola, and John Crotts are also based in the United States. All have distinguished academic careers and together their interests and achievements effectively embrace the tourism–hospitality link, recreation, parks, and tourism interests, and marketing and tourism advances. Two contributors come from Europe: Josef Mazanec is from Austria and Ton van Egmond hails from the Netherlands. Their contributions trace different but very active careers in tourism showing strong links to their home bases but offering much work of international interest.

Chris Ryan and I work from bases in the southern hemisphere (in his case, New Zealand, and in my case, Australia). We share the fact that we both did postgraduate degrees in England and now have ongoing interests in tourist behavior and experience in Asia as well as our own countries. Taken together, the 10 contributors provide an overview of scholars' careers across continents where those careers blend studies in tourism and foundation ideas from psychology and allied fields.

Not surprisingly, many of the careers and publications of these 10 authors are interconnected. For example, Mazanec and Crotts have co-edited some of the volumes in the CABI series *Consumer Psychology of Tourism Hospitality and Leisure*. O'Leary and I have been joint authors on a number of multiauthored papers. Other scholars have published together and nearly all of us have shared editorial roles and conference speaking engagements.

It is a pleasure to read their autobiographies and be involved in the task of bringing some stylistic consistencies to their very individual efforts. Regrettably, not all of the people one might want to involve in this kind of exercise were able to contribute. For some, it was a matter of time, for others of failing health, and other authors thought they were a little too "young" in their careers to be included with some of the very senior and older figures in the field. Pioneers, such as Krippendorf, who might have been included have passed away, while other figures with occasional interests in psychology, marketing, and consumer behavior have provided autobiographies in the parallel editions in this series documenting economic and geographical underpinnings of tourism.

There is also the issue of the productive scholar providing a transient influence, effectively producing one or two publications and then not resuming activity in the tourism arena. Examples include the work of Reason (1974) on travel sickness, Stringer (1984) on small group behaviors, and Furnham (1984) on culture shock. These figures were not invited to be a part of this career review process, but their individual contributions are quite well-cited historical pieces. I have an appreciation that there are undoubtedly many fine contributions to tourist behavior and experience study reported in Spanish, French, German, Arabic, and Asian languages. There is no desire to downplay such contributions; if this monograph was being constructed a decade later, then a more international overview might be achievable. The influences of these writers have not at this time been widely influential in the English-speaking world of tourist behavior studies. I encourage readers to savor the contributions that follow and compare their own reflections about these careers with my own in a later and concluding section of this book.

SECTION 2

AUTOBIOGRAPHIES

Chapter 2

And Then There Was Tourism

John D. Hunt
University of Idaho, USA

John D. Hunt <jhunt@kayenta.net> is emeritus professor of sustainable tourism, College of Natural Resources, University of Idaho, USA. In retirement, he lives in Southern Utah among some of the most spectacular national parks in the world. He taught and conducted research in four US universities and many countries around the world. The author of many publications and presentations, his interests have covered subjects such as tourism destination image, planning, and marketing. He was the first person in the United States to be appointed a Distinguished Professor of Travel and Tourism. His awards included the Lifetime Achievement Award of the Travel and Tourism Research Association, Travel Industry Hall of Leaders, University of Idaho Alumni Hall of Fame, and others. He is a founding member of the International Academy for the Study of Tourism.

INTRODUCTION

I never dreamed I would be invited to write my autobiography. I have always wanted to write a short self-help book (hopefully, a best seller) around many of the humorous things that have happened to me in my lifetime; but an autobiography? Never! The autobiographies I have read are by truly notable, prestigious, famous, or infamous individuals. To be invited to be a part of this endeavor is an honor, albeit a daunting one.

The Study of Tourism: Foundations from Psychology
Tourism Social Science Series, Volume 15, 25–43
Copyright © 2011 by Emerald Group Publishing Limited
All rights of reproduction in any form reserved
ISSN: 1571-5043/doi:10.1108/S1571-5043(2011)0000015005

One of Life's Early Lessons

I would be inclined to say I am humbled but for the fact that one of the first, and most profound, lessons I learned as a very new and very young professor was that one cannot truly be humble unless he or she is independently wealthy. I was attending my very first professional conference: "The First National Conference on Research in Outdoor Recreation" in Ann Arbor (USA) in 1962. By happenstance, the first evening I ended up with two people—one a prominent textbook author and the other an attorney, quite skilled at his trade and large in both professional and physical stature. After enjoying a couple of cocktails at a nearby bar, we ended up in the hotel room of one of my newfound friends for a night cap in order to discuss some of the deliberations of the first day of the conference. When it was my turn to speak, I started by first expressing how humbled I felt to be among all these famous people and treated as an equal—I was nearly brought to tears. That was the first and the last thing I was to say that evening.

Before I got the whole thought out of my mouth, my attorney colleague had risen, towering over me—and I'm not particularly small—and said "bullshit!" He proceeded to give me my lesson on being "humble." After telling me that only independently wealthy people could "afford" to be humble, he told me that despite my clichéd statement I thought (perhaps typical of recent graduates in general) I was just as good, if not better, than anyone at the conference, but in fact, I was not. He added that he was better than me and that I should stay out of his way because should I not do so he would chew me up and spit me out. He ended my lesson by loudly exclaiming "humbled," followed by the same expletive he had used earlier and added a few others. I have remembered that lesson to this day.

Today, nearly a half century later, I am not so sure I agree that that early lesson applies. Now in the middle of my seventh decade, I have the right to say I am humbled. I am neither independently wealthy nor famous, but I need not fear a reprisal for I am almost certain my early teacher, the attorney, is now dead. I have been humbled many times, more so as I have grown older. However, at the time the lesson probably did apply to me and I believe it sometimes applies to the younger members of our academic community, particularly those who are just hitting the street with a newly acquired PhD in hand. Having said all of this, to repeat, I have earned the right to say that not only am I humbled but also honored to be invited to join my esteemed colleagues in this somewhat unique tome.

During my early graduate education while participating in a rather heady seminar, the professor accused me of being flippant. At the time, I was so naïve that I did not know what it meant until I got home and looked it up in the dictionary. At the time, I was somewhat chagrined and offended. However, in retrospect the professor was correct. To this day, I have never taken myself or my teaching and research too seriously. I have tried to approach this treatise with similar belief and some levity. As tried and worn as the statement may be, the academic study of tourism is not rocket science. Rather, it is the observation (both qualitatively and quantitatively) of mankind in a wonderful, usually fulfilling, social phenomenon; a wonderful dance of humanity—one with rewards and costs to most everyone who comes to the dance—tourists and hosts and the places they live or visit. Nonetheless, I hope that I have made a contribution, albeit small, to the understanding of this dance.

As I have read the autobiographies of others, it is easy to note that they have a beginning—a rather obvious observation—a journey, a bit of retrospective observation, and an epitaph, usually written by someone else or included in the epilogue, written as well by another person. I will follow that pattern here, leaving the epitaph for someone else to write; most likely in my obituary in, what I hope is, some rather distant time in the future.

LIFE IN THE WOODS

I was born in Southern California. My father worked as a ranger with the national forest service, while my mother was mostly in a stay at home role but not a particularly conventional person. It was a period when professional employees of the forest service were transferred quite frequently, much like the military. Although I was not a military brat, I have often referred to myself as a forest service brat. I lived from San Diego (the southernmost city in California) to Redding (the northernmost) and many small, rural places in between. I went to eight different elementary schools, two small high schools, and a small community college before I left home. My schools ranged from a moderately sized city school to a one-room-one-teacher-eight-grade, very rural school with a total of 13 students. I really do not think all of this movement got me interested in tourism, but it did make me socially adaptable and easy for me to meet people. I was forced to reach out because once I had found and become acquainted with friends it was time to move on to find new friends. This pattern of repeated movement generated a great deal of fear that served me well. Another bonus was I got to live in some of the most gorgeous places in California long before they were overrun with people.

I did a few things in high school and community college before I left home. I played American football, performed in various school theatrical productions, and chased girls only to have my heart broken on numerous occasions. I was an OK student. When I started college, I felt it necessary to choose a major and career direction. I wanted to major in theater, but being a conservative youth of the 1950s, I felt it was necessary to do something more practical, productive, and down-to-earth. Thus, I decided to follow in my father's footsteps and study the biological sciences and forestry. In retrospect, it may have been a mistake but I did get a strong, scientifically based education—no social sciences to speak of or humanities, but a good biological/ecological/science foundation.

Although, at the time, it was not evident, this foundation began that part of my journey leading to my discovering tourism. It was a circuitous route, but one in which I can still identify the most critical and influencing events, most of which were serendipitous. It is not, however, one that I would recommend to anyone. Nonetheless, it eventually took me all over the world and through a most rewarding and fulfilling career.

In 1956, I left California and never returned to live in that state. Nevertheless, I have had lots of visits to family and friends who continue to live there to this day. I ended up at the University of Idaho, another serendipitous event. My football coach in the community college had attended a workshop held by the head coach at the university and thought he might be able to get me an athletic scholarship. This possibility coupled with the fact that the university had a good forestry program sealed the deal for me. Fortunately, the football scholarship did not work out. Had I played football, I am sure my life would have taken a decidedly different path. I was about to get married and it was either play football on a funded, athletic scholarship or get a job. I went to work, got married, started a family, and became an above average, but not stellar, student. During this time, my wife gave birth to two of the three beautiful daughters we would eventually have.

My jobs were varied including work in a greenhouse and tree nursery, as a newspaper boy (this one was tough on my ego, but every little bit helped), and a taxicab driver. While some have suggested that the latter job may have led to my interest in travel, I highly doubt that to be the case. However, it did serve as the foundation for some of the most humorous events in my young life. Today, they still make good stories. I can see how HBO (Home Box Office television network) made a successful series around taxi driving events not too many years ago.

The Early Significant Events

I began taking my studies pretty seriously as well as participating in a variety of extracurricular activities. It was one such extracurricular pursuit in the last couple of months of my senior and final year that was probably one of the two most important events to shape my future. To this point, my direction was pretty well defined. I had already accepted a permanent, professional job as a farm forester in a nearby western state to commence after graduation. However, before the end of the term, I volunteered to be the chairman and master-of-ceremonies for the school's annual Foresters Banquet. Even though the event was held annually, there was not a good archive of past programs and activities to guide me. Innocently, I really dove in and did things that had never been done before, which ended up making the event a major success.

In addition, I have always been pretty good on my feet either in presenting prepared or extemporaneous remarks—in part the results of my theatrical and public speaking experiences coupled with possibly some inherited or learned behavioral characteristics. Regardless, the night of the banquet I waxed eloquently. Programmatically and entertainingly, everything fell perfectly into place.

The next day I was called into the Dean's office. Not knowing the Dean well or knowing why he wanted to see me, I feared a few of my quips the night before had been a bit too off color. He was a stern, gruff man. He started by informing me of something I already knew that I was just barely an above average student, in no way the best or the worst who had or would graduate in the future from the program. But then he said he felt I had some characteristics in organization and presentation that really were above average. In the next breath, he offered me one of the first three doctoral fellowships funded by the National Defense Education Act to be awarded in forestry in the country. For that time, they provided a relatively large stipend, including additional compensation for a family. The fellowships also did not require any work obligation in the form of teaching or research assistance. Followed by a brief discussion with my family, I accepted the three-year fellowship and called the employer with whom I had just accepted a job that I would not be able to accept the offer.

The following school year, I entered the graduate program not having any idea what I wanted to research or had the aptitude to study. So, I took more biology and forestry courses—actually the last subjects in the world I really needed. At the end of the year, I had the opportunity to interact with a very successful forestry professional role model. I confessed to him that I really did not look forward to facing trees the rest of my life and was far more interested in people. Without missing a beat, he told me that there was a relatively new phenomenon taking place in the forests and outdoor places in the country that presented some real challenges to biologically trained foresters, essentially understanding what brought people to forests.

Across the western United States, the forests environments were being sought for new purposes. In the old uses of forests, the forester was separated from the final consumer by many other producers and seldom came in contact with the final customers. Rather, foresters were responsible for growing, cultivating, and harvesting trees for timber, which was then delivered to millers who cut them into pieces for delivery to retail lumberyards who sold to builders producing houses, furniture, and other wood objects that were the end products for consumers. The new element in the forester's world was the growing demand for consumer experiences whereby people were coming to the outdoors and to the forests to take part in various leisure activities (basically to consume a product *in situ*). Foresters knew their trees but, unfortunately, they did not know human behavior and people's needs. They did not know what brought these people to the forests. Or, what they were doing there and in surrounding areas. Nonetheless, they attempted to cope with this new trend, albeit not too effectively. In the early days of the post-World War II and the emergence of outdoor recreation, we used to say that foresters were planning and developing recreational opportunities and facilities for people and "foresters just ain't [sic] people."

LIFE OUT OF THE WOODS

During my next two years in graduate school, I did everything one could to shape what I believed might be a good course of study to become a planner and researcher of the rapidly growing mass outdoor recreation movement. I began loading up on the social sciences, particularly sociology, economics, and psychology. I sneaked across campus to take a course or two in leisure studies that my biology/forestry professors did not regard as a particularly heady, academic topic. The last two years of my doctoral study and fellowship went by pretty fast, and at the end of which I had no PhD degree. I had slipped in a master's degree (in forestry of course), when I realized there was no chance I would finish the PhD. It was clear that neither the university's forestry program nor I were quite ready to undertake doctoral studies. Nonetheless, I had become the resident expert in the field of outdoor recreation and the college offered me a temporary instructor's position enabling me to return the following year to teach their first course in outdoor recreation.

As well as beginning to study the social sciences in my last two years, I accepted summer seasonal jobs working on an early outdoor recreation research project with one of the US Forest Service's Experiment Stations. The project was a cooperative one with Utah State University's College of Natural Resources. Probably I impressed another Dean; he offered me a teaching and extension job at Utah State University—tenure-track, assistant professor and $1,000 more than the job at my alma mater—raising my annual salary to a whopping $7,000. That Fall I returned briefly to Idaho to move and tell my Dean that I was going to go to Utah State and would be leaving the position there. This news was not well received. I was marched to the university president's office and rightly scolded for pulling out of the job at such short notice. I was told I would never be able to work for that university—banned for life. Fortunately, institutional memories often fade as will become evident toward the end of this chapter.

Discovering Tourism

My role at Utah State University was to teach a couple of courses and head up an outreach program in forestry, parks and outdoor recreation. I ran all over the state studying and exploring small, economically struggling communities amid some of the most splendid outdoor environments in the world.

At the end of my first year, a colleague left to take up a job in another state. He left behind a funded but uninitiated research project. I really did not have any research experience other than my seasonal jobs with the Forest Service, still I was asked if I wanted to assume leadership of the project. It was a relatively simple study of a fairly important recreation destination on the Utah/Idaho border accessible by only automobile. Our goal was to study the people visiting the destination, inventory resources for development, and then recommend a development plan for the area.

Shortly into the project, it became clear that the area was visited by two very different groups of individuals. There was a relatively large group of local people who lived within 100 miles of the area that visited the area primarily on weekends and holidays to participate in a variety of outdoor recreation activities such as swimming, camping, fishing, boating, hunting, and other active leisure pursuits. The other group was primarily a transient one comprising families whose residences were well beyond 100 miles and who stopped only briefly to enjoy a scenic overlook or snap a photo. They were passing through an area that lay between prominent destinations in the western United States—Las Vegas, Southwestern National Parks, Salt Lake City, Utah, and Grand Teton/Yellowstone National Parks in Wyoming. To this day, I claim that I inquired as to what this group of people was called and was told they were "tourists." They interested me much more than the local group. I became fascinated with their travel behavior and set out to learn more about them. Clearly, I was hooked; and through a long history of trial and error, I ended up devoting the remainder of my career to studying tourists: their behavior, their impact on economies, natural environments, and communities, as well as the planning, development, and marketing of host places for tourism.

While working on this project, I noticed a behavioral pattern of the transient tourists that fascinated me. Given that our location was about halfway between two major attractions, and overnight destinations approximately a day's drive apart, it appeared the anxiety of tourists seemed to increase as the day progressed. When told the distance to either destination, their behavior, as compared to people arriving in the early or first part of the day, appeared to change dramatically. It was as if they had an airplane flight to catch and believed they would be late and miss the departure. They were less willing to take the time to participate in our personal interview. Their stops were shorter in duration than those arriving earlier in the day. For some, their anxiety seemed to manifest itself in a level of irritability and discord among the members of their family or party.

As a result, we began inquiring about the tourists' trip planning, scheduling, activities, and progress. Some very interesting trends emerged. These were automobile travelers, many of who resided in the largely populated Southern California Region or various midwest population centers. They were taking a grand, family automobile tour of major western attractions. At that time, the foreign market for the western United States was small with visits concentrated mainly in the major port-of-entry cities. In those days, there was not a large fly-drive market. These were mostly families that piled into the family station wagon and visited, or sometimes better described as "collected," as many national parks, cities, and other well-known destinations as they could. For some, it appeared that they were trying to visit more places than was feasible in their scheduled vacation time.

We learned a lot. In those days (mid-1960s), most auto travelers in the West planned their vacations before leaving home, including a daily itinerary that they perceived required them to be at certain places at certain times. Even though a large portion did not make reservation for specific accommodations, they expected to adhere to their preplanned itinerary, including spending their overnights in preplanned destination areas. Trip planning was aided by major travel organizations, such as the American Automobile Association. They relied to a lesser degree on state tourism offices and significantly less on local area visitors' bureaus and chambers of commerce. In the final analysis, short of a major emergency or automobile breakdown, the majority of auto travelers maintained a preplanned route and rigid schedule. They were reluctant to leave the route in search of other lesser attractions or accommodations. As astutely observed by John Steinbeck during his grand auto tour of the United States with his dog Charles le Chien affectionately called "Charley" and reported in his book *Travels with Charley in Search of America*, published in 1962 by the Viking Press. "I know people who are so immersed in road maps that they never see the countryside they pass through, and others who, having traced a route, are held to it as though held by flanged wheels to rails." Fifty years later, the observations Steinbeck made about travel are fascinating and astute. His book should be read by every new student of tourism.

These and other findings in our study were reported in an obscure Utah Experiment Station bulletin, entitled *Tourist Vacations—Planning and Patterns* (Hunt 1968), and, unfortunately, never made it into a major journal. Of course, at the time there were really none in tourism. However, in the final analysis, the information afforded me considerable fodder to reach out to the emerging tourism industry in my state, the region, and eventually the country. At this point, my journey began to go in many directions—too many to document here but personally rewarding and in a way that I hope may have made some contributions to the growing phenomenon of tourism.

I became a member of a team with state and regional tourism leaders who began barnstorming the state on behalf of tourism as an emerging economic development tool. This led to an increasing role in research and intelligence gathering to assist state leaders in developing tourism marketing programs. Most of the research was applied in nature, focusing on and directed to meeting the needs of organizations that were willing to fund data gathering for their marketing activities. Our more basic research, the fun and probably more valuable outcome, was bootlegged from the limited financial resources and the infrastructure we built to provide these services.

One of our very early endeavors was motivated by expediency. That is, as my involvement with the tourism industry began to develop, I needed a vehicle to represent our interests and to communicate with our new clientele. I was housed in the Department of Forest Sciences in the College of Natural Resources. My affiliation with this department and my efforts to communicate, and thus seek an expanded role away from the campus, led to confusion and misunderstanding among the groups I was eager to serve. Most people could not understand why someone in a forestry department was doing tourism-related activities. As a side note, about 20 years later, I conducted a survey of known academic programs in tourism in the United States to determine their academic homes. I wanted to know where they were housed in their university administrative or collegial organizational structure. Interestingly, there was no logic to their location. They were found in various departments ranging from natural resources and parks and recreation to human kinetics, physical education, and leisure studies. It seemed that they were more often than not in programs where an individual was when they developed an interest in tourism. Most of these people had come to their respective universities for other reasons and subsequently "found" tourism as a new and fascinating field of study. Ironically, there were virtually no programs in colleges or department of business, even though most tourism development was primarily justified for its economic development benefits. However, back to the problem I faced in communicating with my new target audiences. Basically, we had an image problem.

Consequently, in 1968, we created the Institute for the Study of Outdoor Recreation and Tourism. Our primary motive was to get a new letterhead that seemed to better represent our new and expanding activities. Generally, it worked. Historically speaking, it was one of the first university-supported centers devoted to tourism in the United States. Bureaus of Business Research at various universities had been gathering tourist use and expenditure data for a period of years before, but their work involved a much broader range of interests beyond tourism.

The name was eventually shortened to the Institute of Outdoor Recreation and Tourism. The Institute reached out across the campus to bring together faculty and graduate students from a variety of disciplines and academic centers with interests in tourism. We worked together to pursue grants and contracts, coordinate teaching efforts, and provide service and education to off-campus public and private organizations and businesses. Essentially, we became one of the major academic "go-to" institutions in the state and region. Eventually, we reached organizations, universities, and individuals in other states and some other countries. It was not easy either inside or outside of the university. My Dean was highly skeptical of tourism as an area of academic study and research. Even though his field and that of others in the college were primarily applied fields that had drawn on the more traditional disciplines to create their focus, much the same as tourism, he was skeptical. He kept saying, "... show me your textbooks...show me your journals ..." I would turn to my bookcases, and frankly, there were none. Of course, today there are an overwhelming number of texts and journals. There is one for virtually every facet of tourism—I would guess they number in the hundreds.

As I alluded previously, my efforts were going in many different directions. We had convinced our state tourism office to fund various marketing and inventory studies. We looked at automobile travel, airline travel, skiing, and many other activities. Basically, we fed the central government tourism office and various associations and businesses with the data needed to develop their marketing efforts or justify their programmatic activities. We developed rather innovative ways to gather this information.

We recognized that many, actually most, of our "visitors" got through our state without seeing a single attraction or spending a night. They represented a huge potential market. In addition, because most survey data were collected at attractions or other places where visitors stopped, we did not know much about the people who traveled through on their way to other places. By missing the pass-through-tourist, estimates of expenditure, length of stay, and other information were greatly distorted. We knew very little about one of our biggest potential markets.

It dawned on us that if we treated our state borders as gates, we could stop people as they entered and learn something about everyone, whether they were destination or pass-through tourists. Thus, we actually blocked nonresident cars as they entered. We asked a few questions and then gave them a diary to complete as they drove through the state. We asked them to return the mail-back diary after they left the state. The diary asked for more detailed information about the trip, such as routes traveled, location of overnight stays, expenditures, and a host of other questions. The few questions we asked of everyone at the roadblocks, which were also included in the mail-back diary, gave us limited information about all types of tourists and a way to eventually identify and correct for nonresponse bias for that portion of our sample that returned the diaries. We adopted this method to studies of other types of nonresidents, viz., airline, skier, and others. The approach allowed us to learn about those visiting attractions and accommodations as well as those who got through the state without stopping. It gave the tourism industry vital information for marketing to tourists who were more likely to be enticed to visit without having to develop new, unknown markets. It was an innovative approach, later adapted by several other regions and states. Unfortunately, today such an approach would never work in most places because the volumes of traffic would generally be so great that it would be unsafe to detain traffic of any type of travel mode.

Tourism and Special Places

These studies and others gave me further entrée to new groups within the tourism industry. However, tantamount to expanding my work in tourism, I continued some involvement with the parks and recreation system. In some cases, I was successful in bringing a balance between issues of environmental stewardship and tourism development. I argued that there could be a symbiotic relationship between special places and tourism. Tourism development and the management of parks and recreation resources did not have to be mutually exclusive. Unfortunately, to most of my colleagues and audiences on both sides, I was a pariah. Some in the parks and recreation movement saw me as a sellout to capitalism and economic development, while some in the tourism industry characterized me as a flaming, radical environmentalist. It was a fine line to walk, but I maintained a foot in both camps throughout my career and brought some understanding of the relationships that generated benefits to both groups. Of course, it was a vital relationship for the tourism industry, as it became abundantly clear that most of the major attractions in the western United States were part of the natural environment—national parks, ski terrain, rivers, lakes, forests, and other outdoor areas. Such a situation is not uncommon throughout the world.

Early in my career, when I was mainly working with forests, parks, and outdoor recreation managers, I could not help but observe that most of the natural resources and attractions were used by both resident recreationists and nonresident tourists. Use patterns and other characteristics of the groups were different, but they both used and sometimes competed for the same resources. In some ways, it was easy for me to make the transition from my forestry training to an interest in tourism. It is also fascinating to recognize that today both groups embrace marketing as a tool to increase user satisfaction, enhance economic and other benefits, improve guest–host relationships, mitigate impacts on communities and special places, and manage sometimes fragile, limited resources. Building the bridges of understanding among public agencies, curators of special places, communities, and tourism businesses created challenges akin to learning another language and intercultural communication.

A good many years later, my consulting partner (spouse) and I were successful in developing the first ever summit on public lands and tourism. It brought together land and natural resource managers with tourism industry leaders from the western United States. It helped to forge a hallmark letter of agreement between the major national resource agencies and many of the state government tourism offices. The movement spread to incorporate even more federal agencies and the states of the southeastern United States. While the bridges between the stewards of our land and special places and the tourism industry remain fragile, there is a much improved understanding of the relationships and how vital these are to our future and our ability to meet our respective goals.

A Community of Academics with an Interest in Tourism

Frankly, it is sometimes hard to sort out the routes and directions my career took. I was going in so many different directions at the same time. I was active in teaching, research, and service in forestry, parks and recreation, and tourism. Working with professional societies was also part of these endeavors. While the first two fields are not particularly relevant to this discussion, my involvement with professionals and academics in the tourism community in general and, specifically, the research arena took on an increasing importance as my career progressed. Somehow I found the Western Council for Travel Research that had been organized by a group of directors of university bureaus of economic and business research. It was also the precursor to the Travel and Tourism Research Association (TTRA) that came about as the result of the merger of the Western Council and the Travel Research Association based primarily in the eastern United States.

This association eventually became my primary professional group, providing a platform for learning, exchanging ideas, and fellowship. Although the group remains heavily US centric, it has been greatly enriched over the years by significant involvement of academics and other researchers from Canada and many other countries. This association was good to me in different ways, but one event in particular stands out. One of the principal leaders then and to this day of the organization is Chuck Goeldner. For several of the early years of the Western Council and the TTRA, he edited the *Travel Research Bulletin*. Outside of in-house bulletins and publications and a few professional journals from allied fields, it was one of the few sources in which we could publish and share information with colleagues outside of our immediate realm. But, there still was not a "journal," which by virtue of the name alone carried prestige and academic credibility. I suggested to Chuck that he change the name of the bulletin to the *Journal of Travel Research*, if for no other reason than to give it more status among our academic leaders. After all, getting tenure was as important in those days as it is today. At the outset, and to his credit, he was reluctant because of its quality. Nonetheless, he eventually made the change and for many years it was the only journal of its kind in the world. Shortly thereafter, Jafar Jafari introduced *Annals of Tourism*. Finally, my shelves were no longer bare. Then came a textbook or two and we were off and running. Today, I am sure my shelves could not hold all of the tourism-related textbooks, scholarly journals, and other publications that exist.

The other benefit of working closely with the local public and private sectors of tourism is that it brought me entry to other groups in the tourism industry. During this time, many states were experimenting with multistate or regional marketing, particularly in targeting international markets. My state had joined with three other western states—Colorado, Montana, and Wyoming, in a marketing consortium known as Rocky Mountain West. Among the things we did with this group was to find various commonalities and differences that could be utilized to develop an approach and theme for cooperative marketing, particularly focusing on advertising in the most appropriate media of the time.

A Rose Is a Rose

Early on in our work with this group, we could not help but compare levels of touristic activity. Among other things, I had observed that although Utah had attractions comparable if not superior to the member states in the consortium, as well as to many other states, tourism activity and development lagged behind most places. It did not make sense that while other states were becoming increasingly invested in tourism, Utah's development seemed to lag. I wondered if Utah's unique history and the culture of its Mormon inhabitants might in some way affect potential tourists' perceptions of Utah and thus their willingness to visit and vacation in the state. I had heard that new consumer and media products were not test marketed in Utah because it was believed that it was a unique market that could not be generalized to other US markets. As a sidelight, it is interesting to note that the State of Utah tourism division was using "Discover the Different World of Utah" as its marketing slogan. The slogan was intended to create the impression that Utah had a great variety of outstanding attractions and features, and indeed it did. To this day, it remains a western state with a vast and diverse array of attractions. However, the Utah promoters did not recognize the semantic significance or "bias" of the word "different" and the fact that it could easily be substituted by words such as "odd," "strange," "weird," and other not so flattering descriptions. The slogan probably helped to solidify the perception that Utah was indeed a unique and, perhaps, not so hospitable place.

Drawing upon the limited but mounting body of information in marketing that dealt with product image, I set out to determine if potential out-of-state tourists perceived images or personalities of states or destinations. And if so, what were the images of the four states in the marketing consortium? This preliminary, unpublished work conducted by me and Perry Brown, a new, young colleague in our program, in cooperation with the *Better Homes and Gardens* magazine research department, led to my dissertation research on image as a factor in tourism. I earned a sabbatical leave, a rare occurrence today for someone without a doctoral degree, and went to Colorado State University. The faculty was gracious enough to tolerate my interest in tourism and allowed me to pattern a program that included psychology and sociology.

The dissertation research was subsequently published in the *Journal of Travel Research* (Hunt 1975). It served, along with the work of a few other professional colleagues, as the foundation for an understanding of tourist perceptions and the beliefs they maintained about places that affected their willingness to visit such locations. The understanding of image as it impacts tourists and destination has vastly increased from this early work. Research continues to this day, as it is not uncommon to frequently see papers in different scientific journals that continue to plumb the theory of image and its impact.

During this time, as my work with the tourism industry increased, a couple of other significant events took place for me. I had been appointed as a nonvoting, ex officio member of my state's government tourism office's board of directors. This was unusual for an academic to be in close allegiance with the "real world." The term "real world" has always antagonized me. Then where was I if it was not in the real world; I just happened to work for a university. Anyway, I found myself particularly enamored with the deliberations of the group. There appeared to be marked differences between the official agenda and deliberations, and the informal discussions usually held around dining tables, cocktails, and other social functions. The official agenda dealt almost exclusively with approving or giving guidance to the staff regarding advertising, collateral material development, increasing the budget to do more of the same, and various other sales issues. The informal agenda was almost exclusively devoted to the major challenges the organization seemed to face. Among these were issues of coordination and communication among the many segments of the industry, the seeming lack of support from elected officials, the lack of understanding about the value of tourism among political leaders and the public, needs within the industry for human resources development, poor training of hospitality workers, and many others. None of these seemed to deal directly with the matters to which they devoted their time. They had the sales stuff down pat; the hospitality and airline components of tourism possessed the most brilliant marketing campaigns in the field. However, they all continued to devote their attention to such matters, never considering how they might address those other issues so constraining to the success of their programs and the tourism industry in general.

Later, I came to call this preoccupation with sales strategies, which seemed to be the major focus of most national and state tourism offices (Hunt 1988), "Building a Better Brochure Syndrome." The answer to our challenges and opportunities was simple: build another brochure.

The Pace Picks Up

These observations lead me to another turning point in my career. Since I had the ear of the industry in my state, I began conducting a series of meetings whereby I encouraged the participants to brainstorm issues (mostly problems) impacting the industry. I then asked them to place the lists of issues into priority rankings. In most cases, it was those nonsales issues that floated to the top. We subsequently discussed goals and strategies for meeting those goals. Although I was totally unaware of the concept of SWOT (strengths, weaknesses, opportunities, and threats) analyses, that is exactly what I was doing. My approach was a formative version of the nominal group technique emphasizing participatory research.

About this time, I was due for another sabbatical leave and chose to join the US Travel Service, Office of Research in Washington DC. This was a rather insignificant national tourism office, albeit, probably as good as the United States would ever have. It rose and ebbed for many years until it was eliminated entirely as a stand-alone agency in the federal government. My work with this agency during my sabbatical was of no real consequence (Hunt and Layne 1991). However, most importantly to my future development and professional directions was that while in Washington DC, by happenstance I became acquainted with a couple of staff members of the US Congress. Their congressional representatives were about to embark on the National Tourism Policy Study. A consulting firm was hired to lead the effort. I had a chance to make some input to the data-gathering process and convinced the group that we should conduct a series of regional SWOT analyses (although I still did not know what that technique was). I eventually became a member of the policy study team. We were able to gather a wide array and large quantity of information about the status of the US tourism industry. We produced rather ambitious policy and implementation strategies for a national tourism program. Unfortunately, little came of our work. The United States has never really embraced a federal government role in tourism development and marketing. Most public or governmental involvement has been left to the states and cities.

While very little came of the National Tourism Policy Study, it opened numerous national and international opportunities for me. It exposed me to the nation's tourism industry leadership and took me to a number of countries in Europe, Asia, and Latin America to seek information about national tourism programs. It also led to a partnership with one of the members of the consulting firm that subsequently took me to Southeast Asia where I was part of a World Tourism Organization and United Nations Development Programme team. About this same time, my personal life took a major dip, and after 19 years, I ended up leaving Utah State University. My tenure there had treated me well professionally and academically, but it was time to move on.

I had never lived in a truly urban environment, so I began exploring opportunities in some of the larger cities of the United States. I ended up back in Washington DC, but this time with The George Washington University. Living in the city and being at this university was highly rewarding in many ways. I taught, helped administer its tourism program, and did a little research. I was also exposed to various tourism trade associations based in the area. Among them was the Travel Industry Association of America, which was probably the most representative of the diverse segments of the industry. Its membership comprised representatives from all segments of the private sector, as well as state and regional tourism offices and other public tourism organizations.

I was invited to revitalize an educational program of the association called the Educational Seminar for State Tourism Offices (ESSTOs). The program moved around the country. Our first meeting following a hiatus of a few years was held on the campus of the University of Kansas. While the program was good—a bit academic; most importantly, I met my future and present wife who was the public relations director for the Colorado Tourism Board. I served as ESSTO's "Dean of faculty" for 19 years. I like to think the program got significantly better and much more practical and useful. Not because of me, but due to the fact that we increasingly utilized the practitioners in the program. Once again, I received exposure that led to a strong, ongoing relationship with state tourism offices throughout the remainder of my professional career, both as an academic and a consultant. My role with the states through the seminar series led to numerous opportunities in research, education, and outreach. In addition, during this time, I had many opportunities to conduct short-term teaching activities in many countries of the world.

THE FINAL MOVES

I eventually left The George Washington University and moved to the hotel school at the University of Massachusetts. They anointed me with a fancy academic title and I became the first Distinguished University Professor of Travel and Tourism in the United States. At the same time, my wife and I opened a consulting office that proved very rewarding; but as a generalist "tourism guy," I was like a fish out of water in the hotel school. The place was good to me, but after four years at the University of Massachusetts and a total of 10 years on the East Coast, I needed to head back West where my heart belonged.

I ended up at one of my alma maters, the University of Idaho, as the head of the Department of Resource Recreation and Tourism. As a sidelight, it is interesting to note that very often "institutional memory" fades. Here I was back in the place I had started, the place where I was told 30 years before that I would never be allowed to work. I neglected to refresh their memory. Although I am not quite sure why some of us want to be academic administrators, I had a fruitful time at the university. I was allowed to continue my professional and business activities, which continued to expose me to wonderful people and places. I had an outstanding group of colleagues, but after nine years of trying to "herd cats," I retired from academic life. I continued to consult on a limited basis. My partner and spouse earned a PhD. While much of her focus remains in the tourism arena, she built depth and expertise in a process known as "appreciative inquiry"— a type of SWOT analysis, but with much more positive and productive focuses. Being a bit younger, she has ventured into academia as a communication professor at a local college where we now live. Today, other than being a good pool boy, houseboy, and cabana boy, I follow her around doing "appreciative inquiry" events with a broader array of clients.

Nonetheless, in retrospect and in the final analysis, while my career had no basis of a traditional scholastic discipline or foundation and wandered in many different directions and to many different places, it served me well. It allowed me to meet and know wonderful and interesting people. It took me to some exotic and fascinating places in this world—some places where I wonder to this day how I ever got home or, at least, back to my hotel room. Hopefully, I made a small contribution to the understanding of preserving and protecting special places and providing for sustainable tourist experiences. Had I not hung in with my interest in tourism, I doubt very little of this would have happened. I am ever so thankful to all of those people who influenced my life.

Chapter 3

Tourism Research: A Pragmatist's Perspective

Stanley C. Plog
Best Trip Choices, Inc., USA

Stanley C. Plog <scplog@earthlink.net> is chairman of Best Trip Choices, Inc., a company that uses his travel personality system to help tourists select destinations suited to their personalities. Prior to this, he developed and sold two market research companies, BASICO and Plog Research, Inc., to publicly held corporations (Planning Research Corporation and NFO Worldwide). He received his undergraduate degree in psychology at Occidental College and a PhD in the social sciences at Harvard University, USA. He has written three books in this field; *Leisure Travel: Making it a Growth Market Again*, *Vacation Places Rated*, and *Leisure Travel: A Marketing Handbook*. He has also coedited four books in the field of social psychiatry. He is a current editor of the *Cornell Hospitality Quarterly*, a past editor of the *Journal of Travel Research*, and has written numerous articles in both scholarly and trade publications. In 2004, he received the Alfred E. Koehl Lifetime Achievement Award in Marketing from the Hospitality, Sales and Marketing Association International. He lives in Fallbrook with his wife and has two sons.

The Study of Tourism: Foundations from Psychology
Tourism Social Science Series, Volume 15, 45–62
Copyright © 2011 by Emerald Group Publishing Limited
All rights of reproduction in any form reserved
ISSN: 1571-5043/doi:10.1108/S1571-5043(2011)0000015006

WHAT AM I GOING TO BE WHEN I GROW UP

I took so many paths before I settled down to a research career that I often joked with friends that I could not really grow up yet because I did not know what I wanted to be.

I was born in the Los Angeles area but immediately was moved back to North Dakota to live with relatives, because my father left at birth and my mother could not afford to keep me during the depression years. I returned to California at about age eight when my mother remarried. My new dad was a trombone player who worked with a number of dance bands in the Midwest and California. He gave me trombone lessons with the statement that I could avoid the poverty and makeshift life I faced until that time if I became a great trombonist—and did well in school. That was a clarion call to climb above some difficult beginnings. I disciplined myself, practicing trombone religiously, and improved my so-so grades to be among the best in the class. It worked. By my mid-teens, I had my own 12-piece dance band, playing high school and college proms, weddings, bar mitzvahs, parties, the Pasadena Rose Queen Ball, and even coming close to capturing a television show. I joined the Musicians' Union, Local 47 (Hollywood) at 16. By the time I graduated from high school, I counted myself as one of the better trombonists in Los Angeles. On graduation night, I joined Dave Cavanaugh's band for stints that summer at the Salt Air ballroom outside of Salt Lake City and the Boardwalk in Santa Cruz, California.

I completed a year at Occidental College in Eagle Rock of California on a music scholarship, doing casuals (single music jobs), some motion picture, and television work, and juggling the demands of a full academic schedule and part-time employment to cover living expenses. At 19, I got an offer to join Horace Heidt's Orchestra as first trombone (my best music job ever). Heidt had a very popular radio and TV show that featured young talent competing weekly for grand prizes awarded to a finalist every quarter. This job fulfilled all my expectations about how great life as a musician could be. It almost had too many benefits to count.

We toured the country about 10 months a year, working one-nighters seven nights a week with the chance to visit big and small towns in every mainland US state. Each week we did a simulcast radio and TV show, and I was featured on the theme song at the beginning and end of every show ("On the Trail" melody from Ferde Groffe's Grand Canyon Suite). We even toured Europe and North Africa on a US State Department Goodwill Tour, with a special concert in East Berlin when that city was still divided into four sectors. I still remember communist protesters gathering around our bus after the concert and refusing to let us move out. Whenever we hit New York or Los Angeles, we did record dates and rehearsed new production numbers for shows we would take on the road. I never faced a dull moment because each week we inserted routines for new talent into our road show. The size of the crowds added to the excitement. I could not believe Mitchell in South Dakota; a small town then (1949–1950), it had the famous Corn Palace auditorium that could seat 3,200. We filled it for five nights, with more people still wanting to get in. Farm families drove more than 100 miles to see us. On a European tour in 1950, over 10,000 Germans crowded into the hall in Munich where Hitler had planned his big putsch while about 3,000 more listened through speakers set up to the first American music they had heard since Hitler seized power.

Union scale included extras for traveling on the road, playing seven nights a week instead of six, the TV and radio weekly simulcasts, and the recording dates. I added to my take-home pay by driving the show's wardrobe truck. I had to join the Teamster's Union, but got paid only a pittance of scale. But that was fine. I liked to drive, and the money added to everything else I earned.

A special relationship exists among musicians in most cases. They establish closer relationships than in most other professions I have observed. A lot of oddball and offbeat people exist, but all are accepted. Inside jokes are prevalent, often with a gallows humor focused around the difficult lives they face because they live precariously from one temporary job to another—and no pension plans. Those with the most musical talent become the *de facto* intellectual leaders in a band or orchestra. Others look up to them and respect their judgment. But most musicians are very bright and creative.

However, this great life changed when the Korean War came along. I joined the 775th Air Force Band in Tucson, Arizona in late November 1950 that gave me a chance to keep up my Hollywood musical contacts. It was a great choice, too. A bunch of talented young musicians also joined, all having the same idea—to be close to the Hollywood musical scene. The list included five-time academy award winner, John Williams, two future presidents of Local 47, a future arranger and tenor sax player with the Doc Serverinsen Tonight Show Band, and the lead alto from my teenage band. Friendships developed that last today.

After discharge, I returned to Occidental College to continue pursuing a degree in music. I immediately got some good work around town—motion picture studio dates and weekend casuals. Soon I joined Freddy Martin's Orchestra on lead chair, a major recording artist at the time. This job proved a boon, because I was married now with my wife expecting a child soon, and Freddy was a permanent fixture in the Coconut Grove ballroom at the Ambassador Hotel in Los Angeles. I could settle down and continue to attend Occidental. It required juggling my time carefully to meet the demands of a full-time job and a full academic load.

Doubts about a Musical Future

As perfect as everything seemed to be, nagging doubts arose over time about whether I really wanted to continue to be a musician. Even while with Horace Heidt, I noticed that guys 45 or older had trouble landing regular jobs. Bandleaders wanted young, fresh faces on the bandstand. That seemed crazy to me. In most professions, at mid-career one can project future increased earning power, greater job stability, and more respect among peers. The temporariness and specialized roles of most gigs means that one worries about the next job.

In short, I came to the conclusion that I loved music but not the music business. I decided to get out and leave a profession that had consumed my life for so many years but offered a limited future than I had imagined. This was a tough decision, because I had devoted myself to it since I was almost nine and had no idea of what I might want to do. I had to support a family, so I could not just drop everything and not earn a living. It was not made easier by the fact that my Mom and Dad both wished I would stay in music because of my success. My younger brother did and is now the trumpet professor at the Freiberg Hochschule in Germany and a classical composer. He enjoys it, but it's still difficult to make a substantial living for most musicians.

CAREER CHANGING DECISIONS

At Occidental College, I sampled a lot of courses in search of a field that I would like. Many were interesting—biology, physiology, and even philosophy, but which career should I choose within any of these fields? I considered a premed major for awhile, but dropped that. I thought marine biology was fascinating, but opted out after visiting an oceanographic institute and noticing the very limited lives that these people lived. What I seemed to like most was research—of all kinds. It meant discovering new things constantly. I looked into medical or physiological research, since it could combine a couple of my interests. But I came to the conclusion that this was not for me. I noticed that some people spent a lifetime in laboratories looking for a cure for a specific type of cancer, but never came up with a solution. The wasted career in that kind of a situation would seem depressing to me. My background in music to this point had built in a need to find something that could provide a chance to work in an ever-changing environment.

Finally I sampled courses in the social sciences—abnormal and social psychology and sociology. The fields seemed fascinating, although young in history and without a lot of firm conclusions like the hard sciences. But they offered one advantage not available in the hard sciences. The student could jump around within the social sciences easily if current efforts did not seem intriguing or productive. The hard sciences proudly proclaim the precision and controls that define their experiments. For the most part, everything is done in laboratories where all elements of a design can be detailed and reported. The social sciences do not enjoy such luxury. The behavior of people is complex and truly requires a social setting where it is impossible to nail down every variable to test hypotheses. Laboratory experiments using rats, chimps, and dogs never made sense to me. How could the reactions of animals to limited stimuli be interpreted as reflective of human behavior in social settings? To handle these kinds of difficulties, the social sciences developed new and quite innovative research designs and advanced statistical procedures that seemed miles ahead of anything used in the hard sciences.

But I was still unable to make up my mind as to what I wanted to do. Music is such a consuming and seductive passion that it is hard to leave the field. Most musicians stay on and become part-time real estate agents or travel agents to supplement their incomes, while still hoping for a big break. That was not for me. So, I took time off from school to try and reach a conclusion during the year that Freddy Martin decided to spend a winter season at the Boca Raton Hotel in Florida, with a stop at in Las Vegas to be featured with Elvis Presley, and one-nighters in between. I returned to Occidental, and decided to concentrate on a degree in psychology. It would give me the most flexibility in what I could choose later, I believed, but I still had no clear idea of how I would use it. All I knew was that I would need a doctorate because a bachelor's degree would not buy entrance into any credible job.

At graduation I applied to clinical psychology programs at a number of good schools, because I reasoned that I could always cross over to sociology or social psychology if I wished, but not the opposite since clinical psychology required "tickets," my term for certification of psychologists by state review boards. The limitations of being a sideman musician prevented me from having lots of choices, and I did not want that to happen again. Surprisingly, Harvard University gave the best scholarship deal. Their program emphasized training in all of the important social sciences, requiring students to pass qualifying exams both in a chosen field and in social psychology, sociology, and cultural anthropology. I accepted the offer and moved wife and child back to the Cambridge area. From that point on, it took me 15 years to earn the same income in my new field as I did as a musician, not counting inflation, making my choice a bit sobering.

The first year at Harvard was fabulous! Exposure to great minds whose books I had read, deep immersion in multiple topics and fields of endeavor, new ideas through a ton of books we had to read each week, and exposure to fellow students who were so bright that it was scary. It was a challenge just to keep up with the fast pace they established in class discussions and their ability to argue almost any point. I did not play my horn the first year to make certain that I got through the qualifying exams, because we were told that this was the flunk out year. Indeed, and unfortunately, a lot of students did not make the grade.

After the first year, I picked up my horn again to earn money and got the best work in town—the Ice Capades and Rodeos when these came to the Boston Gardens, Boston Celtic games, the North Shore Musical Theatre in the summer, more weddings and Bar Mitzvahs, and the plum job of all: Ruby Newman's Society Orchestra for society coming out parties. Ruby's society events paid incredibly well, all compounded union scale. Jobs started at 10:00 pm with union scale beginning at 8:00 and going only until 11:00 pm. After that point, scale increased to double time until we quit at 2:00 am (we got extra as we had no intermissions). The band played continuously, because Boston society wanted their girls to always have someone to dance with and not have to sit around during band intermissions. We also got travel time—to the North Shore where many of the big homes were located, or even flying to other locales for dates—Charleston in North Carolina, Detroit area (the Dodge family party), and more. I made lots of money while still attending grad school, a fact that also called into question my decision to leave music.

But my schooling from the second year on was a different story. There were disappointments with Harvard. In course work and seminars, I was exposed primarily to more junior professors, many of whom were there on one-year assignments. They had little interest in teaching. Instead they focused primarily on their own research projects, hoping to create a reputation that would land them a good position at another university. They lampooned the older faculty whose reputations they would never achieve. There was even greater disappointment in my clinical training. The psychiatrists who supervised our work seemed like they were from another planet. All adopted a Freudian perspective, and many had a penchant for making wild, speculative assertions about what was going on in the lives of the cases we presented. I blew up in a couple of sessions with these "respected" therapists, commenting that the music field I left allows for free and creative artistic expression, but only within a foundation of understanding chord progression and having facility on an instrument. Psychiatry, in contrast, lacked a foundation for much of its undisciplined and unfettered speculation about people's lives. Surprisingly, I was not kicked out and somehow got through the courses. I thought of quitting and returning to a career in music but finally took a different path. I latched on to the great names and each semester became a research and teaching assistant to luminaries such as Gordon W. Allport, Henry A. Murray, George A. Miller, and Jerry Bruner. Few people could match the personal qualities of Allport, and I chose him as my dissertation advisor.

I served my clinical internship in the Department of Psychiatry at University of California, Los Angeles and, after getting the doctorate, was offered a position at its Neuropsychiatric Institute as a medical psychologist. That was followed a year later by being named the Academic Director of a new program in Social Psychiatry, also within the Department of Psychiatry. The following year, I was invited to establish and direct a new program to study urban social problems. Nevertheless, contentment eluded me. Academic life seemed too confining with its focus on publishing (or perishing), and there always seemed to be a considerable amount of infighting among faculty members. It was not like the music business where players are collegial and accept all kinds of less than ideal conditions in their quest, just to play their instruments. I decided to get into business for myself. But what kind of business? I could not just leave and say to the world, "I'm here. Hire me to solve your problems!" All I could do now was think of ideas about businesses I could start.

New Career Beginnings

It helped that I found a compatriot at my last university whose attitudes were similar to mine. We had discussions about what entrepreneurial ventures we could undertake. At first, we thought of developing a counseling center, but, after looking at office space, vetoed that idea. We did not want to handle a caseload that would be made up mostly of neurotic adults and acting out teenagers. If we did not think that highly of psychology/psychiatry in general, why go into it? Then one day, I had an interesting case to work on. While still a medical psychologist in the Neuropsychiatric Institute, a case was referred to me for psychological testing of an eight-year-old blind girl who had fallen far behind in school. The school psychologist's report stated that she had a low IQ and the request was to determine what kind of mental disability she had. I gave her an individual intelligence test (I do believe in some of the testing procedures developed within the field of psychology) and a battery of cognitive function tests. I discovered that she was not retarded; she had an IQ of at least 125. So I interviewed the parents to learn more. The girl was the product of an intercultural marriage. The father was a World War II G.I. stationed in Japan who married a Japanese girl. Both sets of parents were strongly against the marriage. Their child, who was born in Japan prematurely, was put in an Air Force hospital incubator and excess oxygen in the incubator broke the blood vessels in the back of her eye (retrolental fibroplasia, now called retinopathy of prematurity) that caused permanent blindness. The parents assumed that they had sinned by marrying and this was their burden to bear. Through counseling sessions, I convinced the parents that they had not sinned, their child was bright, but had been misdiagnosed and wrongly placed in classes for the retarded. It was the Air Force hospital that had erred medically. I referred them to the Braille Institute and centers for blind children, and the girl progressed beautifully, ultimately proceeding to do well in all of her studies.

But this case also carried a message to me. The problem and the solution both seemed so simple, why had not the school psychologist picked this up? I decided that it was difficult to get competent psychologists in school districts and maybe my associate and I could offer services that would help fill the gap. We formed a company, University Consultants, which provided psychological testing services to small, outlying school districts where we would not face in-house resistance. We offered a win-win situation. Most of the cases that would be referred to us could qualify for California State special education funds, both for the assessment and for follow-on special education classes. Thus, it would not cost the district anything, and they would actually increase their revenue. We hired university psychologist friends to do the work and took a cut of the action. In a short time, we had a half dozen districts signed up, while still holding down our university positions.

But this is not what I ultimately wanted to do. I had developed a background in survey research on my dissertation work at Harvard and was more interested in pursuing this form of research. The school districts supported us (we did not even need office space) while we searched for new opportunities. We changed our name to Behavior Science Corporation to reflect our broader business interests, and I began calling on ad agencies and corporations to offer our services. We got only small contracts at first, but it was a beginning. All we could do was slog it out until we got a break.

A Big Break Leading to a Self-fulfilling Career

Sir Winston Churchill said something that always stuck with me. I do not have the direct quote but it was to the effect, "Opportunity may knock but once in a lifetime; pity the poor soul who is not prepared." I took that to heart and lived by it from early on. It helped in my music career. I never lost an audition because I always came well prepared. Not only did I have competency on my horn, but also I would listen to records of the band to learn their style and how they used trombone. With my young company, a great opportunity occurred that I did not want to lose. A client, Planning Research Corporation, was bidding on a large project for 16 sponsors— 10 major airlines, the three airframe manufacturers (Boeing, Douglas, and Lockheed), and three magazines (*Life, Reader's Digest*, and *R. H. Donnelly/ Official Airlines Guide*). Planning Research Corporation did not have the in-house skills to win the contract. They asked me to write the proposal.

I met with the sponsor group to learn more about the requirements, wrote a proposal that matched their criteria well, and we won the bid. The task was to get more people to take flights on commercial airlines. The year was 1966 and only a quarter of the population had ever flown commercially, quite a different story from today. Airlines were taking delivery of jets that increased their capacity at 20% a year, but traffic was building at only 8% annually. They desperately needed to make up that shortfall. I saw a big opportunity. If my company directed the project, I knew that I would establish credibility with all the sponsors and could expand to other clients after it was completed. I went to Planning Research Corporation and told them that they did not have internal capability to handle the assignment, so I would have to direct it. But it would not do me any good to be just a hired hand on the project, since my focus was on growing my own company. I wanted to buy the project from them. After some discussion, they agreed, but at a steep cost—20% of the total project price. I accepted their offer even though that put us in the hole because we could not expect to cover our costs with that much taken out of the contract. I just knew, however, that this was a great entry into the world of travel—airlines, magazines, and airframe manufacturers. I could build from there.

Their basic questions centered on who does not fly, why not, and what could be done to get them to fly. Today, those ratios have reversed as a result of some of the programs initiated from the research and other events in travel. Now, over 80% of the population has flown, and about a third takes to the skies every year. What a change in a relatively short period of time. Travel has become a huge business, growing from about the 15th largest industry, at the time of the original research, to the largest in the United States and the world, according to the UNWTO.

The original study provided several research luxuries that facilitated developing new ideas that are not common in today's fast paced, slimmed down research environment. We had the freedom to pursue offbeat ideas, the time and money to be more thorough in testing concepts, and the opportunity to employ several research approaches to ensure that the conclusions are justified. My associate, Holden, and I decided that we had to understand the psychology of travel—why some people travel and others do not—in order to provide recommendations to our sponsors on how to get more people into the air. To do this, first, we conducted an extensive literature review on what was known about why people do not fly (not much), and investigated a number of psychological theories to determine their applicability to our research needs. Second, we completed over 60 in-depth, two-hour interviews with people who did not fly but had sufficient income to travel whenever they wished. These interviews proved to be invaluable, because we explored life histories, from childhood to the present, to determine common life patterns or psychological characteristics that might be common among this group of nontravelers. Third, a team monitored 1,200 telephone calls at airline reservations centers from naïve travelers to learn about the kinds of questions these novices asked of reservations agents. Some of the questions from first-time fliers proved to be humorous and showed their lack of understanding of the basics of air travel ("If I feel sick, can I open the window?" "Are there bathrooms on board?" "Do I tip the stewardess?"). Fourth, we completed 1,600 in-person intensive interviews on a door-to-door random sample of the US population. The questionnaire examined a number of psychological concepts that grew out of our exploratory research. Analysis of the data indicated that a constellation of three primary personality characteristics defines the nonflier personality: generalized anxieties, a sense of powerlessness, and territory boundedness (an emphasis on local horizons).

At the time, we called this person a "psychocentric" to reflect the fact that so much of their personal energy daily focuses on the small events in their lives, leaving little time to face up to and manage the larger problems we all encounter. I later developed a more "user friendly" term for the consumer travel website I developed <http://www.BestTripChoices.com>, calling them "authentics" instead, since so little is hidden or masked in their daily lives.

The original report was well received and resulted in the airlines following a number of recommendations that helped change the industry and put them on a path to growth, including: develop advertising campaigns that emphasize the safety of air travel, especially comparing it to car trips; promote discount flights (not common at the time) and point out that flying can be cheaper than driving; initiate fly/drive programs (also not current at the time). Now airlines routinely try to sell car rentals at the time of a booking since they can pick up added commissions and train staff at call centers on how to handle questions from naïve and first-time travelers.

Reader's Digest picked up on the results and sold a two-year eight-page insert campaign to the airlines and airframe manufacturers to convince nonfliers to take their first trips by air. It was their second most successful insert campaign ever up to that point, with over 25% of the readers browsing the inserts. But my good luck did not stop with this initial project. *Life Magazine*, one of the sponsors, called and asked for a study to define the psychological type that fits at the opposite end of the spectrum—someone who uses commercial airlines for leisure trips. They believed that their readers were very different from the constellation we found. Without going into detail, the results pointed to persons whose personalities were the opposite. They are free of "generalized anxieties." They make decisions easily and without worrying about the consequences, because they know that not all choices in life can be right, even for the smartest people. Rather than feeling "a sense of powerlessness," they are self-confident in life, a quality that allows them to advance more rapidly in their jobs than their more timid peers. Rather than having a background that included "territory boundness," they traveled more as children and explored the world with their parents.

This type of person I originally labeled as "allocentric," from the root Latin word "allo" to reflect their varied interests. For my website, I now call them "*venturers*" to emphasize their exploring nature. Now I had a full psychographic spectrum. On a nationwide sample, I found that it distributed beautifully across a normal curve and I divided it into six segments. With a 15-item scale, I could classify people into these segments. Various studies for clients indicated that media habits varied across these groups as did the types of products they purchased and their interest in new technology. I was able to use the system to help position and change the products and services offered by travel providers and destinations, and change the focus of their advertising campaigns. The benefits from this research increased. I discovered that the concept was generic and could help other types of clients that I had now picked up, such as car companies (repositioning BMW and Saab), beverage companies (used by Molson's Brewery world-wide), and others.

The psychic rewards of this effort were great. I found a vocation that challenged me and captivated my interests to the same level as music. I loved doing client-focused studies. Each project was unique, the challenges to understand complex issues in the marketplace and come up with suitable answers were considerable, and one could see the results put into action. Some clients won advertising awards based on research I had done (Hong Kong, BMW, FedEx), another psychic benefit. The system and its uses for travel providers are explained more completely in my book, *Leisure Travel: A Marketing Handbook* (2004).

Building a Stable Company

Small businesses confront risks and challenges not faced by larger organizations with long histories and sizable staff. To borrow a phrase, I was a one-man band at the beginning. I had to go on marketing trips and sales calls, do the research, write reports, stay on top of expenses, look for office space and furniture as we grew, hire and fire, handle legal issues, deal with the Internal Review Service (I will never know why they target small businesses so much), oversee accounting, and much more. The biggest challenge is always keeping new business coming in the door. After you have sold some projects, you have to work on these, leaving little time for marketing and sales. But if you do not continue to market your company, you will face a drought very quickly. I would remind my staff that we had a three-month-old company, by which I meant that we had enough business to keep our doors open for three months, but we had to develop new business to survive beyond that point.

Because of the airline project and the client contacts it provided, travel dominated my company early on and it continued that way until I left. Ultimately, I worked for more clients across a broad spectrum of the industry than any other organization. We also became an important supplier to automobile companies, conducting car clinics and image/positioning studies, and picked up some media, retail, and food/beverage companies. The life was not easy—constant 60–70-hour weeks, lots of traveling to call on clients, and many disappointments when we lost projects on which we bid. But I was my own man. Quite different from my life as a musician where

I had lots of free time but was subject to the whims of a band leader or orchestra conductor. An entrepreneurial research career was still a great choice in spite of the challenges.

My company was acquired by Planning Research Corporation, and I spent several years in an extremely happy environment. It had a stable of companies that focused on economics research, human resources, transportation studies, real estate research, and its core business of software development and operations research for the federal government. We were able to bid jointly on projects that required multiple skill sets, and I learned much from these other disciplines. But the biggest benefit was being around Robert W. Krueger, the founder of Planning Research Corporation, the first private for-profit government service supplier. I considered him an absolute genius, and I learned about how to run a company more effectively, ways to control and manage expenses, use a cash basis accounting system rather than the more common accrual method, and how to cost bids when some variables are unknown. But all good things must come to an end, it seems. After I had completed my obligation period (about four years), I had a disagreement with Krueger on how to manage a large New York-based advertising research company over which I had been put in charge. I worked to control their wild spending habits that cut into profits without producing benefits. The senior people of the company did not like these restrictions and secretly approached him to object to changes I had put into place. Unfortunately, he agreed to some of their demands on the spot. I told Krueger that he had made a classic management mistake by undercutting my effectiveness with his actions. He refused to change; so after considerable thought, I gave notice and left the company. We maintained our close relationship through the remainder of his life, and I even used him as a consultant at various times. Our disagreement was on management philosophy and was not personal.

I took a year off to recover from years of a strenuous schedule and spend more time with my family (now two sons). But I got bored tending to the garden. I missed the intellectual challenges. I had no plans to return to the fray until one day I got a call from Molson's Brewery in Canada. They said that they were not getting what they wanted from my old company or other suppliers they used after I left; they asked if I would take on a new project for them. I traveled to Toronto and agreed to do the study. This set the stage for a new company that I simply called Plog Research, Inc., to make it easy for clients to identify and find me.

With the new company, I chartered a different course based on what I had learned from my previous experiences. One, it became a full service company (most operations would be in-house). Ultimately, we had our own computers, a large coding operation to handle questionnaires, and a center to complete telephone surveys. When I found that I could not control coffee klatch discussions in the coding room, I let the best coders work at home on a piece rate basis. We sampled and double-checked their work in-house. Two, staff now had more specialized functions than before. My previous model assumed that I could hire enough professional staff that could do all the things I did—write proposals, make sales calls, direct the studies, write the final reports, and present results to clients. But, as I discovered, few persons possess this array of skills. In the new organization, some staff focused on client contact, others wrote reports, and still others might present results to clients. Three, I purposely took on more speaking opportunities at associations and meetings of professional groups. These provided access to new client prospects and helped to build a reputation. Finally, most important, I focused on syndicated projects with a goal of building this to at least half of our business mix.

Syndications, in a research setting, are multiclient frequent projects that provide trend data over time. I learned from a previous recession that custom studies quickly get cut from client budgets in difficult times, but not syndicated projects because these provide trend data that clients consider essential to their yearly planning efforts. Thus, syndications provide stability during uncertain times. They also offer another big benefit. After a sufficient number of clients have been signed to cover costs, every new client contributes heavily to profit. Ultimately, they require very little marketing, since clients tend to sign up year after year. I was able to develop several of these for airlines, including a survey of 90,000 US airport distributed mail back questionnaires ("TravelTrak"), a 60,000 in-airport mail back questionnaire for international airlines ("International Travel-Trak"), a twice a year survey among frequent fliers of their perceptions of the competitiveness of the major airline frequent flier programs, and a 10,000 annual sample of an intensive study of the travel habits of a random sample of the US population (American Traveler Survey). Obviously, not all attempts at syndications were successful, but these efforts were still a great way to build a more stable and growing business.

I also developed a number of new approaches to measuring common problems. These were not syndications, but the same approach could be used with multiple clients and success in past efforts helped in the selling process. Several examples come to mind: *The Immersion Index*. Primarily used for magazines, this approach presented a list of active vs. passive adverbs to respondents and they were asked to select which of these applied to specific magazines. Active adverbs demonstrated a higher degree of involvement by readers in a magazine such as engrossing, stimulating, captivating, exciting, and engaging. Passive adverbs implied a more casual attitude in reading the publication, as relaxing, interesting, soothing, and intriguing. For *Time Magazine*, I was able to demonstrate that it scored higher on the Immersion Index than its chief competitor, *Newsweek*, an important criterion for advertisers who constantly need assurance that their ads are in a publication that engages its readers to a high degree.

A second approach was labeled *AutoTrak*. This scale addressed the problem of most measures of loyalty and involvement of car owners with their new cars overlooked. The typical approach asked the owners to rate various features of their new cars and then summed up the total to get a score that ranked cars on how well their owners liked them. But, it had a critical flaw. Not all elements are equally important to different owners. For example, gas mileage ranks high in importance among buyers of economy cars, but much less so among owners of luxury vehicles. Performance and handling score higher in importance for import buyers than for those who purchase domestic products. The approach I used required respondents to rate a long list of features in different categories, including *external* design, interior design, quality of fit and finish, performance and handling, gas mileage, amenities, and more. Then I required respondents to rate the importance of each item in their buying process, and finally rate the overall categories in importance. Now it is possible to develop a final index based on factoring in the relative weights of these variables—an index that is far less arbitrary than simple summing up of individual scores. The same concept, obviously, can be applied to a variety of research settings.

A third approach was entitled *PriceMax*. This approach is based on the work of two Dutch economists and had the purpose of determining acceptable price levels for products. They developed a scale that asked respondents to indicate at what price a product seemed so expensive they would no longer consider purchase, and at what price it seemed so cheap that they would doubt its quality. It offered a considerable advantage over commonly used questionnaire-based approaches to pricing in which people were simply asked their degree of likelihood of purchase at a particular price level. With this approach, only a single price point could be offered to a respondent, because any other price point (whether lower or higher) would be biased based on their first response. Thus, large samples were required to achieve reliable results. As can happen, the researcher may misjudge appropriate price points, either starting too low or too high in the questionnaire, further wasting the results. The Dutch index used every respondent in a highly efficient manner. But, their results were variable and not usable in projects without some modification. Through some testing, I was able to put tighter limits on the parameters and ultimately show clients when their products were underpriced and they could increase pricing or that their goods or services were now overpriced. Extremely useful also was the fact that the index allowed playing with the numbers to determine overall revenue and profit totals based on how many unit sales were lost as prices increased. Thus, clients could determine at what pricing level they could maximize profit even if they sold fewer units. Car companies used it and Marriott Hotels adopted the system to continually monitor the pricing of their rooms.

A final and fourth approach employed was the *Relative Value Index*. This approach handled pricing issues in a different way and was particularly useful when questions of pricing were more limited. For instance, a hotel in Times Square wanted to know if they could move their pricing up to equal that of the large nearby Marriott. From my extremely large Survey America sample (about 600,000 previous respondents), I identified business travelers who visited New York City. The questionnaire asked them to indicate a price at which they would consider staying at a half dozen New York City hotels, including my client's and the Marriott. The results pointed out that my client would have to price from $12 to $15 a room night cheaper than the Marriott or it would lose clients.

Other indexes, scales, and approaches were developed to serve clients based on individual needs and circumstances. My feeling was always that I would have to be creative in order to capture new business, and never sit on past laurels. The marketplace is too fast paced to allow slow adapters to do very well.

CONCLUSION

The consuming passion of music—even with its problems related to bad gigs, domineering leaders/conductors, bad contractors, and terrible hours and working conditions—made it difficult to find another field that could capture my interests to the same degree. The vast majority of my friends stayed in the business and tried to talk me out of leaving. Since I had dedicated myself to a musical career from the age of about eight and had so many great experiences, it made the choice even more difficult. Why would I want to throw away something for which I had practised hours every day for years and had competed with some of the best to earn my position and acceptance among fellow musicians?

But in retrospect, it was absolutely the right decision, and for reasons I had not even imagined at the time. The music business has since deteriorated to the point that it is difficult to get enough work even for the top guys. Digital music eliminated the necessity of having an orchestra. It is now common to go to musicals and discover that the orchestra is a virtual CD that can be sped up or slowed down without changing the pitch depending upon the pace of the show. Even the chorus singing is typically prerecorded and only actor/dancers appear on stage. The rise of rock stars has elevated electric guitars to a new position of prominence, and there may not be a brass man among the bunch. Major motion picture studios and TV networks no longer have contract orchestras, and hit movies sometimes record with only a handful of musicians on synthesizers (effectively started with the film *Chariots of Fire*). The mental strain on those who have remained is huge because of the uncertainty of finding work. Membership rolls at most local musicians' union headquarters around the country are now about half of what they were at one time. I would have faced these same deteriorating conditions had I remained.

It took a long time of sticking my head into various fields before I finally decided on the career I wanted. But the choice could not have been better. Research is intriguing, especially in the field of travel and tourism, and I never thought that I was not learning something new because this is ever-changing industry. Starting a company with the opportunity to report to noone but myself gave me the freedom to make my own mistakes, rather than having to live with the decisions of others. Working with businesses proved fascinating and rewarding. They need help and they respect quality research. A true joy was seeing recommendations put into action and often on a tight time schedule, an experience very different from academic life where thoughts and ideas may never truly gain wide acceptance or public exposure. I experienced burnout at times, but never boredom. Each day, each study, each client all demanded new approaches and new skills. Contrary to the view of much of the public, I found most business people to be straight forward, honest, and dedicated to helping their companies grow and prosper. When I found a company that did not fit these high standards, or they ignored my recommendations, I dropped them. I stopped working for domestic auto companies; they were not listening. They thought their dominant market share could not be chipped away. So, I just concentrated on import auto companies. They knew they faced big challenges and were open to ideas about how to overcome these obstacles.

Of all the industries with which I consulted, travel was always the most fascinating and interesting. Let us face it: Most of us like to travel, and studying its dynamics and reporting on trends and consumer desires provide interesting insights into the psychology of people. Destinations always ranked high on subjects I liked to investigate. They typically convey strong images of what they offer and the kinds of people they attract. Any attempt to reposition a place had to start with the realization that the ambience it creates in people's minds has to be a contributor to the final recommendations. My only disappointment with the travel industry is that their marketing budgets are small compared to most other major industries. This means that it is more difficult to build a high-volume company if clients have smaller budgets. But so be it; I had a fun ride.

I cannot say if anyone else would have the same psychic needs and goals as I have. There are lots of ways to make a living in research, and most of them quite rewarding. I have always tried to stay close to the academic community, because so many good ideas originate in these halls of learning. I have been fortunate that they, in turn, have allowed me to be an editor of a couple of their journals. So, in saying Auf Wiedersehen, I hope I have not bored too many readers with what is my most personal story ever.

Chapter 4

This I Believe

Abraham Pizam
University of Central Florida, USA

Abraham Pizam <apizam@mail.ucf.edu> was born in Romania and completed a bachelor's degree in sociology and political science at the Hebrew University of Jerusalem. He also undertook and successfully completed a master's degree at New York University and a PhD in business administration from Cornell University, USA. After a period as chair of the Hotel & Tourism Administration Department at the University of Haifa, Israel, he spent some time at the University of Massachusetts before joining the University of Central Florida where he has been a founding chair in the hospitality and tourism program and now holds the position of eminent scholar chair and dean of the University of Central Florida's Rosen College of Hospitality Management. His many publications edited with colleagues include the *International Encyclopedia of Hospitality Management, Tourism, Security and Safety: From Theory to Practice, Consumer Behavior in Travel and Tourism,* and *Crime and International Security Issues.* He has published in many journals including Annals of Tourism Research, Journal of Travel Research, Tourism Management, and Cornell Hotel and Restaurant Quarterly. He also serves as the Editor in Chief of the International Journal of Hospitality Management.

The Study of Tourism: Foundations from Psychology
Tourism Social Science Series, Volume 15, 63–78
Copyright © 2011 by Emerald Group Publishing Limited
All rights of reproduction in any form reserved
ISSN: 1571-5043/doi:10.1108/S1571-5043(2011)0000015007

INTRODUCTION

My journey into the world of hospitality and tourism began accidently, since like some of my contemporary colleagues, I neither studied these fields formally nor obtained a degree in them. In 1968, I arrived at Cornell University to do a PhD in organizational behavior at what today is known as the Johnson School of Business Administration. For the following two years, I spent my time taking courses and doing research in a building that was across the street from the renowned Cornell School of Hotel Administration.

Though I was aware of the fame and reputation of the school, I did not take any interest into what was going on in that building and it never even crossed my mind to visit it or get to know someone who was teaching, doing research, or studying in this field. My lack of interest was instigated by repeated unflattering remarks made by some of the faculty members in the business school who strongly believed that the hotel school was nothing but a "glorified trade school" that had no place in an ivy league university.

While studying in the business school, I took a strong interest in hospital administration and worked with some faculty members who had expertise in this area. Upon completing my PhD in 1970, I joined the faculty of the Leon Recanati Graduate School of Business Administration at Tel-Aviv University, Israel, where I taught and conducted research in the field of organizational behavior and human resources management. One day, a few years into my career as an organizational behavior and human resources management researcher, I was called into the office of my supervisor who made me an offer that I could not refuse. Since both of us were educated in the United States, he chose to make his offer in English rather than Hebrew. He informed me that the university has received a grant from the Israeli Ministry of Tourism to start a degree program in hospitality and tourism. Since no one at the university possessed a degree in these fields, he looked at the records of the junior faculty members to find if any of them have studied something similar to hospitality and tourism. Having discovered that in my PhD studies at Cornell I took a strong interest in hospital administration, he decided to invite me for a talk about making a change in my careers. He then proceeded by saying that since the difference between hospital and hospitality is "ity" I might consider a change in career and return to Cornell University to do a postdoc program in hospitality and tourism management and then come back to Tel-Aviv University to start an undergraduate degree program.

I looked upon this as an opportunity of a lifetime. In 1972, I returned to Cornell University to do a 12-month informal postdoc program under the supervision of Dean Beck of the Hotel School. While there, I took numerous courses both in hospitality and tourism management, but fell in love with the latter. Unfortunately, during my stay, the Yom Kippur War broke and as a result, incoming tourism to Israel came to a standstill. Thus, when I returned to Tel-Aviv University and started a degree program in hospitality and tourism management, there were not enough registered students to justify the existence of the degree program and the university decided to abort it. Faced with the choice of going back to my old field of study (organizational behavior) or join an American university that had a strong hospitality and tourism program, I decided to choose the latter and moved to the University of Massachusetts in Amherst.

Exposure to Tourism

Among the works that I read while attending Cornell University was a book written by Sir George Young (1973) titled *Tourism: Blessing or Blight*. This book influenced my career in a significant manner and was directly responsible for my first stream of research in tourism, namely the social impacts of tourism. Being intrigued by Young's propositions, I decided to empirically test them and conducted a number of studies in Massachusetts intended to measure the residents' perceptions of the costs and benefits of tourism development to their communities. I kept an interest in this subject area and over the years continued to study it empirically in other destinations. Having realized that one of the negative impacts of tourism on destinations is an increase in crimes and other illegal activities, I branched into the subject of tourism safety and security and published numerous empirical and theoretical articles and two edited books on this subject.

For several years, I was engaged in researching and publishing articles on the macro aspects of tourism, such as tourism planning and development, tourist–host social relations, tourism as a change agent, tourism as a promoter of peace, the environmental impacts of tourism, the impact of energy prices and gasoline shortage on tourism demand, rural and farm tourism, citizens' participation in tourism planning, and more. While busy with these, I renewed my interests into its micro characteristics and more specifically into the human resources management, consumer behavior, and cross-cultural aspects of the management and marketing of hospitality and tourism enterprises.

In the human resources management stream of research, I conducted a number of empirical studies on such issues as workers' values and motivations, tourism manpower, employees' job satisfaction, burnout, absenteeism, turnover, employees' alienation, depression, career success, training and education needs, and other related subjects.

In the consumer behavior research stream, I have conducted several studies on tourist satisfaction, expenditure patterns, values as determinants of tourist behavior, effects of destination awareness and familiarity, tourist sensation seeking and risk taking, attitudes toward animal-based attractions, and other topics related to consumer behavior.

Finally, in the last 20 years, I have been and continue to be fascinated by the realm of cross-cultural management and marketing. Thus, I have examined such issues as tourism as a factor of change, the impact of tourism on ethnic attitudes, the effect of nationality on tourist behavior, the role of culture in the management and operations of hospitality and tourism enterprises, the effects of nationality vs. industry culture, and emerging issues in this research stream.

Now, after 40 years in academia, I still continue to do empirical research though at a slower pace because of my administrative responsibilities. But at the same time, I feel more liberated in sharing with my colleagues and graduate students my values and beliefs about our field and its future direction. Therefore, in the subsequent part of this chapter I will share with the readers my true feelings and opinions on a range of subjects that I call "In these I believe." I borrowed this title from a US National Public Radio program called "This I believe" in which US listeners discussed in an essay format the core beliefs that guide their daily lives.

THIS I BELIEVE

The Travel, Tourism, and Hospitality Industries Are Not One and the Same

In my opinion, the travel industry is made up of all those businesses that move people (passengers) from one place to another via various modes of transportation. The tourism industry is composed of all businesses that provide goods and services to tourists. The hospitality industry is made up of businesses that provide accommodation, food and beverage, and meetings to tourists, travelers, and local residents.

When closely examining the above definitions, I quickly surmised that the travel and tourism industries are not one and the same and tourism is not a subset of the travel industry. While it is true that the travel industry provides transportation to tourists and nontourists alike, the tourism industry comprises businesses such as accommodation, food and beverage, meeting and events, that provide nontransportation services and goods to tourists; thus, the tourism industry is at the same time more and less than the travel industry. It is more than the travel industry because it also provides nontravel goods and services to tourists such as accommodation, restaurants, events, and time-share facilities, and it is less than the travel industry because the travel industry provides many modes and forms of passenger transportation to nontourists (locals) as well. But as can be seen from Figure 1, the two industries have quite a few things in common and overlap significantly.

The tourism and hospitality industries are neither identical nor interchangeable. While tourism is composed of many goods and services that are produced by hospitality enterprises, these hospitality businesses provide goods and services to nontourists (local residents and nontourists) as well. Indeed, in some communities where tourists do not visit, the hospitality industry provides goods and services only to locals. Furthermore, a number of these businesses, such as clubs, institutional foodservices, and assisted living facilities, provide goods and services to locals only and have absolutely nothing to do with tourists. Thus, as shown in Figure 1, the hospitality industry is at the same time more and less than the tourism industry. It is more because it consists of many businesses that are strictly for locals, such as institutional foodservices, clubs, and assisted living facilities, and less than the tourism industry because the tourism industry is composed

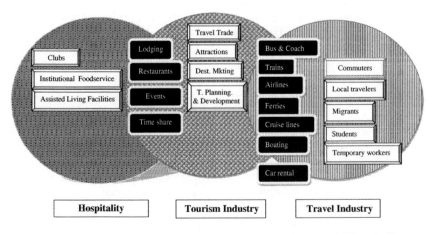

Figure 1 The Relationship among Travel, Tourism, and Hospitality.

of many nonhospitality businesses, such as travel trade (travel agents and tour operators), tourist attractions (built and natural sites and events), passenger transport companies (airlines, coaches, cruise lines, rental cars), and macro issues at the destination level (destination planning and development and destination management and marketing). As was the case with the relationship between the travel and tourism industries, the hospitality and tourism industries overlap in numerous ways.

Academic Programs Should Focus on the Micro, Not the Macro Levels

While I fully admit that the study of both hospitality and tourism is multidisciplinary and both have their roots in various disciplines, such as economics, sociology, anthropology, psychology, geography, engineering, regional planning, food science and nutrition, political science, and more, it is my conviction that the main focus of our research and teaching should be on the management of hospitality and tourism organizations, be they in the private or public sectors. Therefore, in my opinion, hospitality and tourism studies are *mainly* organizational studies conducted at the micro level rather than social studies that examine the tourism or hospitality phenomena at the macro level. To this extent, I disagree with the "hospitableness" approach suggested by colleagues like Lashley and Morrison (2000) who refer to hospitality as a set of transactions between hosts and guests, together with cultural and religious obligations associated with the two roles. Such colleagues (e.g., Lashley 2000) suggest that commercial practitioners who provide professional hospitality services, such as food, beverages, and accommodation, should be inspired and influenced by the other two spheres of hospitality: the social/cultural and the domestic/private spheres. This view has led its followers to advocate the "liberation" of hospitality management education from its vocational and management orientation (Morrison and O'Mahony 2003).

To me, modern hospitality is a set of commercial transactions between sellers and buyers: one that has very little relevance to the private domain of "host–guest relations." Therefore, hospitality and tourism management curricula should be applied to business curricula that provide the students with a set of skills and knowledge to operate and/or manage hospitality or tourism organizations. Though there should be room in the typical curriculum to discuss macro issues such as the social and economic impacts of tourism on the society, or principles of tourism planning and development at local, regional, or national levels, the majority of the curriculum should be devoted to such subjects as the operation, marketing, human resources, accounting, and finance of hospitality or tourism organizations. Our duty as educators should be to prepare our students for managerial positions in the hospitality and tourism industries, the absolute majority of which are in the commercial private sector (Pizam 2008b).

The Subject in This Field Should Be Management—Not Education

I strongly believe that hospitality academics ought to study the hospitality or tourism industries and not themselves and/or their institutions. I have no objection to educational-oriented studies being conducted by school officials and administrators for the purpose of setting benchmarks and improving academic performance in their institutions. What I object is when these educational-oriented studies become the main areas of research and investigation for hospitality or tourism academics and PhD students and when our professional journals become inundated with articles reporting their results. If our mission is to prepare students for successful careers in these industries and help them to solve their problems, then our research efforts should be aimed in this direction. I suspect that the motivation of academics and PhD students who are engaged in the conduct of studies that focus on faculty and students is simply convenience and ease of data collection. After all, it is much easier to get a sample of educators or students to respond to a mail or Web survey than a sample of managers and/or customers. But, this is not a proper excuse. We are hospitality and/or tourism academics—not educational experts, we grant degrees in our field— not educational management degrees. Therefore, it is best to leave the study of pedagogy and educational institutions to our colleagues in schools of education and concentrate our research on the hospitality and tourism industries; that is our *raison d'être* (reason for existence) (Pizam 2003).

Academics and Their Industry Counterparts Should Dialogue

Having been part of the hospitality and tourism academia and interacted with thousands of practitioners over the last 40 years, it has become evident to me that an absolute majority of the practitioners did not read any of the main journals or research reports that academics and researchers use for publishing the results of their studies. If this is so for the industry as a whole, it is no wonder that the knowledge and information that are generated in the laboratories and offices of academic and research institutions never find their way to the shop floors of hospitality and tourism enterprises. When privately inquiring as to why practitioners do not read the research reports published or presented at conferences, I was politely told that these reports are lengthy, boring, and written with a heavy dose of technical jargon that "puts people off."

If this is indeed the case and practitioners are not reading or listening to what academics/researchers write or say, and academics/researchers do not really care if their work is being read or applied to real-life situations, then both sides are to be blamed for not talking, listening, and learning from each other. I believe that academics/researchers should study issues that are of importance to the practitioners and should make a concerted effort to write their reports in a succinct and business-oriented style. The practitioners, on the other hand, should take an interest in what the academics and researchers do and recognize the potential value of the knowledge that is generated from these research reports to the successful operation of their businesses. After all, that is exactly what happens in the life sciences, physical sciences, engineering, and education fields, where academics, researchers, and practitioners talk and listen to each other regularly and benefit from each other's work and wisdom. This is what should happen in our field as well (Pizam 2006).

Consumer Research Should Be Done with Real Customers—Not Students

Unfortunately, during the last three decades, I have noticed a growing trend in using students as proxy for real tourists or consumers of hospitality products and services. This practice is so prevalent that in some courses the instructors incorporate the collection of data from students as an integral part of their curriculum. This is done not because the instructors/researchers believe that students in hospitality or tourism programs are true representatives of real tourists or customers, but mostly because it is convenient and cheap to use them.

I perfectly understand that our faculty members are under pressure to "publish or perish"; reports of empirical studies are more publishable in top-tier journals than theoretical ones; conducting empirical research with real tourists or customers is very costly and it is very difficult to obtain grants and contracts to do empirical research in the hospitality and tourism fields. However, none of these in my opinion justify the use of student subjects as proxies for tourists and customers and then claiming that the results obtained in these studies are applicable to other tourist populations. If this trend continues, then our entire body of knowledge of consumer behavior in tourism and hospitality will be built on the results of studies conducted with subjects who were induced or coerced to participate in these studies and hence did not express real opinions. But most importantly, the results of these studies will be flawed and nonrepresentative of real tourists or customers.

Therefore, I advocate placing a moratorium on the publication of consumer behavior studies that were conducted with student subjects and claim that their results are representative of other populations. It goes without saying that studies that are conducted with student subjects for the purpose of understanding their behavior as consumers or tourists are fully legitimate and should not be placed under such a moratorium.

Academic Research Has Advanced to the Level of Respectability

In the last century, hospitality and tourism research has advanced from being Rodney Dangerfield—an American Hollywood actor whose "shtick" (show business gimmick or gag) was "I get no respect," to becoming Aretha Franklin a major artist who is getting a lot of R-E-S-P-E-C-T (which happens to be the title of one of her most famous songs) from peers and fans alike. During these times, academic research in hospitality and tourism has gone through four phases as follows.

Storytellers: My Life in the Hospitality/Tourism Industry. The researchers in this period were ex-practitioners who retired into academia. Their main objective was to teach "college kids" how to perform jobs in the hospitality or tourism industries by sharing stories from their own experience in one or several jobs. Their writings were descriptive and in most cases lacked any systematic analysis. Because of the above, these stories (or case studies) could not be generalizable to other situations.

Profilers: Who Does What for Whom? As time went by, the ex-practitioner academics came under pressure from their university peers and/or supervisors to do research and "publish or perish." Having little or no training in research methodology, they turned to survey research and conducted studies that identified various profiles of individuals or organizations in the hospitality or tourism industries. These studies had no theoretical underpinnings and did not state or test hypotheses. The statistical methods used in these studies were descriptive rather than inferential.

Copycats: Let's Borrow from Our Big Brothers in Social Science and Business Administration. The "copycatters" were newly minted graduates of business administration, social science, or education doctoral programs, who moved into hospitality or tourism departments at major universities. Having been trained in research methodology and various scientific disciplines (food science, marketing, management, geography, and other related fields), they borrowed the theories and concepts developed in those disciplines and used or applied them in the conduct of empirical inferential research in hospitality or tourism settings. The research methods used are for the most part advanced and up to date. Though these studies extended our knowledge into the realm of hospitality and/or tourism enterprises, they lacked originality.

Innovators: Let Them Come and Learn from Us. The innovators are the third or fourth generation of hospitality or tourism trained academics. They have a high level of comfort with up-to-date statistical methods of analysis, are pressured to publish in top-tier journals, and make significant contribution to knowledge. But most importantly, many of them have made successful attempts to develop completely new theories that apply not only to hospitality or tourism enterprises but also to other service organizations such as hospitals, religious, and voluntary service organizations.

In conclusion, as indicated above, hospitality and tourism research has moved from the position of being a Rodney Dangerfield to being an Aretha Franklin and thus commanding full R-E-S-P-E-C-T from our colleagues in other disciplines. Therefore, paraphrasing a 1980s' Virginia Slim cigarette commercial: "You've come a Long Way Baby" (Pizam 2008c).

Every Tourist Is Like All, Like Some, and Like No Other Tourist

As some readers may recognize, the above statement is a paraphrase of a famous quote by Kluckhohn and Murray (1967), which suggested that "Every man is like all men, like some men, and like no man." This quote is highly relevant to the tourism and hospitality settings. In some aspects, all tourists are alike; in others, they are similar to some groups but different than others; and in a few aspects, tourists are unique individuals.

First, all tourists regardless of their demographic profile, national or ethnic culture, motivation, purpose of travel, and/or other characteristics have several things in common, beyond the desire to satisfy their lower level needs for food, drink, and shelter while away from home. As has been suggested by various tourism researchers such as Cohen (1972, 1979), Crompton (1981), MacCannell (1976), Nash (1981), Smith (1977), Turner and Ash (1975), and others that tourists, and especially leisure tourists, share common beliefs, values, attitudes, meanings, motives, and knowledge which means that they possess a common "tourist culture" that affects their cognition and behavior while on trips.

Second, tourists can be similar to some but not to all other tourists. We know by now that tourists belonging to certain demographic, ethnic, national, purpose, or motivation groups share some common beliefs, values, tastes, preferences, and behaviors. Thus, they can be segmented accordingly and products or services can be specifically designed to satisfy their needs.

Third, every tourist is like no other tourist since the interaction between his/her physical and psychological characteristics, personality, upbringing, heritage, life, travel experiences, and numerous other factors, make him/her a unique individual. Thus, no matter how much we know about the "tourist culture" and the taste and preferences of each market segment, we will never be able to fully predict the behavior and ultimately the satisfaction of each individual tourist.

Academics Should Play an Advocate Role in Promoting Citizen Participation

As researchers and students of tourism, we have known for quite some time about the possible adverse social and cultural effects that tourism development *might* have on the quality of life of the local residents. We have also known that these negative impacts can be mitigated, if not completely eliminated, by the active participation of the local residents in the process of planning and approving the proposed tourism development projects. But with the exception of doing research on this subject and publishing results in academic journals, we academics chose not to get involved for fearing that in doing so we might alienate the industry that supports us. I consider myself guilty of this passivity; I believe now that being an advocate for citizens' participation in the process of tourism development is good for the local community but is in the best interest of the tourism industry. Therefore, I am proposing that the academic tourism community becomes a strong advocate for participatory tourism development, not just by talking about it but by action research, demonstration projects, and training of citizens.

It Is Duty to Sensitize Students to the Possible Adverse Effects of the Industry

Like in the previous case, after years of studying the hospitality industry, my colleagues and I are aware of the difficult working conditions for many of its employees and the effects that these may have on their quality of life. We know that many of its low-skilled or semiskilled employees work in unpleasant physical surroundings, such as hot, noisy, and poorly ventilated areas, or standing on their feet eight hours or more a day. They have inconvenient night shift, weekend, and holiday working hours, work under constant pressure, and in many instances have to satisfy the whims of hard-to-please customers. For many of them, there are very few, if any, career progression opportunities; further in a majority of cases, their wages are low and significantly below those in other industries. On top of these hardships, employees are required to hide their true feelings of frustration and anger and instructed to manage these emotions so that they are consistent with their job rules, regardless of whether they are discrepant with their internal feelings (a phenomenon that is called emotional labor).

These combined factors cause significant organizational problems, such as low labor efficiency, high labor turnover, and high absenteeism. For employees subject to poor working conditions, the consequences may be physical and emotional ailments, including high blood pressure, chronic depression, alcoholism, marital problems, and high rates of divorce.

Yet, despite the numerous published articles on this subject in the last 50 years, we have failed to teach, inform, and demonstrate to our students and industry partners that these poor conditions still prevalent in many parts of the hospitality and tourism industries are not a "fact of life" and that it is possible to change them and create decent quality conditions for all employees.

Social Responsibility Is Quickly Taking the Center Stage

At present, there are numerous hospitality and tourism enterprises that falsely claim to be socially responsible. For these organizations, putting on the mantle of social responsibility is a marketing ploy aimed at attracting good-natured and concerned consumers by claiming that their businesses embrace full responsibility for the impact of their activities on the environment, consumers, employees, communities, stockholders, and all other members of the public.

Other enterprises join the movement of "responsible tourism/hospitality" or "green tourism/hospitality" because they see a significant economic advantage, such as cutting costs through water and energy conservation, reducing solid waste, rising the productivity of their employees through increased satisfaction, and improving the social and political status and reputation of their organizations in the community. But most importantly, they do this for gaining an advantage over their competitors.

Yet, there is another rapidly growing group of enterprises that are truly socially responsible—not because it is economically or politically advantageous, but because it is the "right thing to do." The number of these companies in the hospitality and tourism industries, though relatively small at present, will continue to grow as they start feeling good about themselves and experience the economic, social, and political rewards of their actions. As their numbers continue to grow, all others will have no choice but to join them or otherwise be out of business (Pizam, 2008a).

Professionalism Is a Necessary Ingredient in this Field

I am fully convinced that to prepare students for successful careers in the hospitality and tourism industries, it is not sufficient to equip them with the knowledge and skills required to manage businesses and organizations in this field, but it is equally important to impart upon them the right and proper attitudes, values, and beliefs that relate to their chosen professions. If I had to summarize these in an all-encompassing concept, the word professionalism would come to my mind. Professionalism can be defined in numerous ways, but the simplest and most enlightened one that I found was by an unknown author who said "Professionalism is not the job you do, but how you do it." I realize that though this definition is impressive and catchy, it still does not say much about how one "should do one's job" in a professional manner. Therefore, I searched for more specific definitions and I found a few in the fields of medicine and law. According to some authors and professional associations (Association of American Medical Colleges 1999; New Mexico Commission on Professionalism 1999), professionalism is an amalgamation of an array of appearances and behaviors, such as neatness, good grooming, good manners, good taste, civility, proper speech, and the like; an assortment of technical and conceptual skills and a commitment to maintaining competence in a given body of knowledge; and a set of internalized character strengths, values, and attitudes directed toward high-quality service to others, including ethical and moral conduct, concerns for others, honesty, integrity, fairness, sound judgment, respect for the rule of law, and commitment to excellence.

The above authors uniformly agree that professionals demonstrate these characteristics both on and off the job. They further suggest that character and values of professionalism are built up first in childhood and then strengthened in adulthood through study, training, and work experience. If this is indeed the case, then professionalism needs to be strengthened, as well as taught and practiced, in all of our institutions of higher learning. Talking to many of my colleagues in hospitality and tourism schools about this subject, I found that a majority of them recognize the importance that professionalism plays in the success of their graduates in the hospitality and tourism industries, but very few, if any, incorporated the teaching of professionalism in their curricula and, further, had no formal methods for assessing the professional behaviors of their students.

In other words, most of us recognize the importance of professionalism, but we neither teach it nor verify that while in school or in internships our students practice it. But this situation is not much different in medical or law schools, where the subject of professionalism, according to many faculty and veteran attorneys, is paid only lip service within the curriculum and the professional behavior of their students is hardly, if ever, formally assessed. Thus, I strongly advocate that we revise our curricula and incorporate in them a healthy dose of professionalism that at the same time ought to be practiced and formally assessed while in school or in internships (Pizam 2007).

Our Customers Are Industry and the Society at Large—Not Our Students

In this day and age of assertive consumerism, "entitlement generation," and "helicopter parents," there is a growing danger of misperception as to who the customer in higher education is and what the rights of this customer *vis-à-vis* the duties of the education providers are. Some students perceive the educational process as a commercial transaction between sellers and buyers. The students and their parents are the buyers and the colleges and universities are the sellers. This belief leads them to demand full control over the services they purchase and require "total satisfaction or money-back guarantees." The logical conclusion of this argument is that since they pay for these services through tuition or taxes, they have the right as consumers to determine the makeup and delivery of the curriculum, the individual course requirements, and even the grades that they are entitled to receive. Thus, over the last few years, my colleagues and I have had numerous student grievances over grades, complaints about faculty members who are requiring their students to do "too much work." We heard such demands as eliminating mandatory attendance requirements; deleting mathematics or other general education courses from the curriculum, since these are not relevant to their future jobs; allowing students to enter and leave classes anytime they wish; abolishing internship requirements; replacing existing textbooks with cheaper or friendlier ones; and terminating instructors who are "too tough and demanding" or "stingy graders."

It is my strong belief that the customer in hospitality or tourism education is not the student but the two industries and society at large. The student is the "product" that we shape, mold, and prepare for leadership positions in our field. If this product is imperfect and does not satisfy the needs of hospitality and tourism businesses and society at large, our students will not be hired and ultimately we will be out of business. Therefore, students should have little if any "entitlement" to control the process of "production." But, since they are human beings, let me clarify my position and state that all students should possess all the rights that every citizen possesses in a democratic society. But these rights should not be confused with consumer rights that exist between sellers and buyers.

CONCLUSION

A synthesis of the remarks and belief asserted in these previous paragraphs represents a way of concluding my advice and perspectives to the future tourism and hospitality educators, researchers, and students. I have argued that the travel, tourism, and hospitality industries are not one and the same and offer areas of exclusivity in their operations as well as areas of overlap. I consider that academic programs in hospitality and tourism should focus mainly on the micro skills, which are the highly useful and in demand technical and functional attributes of tourism and hospitality education, rather than the broad overarching sociological and macro concerns. For research, the emphases should be the hospitality and/or tourism management activities, businesses, and practices rather than hospitality or tourism education. There is a strong belief I have that hospitality and tourism academics should talk and listen to their counterparts in the industry but there is a reciprocal need to develop a two-way interchange in these interactions.

Consumer behavior research in hospitality and/or tourism settings should be done with real customers and not with college students. I believe a good case can be made that academic research in hospitality and tourism has advanced to an acceptable level of respectability. I believe that every tourist is like all tourists, like some tourists, and like no other tourist; an important implication of this view is to see commonality but respect differences in research investigations and in the interaction that graduates should have with tourists. Academics have several duties to their students, some of which are consistent with the growing importance of sustainable, ethical, and professional behavior throughout the sector. In particular, hospitality and tourism academics should play an advocacy role in promoting citizen participation in the process of tourism development. Additionally, it is the educator's duty to sensitize students to the possible adverse effects that the hospitality and tourism industries might have on the quality of life of its employees and their families. For us as academics, our customers are the hospitality and tourism industries and the society at large not just the students themselves.

This book has given me the opportunity to express and share my values and beliefs for the benefit of those who are currently pursuing or will pursue the academic study of hospitality and tourism management. I hope the beliefs are valuable to some and are at least considered as topics for discussion by coming generations of tourism researchers and practitioners.

Chapter 5

Marketing Science Perspectives of Tourism

Josef A. Mazanec
Vienna University of Economics and Business, Austria

Josef A. Mazanec <josef@mazanec.com> is emeritus professor of business administration in tourism and was head of the Institute for Tourism and Leisure Studies, Vienna University of Economics and Business, Austria (1981–2010). Currently, he is full professor at the Department of Tourism and Hospitality Management, MODUL University Vienna. His research interests are in marketing and management science applications to tourism and leisure operations, consumer behavior, and multivariate methods. He has (co)authored numerous journal articles, contributed articles, and books in the fields of marketing and tourism research. He serves on the editorial boards of a dozen tourism and management journals, holds membership of the major marketing and tourism research associations, and is also a founding member of the International Academy for the Study of Tourism. In the last decade, he has been heavily involved in working with international colleagues as well as researchers in his own country and has been a key figure in producing the CABI volumes *Consumer Psychology of Tourism, Hospitality and Leisure*.

The Study of Tourism: Foundations from Psychology
Tourism Social Science Series, Volume 15, 79–92
Copyright © 2011 by Emerald Group Publishing Limited
All rights of reproduction in any form reserved
ISSN: 1571-5043/doi:10.1108/S1571-5043(2011)0000015008

INTRODUCTION

Involving the reader in an autobiographic exercise is not a high-flying goal, unless it is linked to the ambition of demonstrating one's personal learning experience. By doing this, I hope to create surplus value for both the senior and junior readership. My senior colleagues may derive satisfaction from being quoted or receiving acknowledgment and confirmation; the junior researchers will certainly benefit from a report about research strategies that were sometimes successful and sometimes ended in failure.

EVOLUTION OF A RESEARCH STRATEGY

For a doctoral student in the 1970s, the *Hochschule für Welthandel* (School of International Trade) in Vienna, now University of Economics and Business (WU), founded in 1898 (similar in spirit to the *Grandes Écoles de Commerce* in France), was an exciting place. Classical traditions of thought such as the Austrian School of Economics met with the holistic approach of Othmar Spann and formed an infant discipline named business administration. For a long time, the approach struggled for scientific awareness and recognition. There was little teaching or guidance on finding a personally convincing position of philosophy of science. We had to explore the literature on our own initiative and discriminate, evaluate, and decide by our own judgment. As I see it today, the variety of scientific approaches with all their diversity of perceived usefulness and problem-solving capacity assist students and scholars in establishing tolerance and humility. One concludes that eclecticism by itself is not evil. The phenomenological and even the most speculative mode of reasoning may serve the purpose of discovery. Some ideas arising from these sources may even later be transformed into empirically testable hypotheses.

In the 1970s, business research in the German-speaking countries stressed the beneficial and purifying effects of critical rationalism on a broader scale. Empirical investigations were gaining importance and started penetrating all subfields of business research. Personally, I became deeply impressed by the precision of language practiced in the writings of Karl Popper, particularly the *Logic of Scientific Discovery* first published in German language in 1934 (my own copy is the 3rd edition, 1969, and I still cherish my little booklet *A World of Propensities*, 1990, with a personal dedication by Sir Karl). One of the most powerful propagators of Popper's philosophy in the intersection area of sociology and economics was Hans Albert. He also became highly influential for my future choice of readings (Albert 1967). This personal influence as well as further literature prepared the ground for my later interest in analytical philosophy and the structuralist "nonstatement" view of theories introduced by Joseph Sneed (1971) and popularized in the German-speaking world by Wolfgang Stegmüller (1969, 1974). I never doubted that the principle of falsifiability provided the "candle in the dark" (Sagan 1996) needed for differentiating between science and metaphysics. This attitude, of course, represents a basic value judgment that found its early expression in a paper on the epistemological position of advertising research (Mazanec 1972). The quest for getting exposed to observation and experience applies to the simplest hypothesis as well as to the more complex, and even serves the "ugly" systems of hypotheses in business and marketing research that many see as lacking the "beauty" and "elegance" of theories in physics (Weinberg 1994). With regard to tourism research, plainly, there is nothing more to say than what Dann, Nash, and Pearce noted in a cogent 1988 *Annals of Tourism Research* article: "… a theory which is not falsifiable is really of little value …" (1988:11).

The nonstatement view of theories became a prolific source of inspiration during the time I was working on my habilitation (Mazanec 1978). If, in physics, a (mature) theory may be considered as consisting of a formal, logically true, and empirically unfalsifiable kernel, plus a set of intended (empirically testable) applications, why not approximate this line of reasoning in business or marketing research? If, for instance, the stochastic process of Brownian motion lends itself to predicting stock prices, or the Newtonian gravity model nicely mimics tourist flows among population centers, many more analogies must be out there. It was the beginning of a research strategy driven by exploring analytical tools that seemed to promise problem-solving potential.

In 1970, John D. C. Little of the Sloan School at MIT published a famous article on "Models and Managers" that changed how management science dealt with "hard" versus "soft" (judgmental) data. At that time, I was enthusiastic about Little's ingenious ADBUDG model for setting advertising appropriations, which he employed to illustrate his point. I was slow in grasping the paper's grandness from an epistemological point of view. While immersed in the process of getting oriented, ideas are sometimes already puzzling and foggy. However, with the hindsight of 35 years, the fuzziness goes away and bits and pieces glue together. Much later, I came to apprehend that Little's notion of the manager's "intuitive model" is just a metaphor for human problem solving in everyday life, *Alles Leben ist Problemlösen* (All Life Is Problem Solving) (Popper 1994); decision making is a life-sustaining activity based on learning by trial and error or, in scientist's parlance, hypothesizing. One may conclude that humans experience the world through their models. Hence, there is a gradual but no fundamental difference between naïve trial-and-error behavior and a model-based approach to business, marketing, or tourism research. Liking it or not, one is a modeler; once realized, one appreciates the position of an "unashamed reductionist" (Hawking 1997). "It is no good appealing to reality because we don't have a model independent concept of reality" (Hawking 1993:38).

From Marketing and Advertising to Tourism

Endowed with a school leaving certificate and a vivid interest in social psychology, my question became what kind of study to choose? A degree in psychology may limit range of options on the labor market and may soon elicit postdecisional regret. Fortunately, WU offered a business specialization in market research and advertising with an apparently strong footing in the behavioral sciences. After diploma graduation, I was accepted as a research fellow and also could acquire practical experience as the Austrian delegate at the European Association of Advertising Agencies. This association held close contact with its American counterpart and a young person could gain an authentic impression of what went on in Madison Avenue. Advertising research of the 1970s was a fascinating blend of consumer behavior, Gestalt psychology, the psychology of emotions, motivation and learning, psychoanalysis, communications research, and the psychology of stereotypes. The last mentioned field would turn out to become significant years later when tourism research, with some time lag compared to consumer behavior, entered serious discussion of destination images and destination branding. Image theory is one of the few topics in marketing research where the literature in German can provide early, highly original, and thoughtful contributions.

On top of my long-lasting memories are two books, Bernt Spiegel's (1961) smart combination of Kurt Lewin's *Field Theory* with Charles Osgood's *Semantic Differential* technique of attitude measurement, and Peter Brückner's (1967) keen treatise on the role of nonverbal information in subliminal expectation building. Before 1980, the German-speaking scholars, and I include myself, committed one big mistake. They did not publish in English. As a striking example, Werner Kroeber-Riel's magnificent book on consumer behavior (1975) would have become a world bestseller, had he written it in English. However, to put things right,

I must state that the most impressive book I came across was *Theory of Buyer Behavior* by Howard and Sheth (1969). I am still convinced that it is the best and most influential book on consumer behavior ever written.

Two articles published in 1979 anticipated applications of analytical methods that resurfaced many years later. In a study of brand image transfer mechanisms, I specified and estimated an advanced version of a Rasch model, Gerhard Fischer's multivariate extension (Fischer 1974; Mazanec 1979a). Many years later, "item response theory" aroused awareness as a rigorous alternative to classical measurement theory (Salzberger 2009) and there is no doubt that contemporary tourism research would greatly benefit from promoting its applications. Another 1979 article reported on a research project that compared the (crisp) partitions gained through a cluster-analytic exchange algorithm with (probabilistic) "latent class analysis" results (Mazanec 1979b). It took 20 more years for an "ancient" technique such as this one to become customary in detecting unobserved (discrete) heterogeneity in explanatory models of consumer and tourist behavior.

The 1980s: Consolidate and Go International

In 1978, I acquired the *venia docendi* for business administration at WU. Three years later, I was promoted to full professor and appointed head of the Institute for Tourism and Leisure Studies. The Institute for Advertising and Market Research, where I had been working as assistant professor, used to maintain regular collaboration with the Austrian National Tourism Organization. Hence, I was involved in their campaign development and pretesting several times. In general, tourism was lagging behind the level of sophistication marketing policies had reached in the branded goods industries, both in central Europe and worldwide. The assessment committee looking for a suitable person to set new priorities, as addressed in two 1979 articles (Mazanec 1979c, 1979d) on target group planning and rational decision-support, obviously shared this view. For a marketing researcher, embarking on a career in the study of tourism, it seemed to be a promising outlook.

The unmistakable mission of the 1980s was internationalization. In Europe, the *Association Internationale d'Experts du Tourisme* was the dominant association of tourism leaders and researchers. Owing to its Swiss origin in 1951, it was focused on the French- and German-speaking countries. Its President, Claude Kaspar, made efforts to extend the service area to overseas regions and strengthen non-European membership. After J. R. Brent Ritchie joined us on the board, the association became better known in North America. The majority of conventions were still organized at venues inside Europe. But I remember well the meeting in Kenya in 1983, and its various debates on tourism development with local policymakers and a visit to the Kenya Utalii College as a particularly instructive example of development aid. In later years, its annual conference also moved to Canada, the Seychelles, Argentina, New Zealand, and Thailand. The Tourist Research Center, a small and club-like subdivision of the association, under the uncompromising and long-term chairmanship of Norbert Vanhove, has been a regular platform for exchanging results and keeping one another updated. With my double responsibilities in marketing and tourism education, I also had to attend the conferences of organizations such as the American Marketing Association, the Academy of Marketing Science, or the European Marketing Academy. Acquiring an international perspective was the common goal of all these associations, but arguably the tourism research community pursued it most vigorously and wholeheartedly. Marketing was definitely second to tourism when appraised for the cosmopolitan attitude of its scholars. The development culminated in the founding of the International Academy for the Study of Tourism in 1988, which we owe to the vision and insistence of Jafar Jafari. Participating in the charter meeting in Spain was an exceptional event and also a lesson in efficient creation of bylaws.

   At WU, a new educational program for a tourism specialization within the business studies had to be conceived and implemented. Given the limited number of semester hours available for teaching the area in the full curriculum, our team chose to build the offerings around the cornerstones of tourist behavior and decision-support for tourism marketing. Our goal was to educate students in core elements of computer-assisted analysis and optimization. We were ambitious in designing a research-oriented program that gradually reduced the hospitality management issues and reinforced the tourism research perspectives. A steady engagement in applied research projects, such as the biennial "Austrian National Guest Survey" with 10,000 personal interviews per year, guaranteed a continuous influx of fresh empirical data. This information of practical relevance provided topical demonstration and case material for educational (learning-by-doing) purposes.

   During the early 1970s, the members of the Club of Rome propagated their view of a finite world. Despite the United Nations World Tourism Organization's regular prediction of continued growth, it was only natural to extrapolate the concept of "limits" to tourism. In an article on the "tourism-leisure ratio," I tried to demonstrate that limits to growth also result from rivaling leisure activities, which curb the consumer's time budget and monetary resources to be invested into travel (Mazanec 1981a). Today, I regret not having pursued these ideas further as they might have contributed an uncommon facet to contemporary sustainability research. Other attempts had longer lasting consequences. When adapting the then novel technique of conjoint analysis to a problem of measuring preferences for savings and investment products (Mazanec 1981b), I did not figure out that conjoint analysis was to become a standard analytical tool in all service industries. As it became apparent over the years, this technique did not only provide decision-support for planning new products and service bundles, it also assisted in solving intricate measurement problems where direct questioning was infeasible. A typical example was optimizing pricing decisions during the period of change from the old national European currencies to the new Euro. When and how during the transitional period should tour operators abandon the local currencies and show their prices in Euro values? Hiding the currency attribute among several other trip product attributes wrapped in a conjoint design leads one to realistic results (Mazanec 2002a). Still later, in an application to city trip products, it turned out that conjoint analysis cleverly lends itself for being combined with log-linear modeling based on paired comparison data (Hatzinger and Mazanec 2007).

The same unexpected development occurred in the field of structural equation modeling that I started exploring (Mazanec 1982, 1983). The beginning of the history of it in marketing research may be dated with Richard Bagozzi's book on causal modeling (1980). It also contained a rare phenomenon with marketing books, a chapter on philosophy of science implications. Given my own dissatisfaction with missing or arbitrary operationalizations, I was excited about the concept of integrating theory (the structural level) and measurement into a unified system of hypotheses that could be jointly subjected to empirical testing. I thought it would relieve marketing and tourism researchers from the temptation of perpetually varying operationalization of their latent constructs. Actually, applications of structural equation modeling in tourism research have risen exponentially (see a recent survey covering 4,627 articles employing 2,086 advanced analytical tools published in six leading journals between 1988 and 2008; Mazanec et al 2010). However, the model did not quite fulfill this promise and there will be more to say about it later.

A study of "how to detect travel market segments" demonstrated the basics of benefit segmentation and argued in favor of using binary measurements of destination or trip product attributes (Mazanec 1984).

The binary data format has gained popularity only recently (Dolnicar and Grün 2007). But the conceptual foundation changed; I abandoned the idea of "detecting" segments and became convinced that the picture of the analyst or manager "generating" market segments is the much better fitting interpretation.

Collaboration with the Austrian National Tourism Organization was particularly intense when Helmut Zolles functioned as a general manager. He was a research-minded person and prepared to experiment with new techniques and procedures. One of them was a nontrivial approach to optimizing the Austrian National Tourism Organization's annual decision on distributing their communications budget to tourism generating markets. For me, this was a unique opportunity to probe the "decision calculus" philosophy in a top-level managerial setting (Little 1970). Basically, it boiled down to the question of how to link the soft data of expert judgments to facts about tourist flows and media survey information. The solution was found in a *Journal of Mathematical Psychology* article to become common wisdom in management science years later. This was Thomas Saaty's (1977) eigenvector method, nowadays known as the analytical hierarchy process that proved to be a promising technique for multiattribute decision making (Hwang and Yoon 1981). Incorporating managerial judgment on market characteristics via this process in an advertising response function framework was the prerequisite for subsequent optimizing by dynamic programming (Mazanec 1986a, 1986b).

Assessing the attractiveness of generating countries is equivalent to portfolio modeling in general management. A destination management organization evaluates its markets in a similar way as a company rates the strengths, weaknesses, opportunities, and threats of its strategic business units. As a consequence, the analytical hierarchy process paved the way for advanced portfolio analysis in tourism. After the WU was invited to join the Community of European Management Schools (now the European top scorer of international management programs in the *Financial Times* ranking), I wrote software and two case studies for its new book series (Hartvig-Larsen 1998; Montana 1994). With updated information on tourist arrivals, bednights, and receipts, they are still in use today.

The 1990s: Method-Driven Approaches Coupled with Services to the Community

The first research initiative of the next decade was a scientific success but a practical failure, too premature to bear immediate fruit. Harald Hruschka, now professor of marketing at Regensburg University in Germany, and I wanted to explore the potential of expert systems for travel counseling. He programmed a prototype in PROLOG. I employed an expert system shell for establishing a PC-based solution very much in line with the standard component parts such as a taxonomy (here of the concepts "trip desired" and "trip offered"), a rule base, and an inference engine (Hruschka and Mazanec 1990). Both solutions were working prototypes with a toy database. When I presented the system at the 1990 Travel and Tourism Research Association Conference in New Orleans, there were vivid signs of interest from fellow researchers and industry practitioners (Mazanec 1990). However, the tour operators we contacted in Europe were reluctant and remained unresponsive regarding a real-world experiment. They shied away from the effort of electronically describing their trip products with a number of key attributes. Years later, when the industry hesitantly grasped the concept of virtual travel agencies, constructing travel recommender systems became fashionable (Fesenmaier et al 2006).

A particularly exciting year was 1992. Earlier I had served on WU-Rector Hans Robert Hansen's advisory board and that role entitled me to apply for a sabbatical. As it worked out, I had the opportunity of spending it as a guest scholar at the Marketing Center of the Sloan School, MIT. More specifically, I gained access to marketing science legends such as John Little, John Hauser, Birger Wernerfelt, and Glen Urban. I also managed to defend Austria's reputation as a wine growing country. John Little had the habit of organizing a monthly wine tasting exercise where participation was mandatory and the team had to guess the quality and price level (both differed widely in this blind test). With good luck, I identified an (unfamiliar) grape as top quality.

A key event during this visit was my presentation of our first experiences with artificial neural network modeling. At that time, the MIT Marketing Group was unaware of these techniques and wondered how an invasive central European came to experiment with such stuff. Regrettably, it was impossible to infiltrate a major US marketing journal with an artificial neural network manuscript before American authors had given sanction to it. But, unsurprisingly, tourism research once more proved its open-mindedness and a neurocomputing approach to market segmentation was published in the inaugural issue of the *Journal of Travel and Tourism Marketing* (Mazanec 1992). Between 1993 and 1999, I published seven more journal articles applying neural network methodology. Teuvo Kohonen's self-organizing map and its derivatives evolved as a particularly intriguing class of methods. Here, I just mention one application example from hospitality management where images of Vienna-based luxury hotels had to be measured and interpreted (Mazanec 1995).

The research focus on classification techniques entailed a marked interest in consumer and tourist typologies. Lifestyles and vacation styles are instantiations of such typologies. The concept of lifestyles became popular in marketing in the early 1970s (Wells 1974) and, since then, has been reanimated several times. The commercial marketing research institutes also embarked on this concept. For example, the Europanel Group generated a unified lifestyle system for 16 European countries. It was tempting to probe the same system in a culturally distant market like the United States. The effort led to an award-winning paper (Mazanec 1993) demonstrating the striking difference in the frequency distributions of lifestyle systems in Europe and the United States.

In 1994, *Association Internationale d'Experts du Tourisme* chose Vienna to be the venue of its annual conference. The general theme was "Tourism Research: Achievements, Failures, and Unresolved Puzzles." But blameful as it is, I cannot remember any details other than the gorgeous ball we organized in one of the grand deluxe hotels on Vienna's Imperial Street.

In 1997, I was appointed the WU's vice rector for research, an obligation that lasted until 2002. This first generation of vice rectors fulfilled a part-time job, besides their usual research, teaching, and administrative duties as university professors. On the top, the WU, for the first time in its 100-year history, succeeded in acquiring substantive funding for a "Joint Research Program from the Austrian Science Foundation." Between 1997 and 2000, I also served as the Speaker of this Program (SFB010) that encompassed three universities and up to 70 scholarly members. The activities centered on "Adaptive Information Systems and Modeling in Economics and Management Science." The Institute for Tourism and Leisure Studies took responsibility for the research initiative on "Market Segmentation and Product Positioning."

The overambitious vision of elaborating simulation models of artificial markets did not quite materialize as the individual interests of the five research initiatives appeared to be too disparate for joining forces altogether. However, there was successful collaboration of two to three initiatives and, with some time lag, publication output increased enormously. Personally, I admit that I never learned more than during the SFB010 period 1997–2002. For anybody inexperienced in large-scale interdisciplinary cooperation, the initial barriers are hard to imagine. It took us one and a half years until each of us roughly understood what the others were talking about, and, most difficult, to be courageous enough to raise uninformed questions in a discourse. Unfortunately, this experience, like my stay at MIT, came 15 years too late to reap full benefit.

At the end of the decade, another international grouping of researchers emerged. On the initiative of Arch Woodside, the first Symposium on the Consumer Psychology of Tourism, Hospitality, and Leisure (1998) took place in Hawaii, USA (Woodside et al 2000). The symposium was next hosted by WU in Vienna (Mazanec et al 2001) and after Australia, Canada, and the United States returned to our venue in 2009.

The 2000s: Gaps Are Widening

The SFB010 left long-term remnants. Collaboration with the colleagues from our Mathematics and Statistics Department, notably Helmut Strasser and Kurt Hornik, opened new avenues of methodology not yet exploited in business, marketing, or tourism research. One was nonparametric analysis and led to a joint book project (Mazanec and Strasser 2000), where we laid out an alternative approach to integrating brand positioning and market segmentation. A second one was detecting unobserved heterogeneity in a data-driven manner in situations where analysts are devoid of theory that guides them in searching for specific causes of heterogeneity (Mazanec 2000). Survey data on tourist behavior are often plagued by heterogeneity, and inattentive analysis easily ends up in spurious findings, a pitfall one can avoid by probing group-specific parameter estimation. The leap of knowledge in adaptive modeling also was instrumental in a European Union-funded project on developing smarter travel recommender systems (Mazanec 2002b) and it also served as a gate-opener into the choice modeling community (Elrod et al 2002).

With some stubbornness and continuity, I worked on applications of vector quantization. An ingenious extension of the self-organizing map by Martinetz et al (1993) and Martinetz and Schulten (1994) made me write a Visual Pascal version of the topology representing network method as well as develop several add-ons. It proved useful in generating partitions (of tourists, trip products, or destinations, for instance) where traditional cluster procedures could detect nothing and came into regular use for research and teaching. Some selected examples are two studies of tour operator images (Mazanec 2001; Mazanec and Strasser 2007), an analysis of competition among modes of transport (Mazanec 2005), and an award-winning paper of marketing professors' conceptual understanding of their discipline (Franke and Mazanec 2006).

When Luiz Moutinho asked for my assistance in launching the *Journal of Modelling in Management*, I continued work with another building block of earlier Science Foundation activities. I used my own Matlab-based version of an artificial consumer market to conduct a simulation experiment with software agents pursuing competing strategies of positioning, pricing, and segmentation. The endeavor paid off, as it resulted in an Outstanding Paper Award (Mazanec 2006). At that time, services to the tourism and marketing communities had accumulated to a dozen editorial board functions as associate or resource editor or coordinating referee. At the present time, a never-ending flow of manuscripts waiting for review captures a significant slice of my work time.

A growing share of review papers has dealt with applications of structural equation modeling. In many cases, I had to diagnose misuse or a wrong claim of having confirmed an explanatory model. It seems that many authors like tinkering with modification indices, *ad hoc* adding and deleting of paths, and introduction of correlated error terms to push the goodness of fit. Very often, the same data are employed for these exploratory manipulations and for subsequent confirmatory analysis. This bad practice has slowed down progress as we seldom get the chance of learning about the original ideas that failed empirical examination. Fitting results to the idiosyncrasies of some specific sample does not build cumulative knowledge. In my experience, a second point deserves even more attention. This point addresses the question of whether or not a causal interpretation is admissible. When becoming immersed in this question, I found the publications of Peter Spirtes and his group at Carnegie Mellon (Spirtes et al 2000) and Judea Pearl's (2001) axiomatic approach to judging causality extremely helpful (Mazanec 2007a, 2007b). Nobody should start playing with structural equation modeling unless they have read the enlightening chapter 5 of his book.

Over the years, city tourism has been one of the substantive areas of research interest at the Institute for Tourism and Leisure Studies. Personally, I always have adhered to strengthening the analytical methods employed in this area (Grabler et al 1996). These ambitions were shared by Karl Wöber who has made an impressive investment in developing and maintaining the TourMis system, now operative for 25 years. It represents the richest source of information on European city tourism currently available and continues to inspire Information Technology (IT) and tourism research (Mazanec and Wöber 2009). Among the most recent research issues at the Institute, two items are noteworthy. The first refers to the fashionable field of destination competitiveness, where my collaborators and I felt that it is timely to make the step from explication to explanation, from definitional subtleties to cause–effect relationships (Mazanec and Ring forthcoming; Mazanec et al 2007). The second was entitled "Interlinking Tourism Research and Marketing Science," which was sponsored by an Austrian National Bank grant, and focused on the role of emotions in tourism Web content and promotion. A typical piece of research was exploring the names of destinations with respect to their Google distance to connotative word items (Mazanec 2009). By doing this, one may unearth facets of the destinations' projected images, including the way they are portrayed in commercial and user-generated Web content.

In our tourism education program and in the diploma and doctoral theses at WU, the ingredients of information technology have gradually increased in importance. Typical e-tourism topics, such as ontologies, domain-specific search engines, analyzing blogs, and log-files, evaluating destination portals and dynamic packaging sites evolved as research and training issues. The Institute for Tourism and Leisure Studies was the only one at WU that managed to acquire scholarships from the industry for its students. The only requirement they had to fulfill was good regular progress and combining tourism with an IT-related second specialization. We also headed the list of graduate students who were awarded the WU's *Talenta* prize for an excellent diploma thesis.

CONCLUSION

Pondering on the relationships between marketing and tourism is not new. Roger Calantone and I once wrote such a state-of-the-art report (1991). Among all service industries, tourism seems to pose the toughest challenges for marketing management. A highly fragmented value chain of service production with widely dispersed contributions from a variety of mutually dependent service providers complicate procedures. Marketing research thus encounters a multifaceted playground. I remember when the Editor-in-Chief of *Annals of Tourism Research* got worried about an imminent preponderance of submissions from marketing. For a while, to my discontent, marketers were discouraged to submit manuscripts and referred to the more specialized journals. Apparently, Jafar Jafari was not alone in assuming that marketing research was not a genuine social science discipline. Considering that influencing other people's behavior is what marketing is all about, this belief is inherently wrong. But, what we really need is more authors writing in the core journals of marketing to publish about applications in tourism and more researchers capable of publishing in first-tier marketing journals.

By now the reader may have become saturated by so many self-references. Again, I regret that I could not avail myself of a means for stirring up memories other than the timeline of publications. So, if we actually learn from our errors, what are the conclusions?

If I were given a second chance, I would change a lot. Regarding a career in academia, the lessons are evident and I would exhort myself—study mathematics and computer science first, before specializing in anything else. If this is done, one has only two more alternatives: muddling through as a lifelong dilettante in advanced methods or becoming a narrative scientist confined by the ambiguity and fuzziness of natural language. Even if the home university will not let the researcher go and offer him or her attractive job opportunities, it may be necessary for the sake of personal growth to choose a different cultural environment and expose oneself to the strange and unknown.

Looking back over my activities during 40 years, I recognize a curvilinear trend regarding the weight of basic research themes compared to applied research problems. Initially, attention was on improving explanatory models of advertising effectiveness and brand choice. After the launch of *Journal of Marketing Research* in 1963, Paul Green and others kicked off the multivariate revolution in marketing. Reliance on advanced analytical methods became customary. Entering the tourism scene brought rising expectations from the industry in tackling problems of their management routine. Down-to-earth research and applied research became dominant. With the SFB-induced strengthening of interdisciplinary collaboration, new elements of basic research appeared and have been fortified continuously. This was in conformity with the WU's explicit ambition of climbing the ladder of university rankings. A lively interest in advanced analytical methods has been conducive to making internationally visible contributions.

Perhaps due to these academic developments, the "cultural" distance between university research and industry practice was bound to grow. Our industry and professional partners had difficulties in realizing that university-based research differs from ordering policy recommendations of a business consultancy. On the other hand, the agencies funding basic research did not view a field such as tourism to be of central importance within their portfolio. "The industry shall pay for it" was an instinctive reaction. To be successful, it was necessary to mask tourism research problems and hide them behind a fashionable facade like "agent-based systems," "sustainability," or "information technology." The process threatens to terminate in a position of suspense between two poles. Personally, I have no solution to it other than recommending a deliberate choice. Cling to one pole or get torn apart.

Chapter 6

Tourism as a Social Leisure Behavior

Seppo E. Iso-Ahola
University of Maryland, USA

Seppo E. Iso-Ahola <isoahol@umd.edu> graduated from the University of
Jyväskylä, Finland with masters degrees in psychology and kinesiology. He
completed his formal education with a PhD from the University of Illinois,
USA. One of his principal contributions to the development of tourism
study was his book *The Social Psychology of Leisure and Recreation*
published in 1980. Papers addressing the tourism topics more specifically
were developed from this core publication. He served for a decade as an
associate editor for the *Annals of Tourism Research*. He became a full
professor in 1984 in the Department of Recreation at the University of
Maryland, where he was also the department chair in 1989 and given the
unenviable task of closing down the department. His career and contribution in the tourism studies area was principally associated with his work in
the 1980s, and subsequent years in his academic life have been shaped by
university funding and circumstances such that he no longer works directly
in the tourism and recreation field. He maintains an indirect interest in the
study of tourism.

INTRODUCTION

Even before I entered the academic world, as a youngster, I was keenly
interested in human social behavior. My father's farmwork had little appeal

The Study of Tourism: Foundations from Psychology
Tourism Social Science Series, Volume 15, 93–98
ISSN: 1571-5043/doi:10.1108/S1571-5043(2011)0000015009

to me, but when his friends came over to exchange stories on Saturday and Sundays, I found their discussions fascinating. Different people had different ideas, opinions, and perceptions, and they even acted differently, each having his own style of self-presentation, as Goffman would call it. It all was intriguing to me. No wonder I later began to gravitate toward social psychology in my academic studies.

I got my first spark for social psychology as an exchange student (from Finland) at the University of Illinois at Urbana-Champaign while working for my master's degree in 1971–1972. After one year back at the University of Jyväskylä (and another master's degree), I returned to the University of Illinois for the fall semester 1973 and finished my PhD in 1976. Those three years made me a social psychologist. I was fortunate to have a research assistantship in Children's Research Center's Motor and Leisure Behavior Laboratory and take courses in one of the best psychology departments in the United States. My dissertation advisor was Robert S. Wyer, known as Mr. Social Cognition. The Psychology Department was populated with great scholars and researchers (including Martin Fishbein and Harry Triandis), and taking courses from them was stimulating, to say the least. These departmental attachments gave me a strong background in research in general and theoretical social psychology in particular. Reading studies on social psychological phenomena day after day, and running my own experiments, was fun. I could not have asked for anything more academically.

My Contributions

Those Illinois years laid the foundations for the knowledge from which I could later make my own contributions. While being interested in the attribution processes at the time, I became enamored by the ideas in Deci's (1975) book on intrinsic motivation. His ideas and findings made a lot of sense and stimulated my own thinking on motivation. The more I delved into this phenomenon, the clearer it became that motivation is a key to all social behavior. Perhaps not surprisingly, I have written more consistently on this topic than any other over the years.

Although I had been interested in pure theoretical social psychology, I found it intriguing that this knowledge had not been applied to various areas of social behavior. Social psychology of work had been recognized, but why not social psychology of leisure? To be sure, work is important, and it is somewhat understandable why social psychology would first have been employed to explain work behavior. But why not leisure as well? Europeans know the value and importance of leisure in their lives as attested to by the

6–7 week paid vacation time a year. Americans, on the other hand, tend to see leisure as trivial, not being an important part of the quality of life. Regardless, I saw a void in the literature and started working on my book, *The Social Psychology of Leisure and Recreation* (1980), which I consider my main contribution to the literature. I was fortunate with the book in that the publisher gave me the freedom to develop it with few restrictions. Thus, I did not have to write a typical textbook that is shallow, only giving a surface type of information. Instead, I could cover a wide variety of topics and do it by reviewing research and integrating findings from different studies. It also allowed me to develop ideas further and even propose theoretical models.

Although I did not specifically write a chapter on the social psychology of tourism, the text became the basis for my subsequent writing on this topic, such as my article concerning the social psychology of recreational travel (Iso-Ahola 1983). The text also included the idea that motivationally people tend to seek intrinsic rewards, both personal and interpersonal, and tend to avoid routine personal and interpersonal environments while engaged in leisure behaviors. This idea was put forward in a theoretical model in a joint 1982 paper (Iso-Ahola and Allen 1982) and was also specifically discussed in relation to tourism (Iso-Ahola 1982). It was further developed and refined in a later chapter on leisure motivation (Iso-Ahola 1989). This theoretical model has since been tested empirically by other researchers with different data sets and has generally been supported. Structural equation modeling allows a direct testing of the model and has successfully been used in recent studies (Biswas-Diener 2008; Snepenger et al 2006).

TOURISM AS A LEISURE BEHAVIOR

To me, leisure behavior is a general rubric that covers all kinds of behaviors and activities, from exercise to movies to bird watching and travel abroad. Tourism is, therefore, a leisure behavior. To understand it, we have to first understand the social psychological processes that underlie leisure behavior in general. Then, we can delve more deeply into this specific leisure behavior, i.e., tourism. While one could argue that each leisure behavior is unique, we also know that there is a common characteristic that determines whether a given activity is a leisure activity (perceived freedom). If there is no or little sense of freedom about an activity, then it does not become a leisure activity in one's mind. This sense of freedom is one of the key intrinsic rewards tourists get from their activity. It is hard to imagine that people could engage in tourist behaviors because they are forced to do so, though it certainly is possible.

There is no question that tourism is a unique social (leisure) behavior (Pearce 1982). It also provides a special setting or field laboratory for investigations of this particular behavior. We (Dunn-Ross and Iso-Ahola 1991) used such a "lab" to study tourists in Washington DC. We gave them a questionnaire before and after a day's tour. This allowed us to study their motivation and satisfaction with the experience. In general, various tourist settings and groups lend themselves readily to this kind of psychological examination of the tourism experience. There are few social behaviors that provide comparable natural settings for a psychological analysis. Thus, those who study psychological aspects of tourism in its field "lab" can easily defend themselves against social psychologists' criticism, "What happened to the study of behavior?" (Baumeister and Bushman 2008).

To social psychologists, a core issue is tourism experience. What is its nature? Is it a leisure experience? What do people think and feel during this episode? What needs are expected to be met and which ones are actually met? What aspects of it determine the overall satisfaction? How will it be remembered? Mannell and I (1987) examined these and related questions in light of relevant research from three theoretical perspectives: "definitional," "posthoc satisfaction," and "immediate conscious experience." While each of these areas can be useful in and of itself for understanding tourism experience, together they provide a theoretical framework for a more comprehensive analysis of this psychological experience. Besides advancing theoretical knowledge, research conducted within this framework can yield practically relevant information as well, the knowledge that might even lead to "tourism experience engineering." Tour operators, for example, aim at providing satisfying experiences for their customers and would, therefore, like to know what they can do psychologically to improve their services. This framework was presented in an article that was part of the special issue of the *Annals of Tourism Research* (1987) on the interrelationships of leisure, recreation, and tourism (Mannell and Iso-Ahola 1987). Anthony Fedler and I served as the guest editors of the issue. The editor of the journal, Jafar Jafari, had earlier invited me to the editorial board on which I served as an associate editor for over 10 years.

END OF CONTRIBUTIONS

With the exception of the article by Dunn-Ross and Iso-Ahola (1991), all my contributions to the psychology/social psychology of tourism occurred in the 1980s. Since then, I have not made one single contribution to the tourism literature. My work has turned to the consideration of such topics as sports, health, leisure, and exercise. The reason has to do with the academic politics. The University of Maryland's Department of Recreation was in turmoil in the late 1980s, and the dean decided to fire the chair of the department. In October 1989, he asked me to serve in that capacity, starting July 1990.

Having served as the chair for about a month, the bad news came. The campus faced big financial cuts because of the state's poor economy. The university president and his associates decided that rather than making cuts across the departments, it is a better idea to eliminate some departments and one entire college. Our department was one of the units targeted for elimination. Faced with this threat, the faculty had no choice but fight it. The academic year 1990–1991 was spent entirely in preparing and circulating documents in our support, attending and holding meetings to defend the department's importance and position, recruiting state legislators and concerned citizens to speak for us, and organizing demonstrations on campus. It was not very pleasant, to say the least. In the end, we lost the battle as all the targeted departments were eliminated. I was given an unenviable task, as the chair, to phase out the department within the next four years. Obviously, the program and its academic courses could not be stopped all of a sudden. Students had to be given an opportunity to finish their degrees. It was a challenging task, but if the success is measured by the absence of lawsuits (administrator's criterion), then we succeeded. In the bigger picture, however, the department's elimination was a dismal failure and a sad outcome. There is hardly anything more dramatic or even traumatic in the academia than one's own department's demise. The process can turn angels into cynics and bitter critics.

I was recruited for the department in 1981 and was soon promoted to full professorship in 1984. The faculty was vibrant and strong with about 20 members. Several young assistant professors were hired and they all were productive scholars, publishing numerous articles and studies in refereed journals. There was, however, one major problem—a rift between the older faculty ("deadwoods") who did not publish anything at all and the new faculty who did. This difference led to infighting among the faculty regarding the direction of the department and its curriculum. Continuous turmoil was noticed by the higher administrators and ultimately cited as one of the reasons why the department was targeted for elimination.

I spent close to 10 years in the midst of this academic politics and turmoil. It took a lot out of me mentally, undermining my motivation and productivity. After the phaseout was completed, I had an option of going to Psychology, Health Education Department or Kinesiology Department. I chose the latter. This, of course, had serious implications for my teaching and research. Kinesiology departments do not teach courses on tourism, nor do they encourage research on it. As a result, I began changing my scholarly interests toward social psychology of exercise and health, and psychology of athletic performance, teaching courses, and doing research in both of these areas. In addition, I have been teaching quantitative research methods for graduate students. While my tourism contributions came to a grinding halt, I still published quite a few papers and studies on leisure behavior in the 1990s and even 2000s, with one of them being a chapter on leisure motivation in 1999 and a couple of chapters on leisure and health. The common thread or theme of my work, motivation, continues as I have published two theory development papers, but now on exercise motivation. The most recent (2009) one is "Exercise and Freedom."

Our college became the School of Public Health last year (2009) and this, of course, means that the department is moving more and more toward an analysis of health behavior and practices, pushing me even more away from tourism. On the other hand, vacation- and leisure-starved Americans could use tourism as a way of getting away from it all, thus restoring their mental health. Well, here is a topic for research and scholarly studies: tourism and mental health. Perhaps, I will return to tourism after all!

Chapter 7

Finding Tourism

Joseph T. O'Leary
Colorado State University, USA

Joseph T. O'Leary <Joseph.OLeary@ColoState.EDU> is professor in the Warner College of Natural Resources at Colorado State University, USA. He was formerly dean of the Warner College and before that professor and head in the Department of Recreation, Park and Tourism Sciences at Texas A&M University (2001–2007), USA. Prior to 2001, he was a senior staff member at Purdue University where he was in the Department of Forestry and Natural Resources. His graduate degrees are from the University of Washington and Yale University, USA. His undergraduate degree is from the University of New Brunswick, Canada. He is a member of Academy of Leisure Sciences, American Academy of Park and Recreation Administration, and the IUCN World Commission on Protected Areas (North American branch). His research has involved knowledge management and the analysis of large national and international studies of tourism and recreation behavior, and his co-publishing with colleagues and his graduate students places him among the most prolific tourism scholars.

INTRODUCTION

The study of tourism was not specifically where I began my work, but it was never far from it either. This reflection was not obvious to me until I began to consider the interesting question Philip Pearce posed to me with his

The Study of Tourism: Foundations from Psychology
Tourism Social Science Series, Volume 15, 99–114
Copyright © 2011 by Emerald Group Publishing Limited
ISSN: 1571-5043/doi:10.1108/S1571-5043(2011)0000015010

inquiry: "Could I write about my evolution and involvement in tourism studies?" In the more than 35 years in which I have worked in academia, I had never really stopped to take stock. For giving me this opportunity, I thank his kind consideration. This autobiographical account of my academic career follows my life from New York to Canada and then back to three different parts of the United States. There are a great many people who have influenced how I think about research and who have helped me identify a research style and opportunities. I can highlight at the outset one such influence—Fran McGuire from Clemson University, USA. It was this colleague who left with me one of those important observations that influences a career and certainly was pivotal in mine. We were writing a great deal, but every now and again after submitting a paper, it would come back rejected from a journal. I remember Fran McGuire being completely unaffected by the rejection. Instead, he made a comment that still resonates with me: "There is no such thing as a rejected paper; there is only the paper that has not as yet found a home." I have never stopped going back to that mantra.

LEISURE, RECREATION, TOURISM

I was born and grew up in New York City until I was 16. Up until this point, I had attended Catholic schools, including riding the subway every day for two and a half years. Then my family moved east, out of the city to Long Island. I finished the last portion of high school in a public school. My father and grandfather were both New York City policemen. My mother was a secretary or clerical worker at various places while I grew up. My mother's father was in the hospitality industry as general manager of several hotels in New York City for as long as I can remember. My grandmother (his wife) also worked in hotels in charge of on-site laundry operations and overseeing maids in the hotel. I can recall visiting the places they worked and getting to the back of the house whenever I visited with my parents. It was quite an experience. They also enjoyed vacationing in the Adirondacks in upstate New York at a resort on Lake George. My sister and I were brought along on these vacations and it was at this time that I learned how much I enjoyed the outdoors. Once presented with the experience, wanting to stay connected to it simply got stronger.

Both my parents worked and my grandparents assumed lots of responsibility for my after-school care. I was good in school, but I was also quite good in sports. I spent almost all my after-school time and weekends in city parks playing whatever activity was available. But my parents also gave me an amazing amount of freedom to travel around the city even before I was in high school. It was never hard to get friends to come with me to baseball games at Yankee Stadium. But I also found myself visiting museums, libraries, art galleries, and almost every other major setting in the city, because they were there and I was curious. To this day, I wonder about this freedom, as I am not certain in this day and age that as a parent I would feel comfortable doing the same for my children. Nevertheless, the opportunities that were presented were exceptional and the chance to explore new things was probably planted during this early period.

None of my family members had ever completed college. My parents lobbied hard for me to attend and I struggled with making the decision about what to study, where to do it, and how to pay for it. This struggle meant I did not go to college right away, choosing instead to work a lot and travel a little. I had run track and played football in high school. One day I was contacted by my former football coach and asked if I might be interested in playing football in college in Canada. In the absence of having better plans, I said sure, packed my bags and flew to the Maritimes where I began at Dalhousie University, but eventually landed at the University of New Brunswick, because of my interest in the outdoors and a decision to study forestry. I "gently" became an international citizen living in Canada on a student visa. I had flown for the first time and gone to another country that was vastly different from where I had grown up. Even more important, the five-year forestry program (and it was really a five-year program) emphasized getting experience in the summers. I had the opportunity to work from east to west and north to south with wonderful people in a truly amazing country. Once I left home for college, I rarely returned.

An interesting part of my learning experience as an undergraduate was that most of the calculations done in courses were done with calculators by hand. At that time, all of our statistics were done by "brute force." But the great value in doing this was that every step was done by hand and understanding how things worked inside a technique has to this day been wonderfully beneficial.

In the fifth year of the undergraduate program, a requirement was to write a senior thesis. I chose to write my paper on small farmer pulpwood cooperatives. That made me consider that in all the material I had learned while I was studying in the program, we had never really discussed the social issues of forestry. The success of these cooperatives was extremely challenging, but it was not because of the biological or physical science aspects of what I had learned. It was a social science issue. While my program had been very good, none of these issues or area had ever been explored. At that point I decided to learn more about that aspect of forestry. So I applied and was accepted at Yale University with the express interest of learning more about this social science stuff for a master's degree. I was the first person to have graduated from university in my family and now I was off to expand that adventure.

At Yale, I was exposed to faculty members (and for me especially William Burch) who expressly worked in this area. Further, I was introduced to reading, theory, and interdisciplinary learning that I had not expected. It was extraordinary. I found myself more engaged in sociology and sociological theory, as it related to natural resources, recreation and leisure, built environments, and even shared classes with architecture students. The opportunity to listen to a very different set of ideas presented from diverse backgrounds was exceptional. I also learned what a "24/7" learning environment was all about. There was never a time when you could not find someone in the school or on campus to discuss, argue, or debate an idea, book, or current event. The Vietnam War was probably at the height of its controversy, Woodstock occurred, the Black Panthers were a large topic of conversation in New Haven, and the first Earth Day took place while I was at Yale. The social fabric was being changed, often wrenched very hard, debate and controversy were the order of the day and one was never sure what would happen next. I also got married and had twin boys.

A major topic of conversation at the Christmas dance held at the school in my second year was about going on to study for a PhD. My wife reminds me to this day that my response was "not me." But six weeks later, I had accepted an opportunity to study for a PhD at the University of Washington, USA. My advisor (Donald Field) was the leader of the social science program in the National Park Service Cooperative Park Studies Unit. I was his first PhD student, the first in the social science arena, and in a circle of activity where there were many important issues associated with National Parks, and a very strong interest in making this program work. I was given enormous opportunities to be involved in research projects beyond my own dissertation and to assist in guiding them to completion. Donald Field was also amazing in getting me involved in writing projects and eventually publications. It was during this period that I learned a core maxim I have carried throughout my career—"if you are going to learn about research, then you must do research."

A major project that occurred while I was at Washington was the North Pacific Border Study, an outdoor recreation participation survey done by telephone and in partnership with the National Park Service and state agencies. Several thousand respondents were surveyed in the study, making the research larger than most efforts at the national level. It was also designed to provide planning, policy and management information, something desperately needed as recreation participation continued to grow. Because it was a multistate regional study, it was also a study of travel and tourism. I was fortunate to arrive just as the project got started, watched the training, listened to the interviews done on the phone, and followed the organization and analysis of the data right from the beginning. To have been given the chance to participate in almost every facet of the research was a wonderful learning opportunity to do and experience research, the outcomes of which I carried throughout much of my career. But it was also controlled by my adviser and allowed me to gain confidence with a few successes early in my program and career.

My dissertation provided me with a different methodological perspective. It was a community study of a town undergoing change next to the newly created North Cascades National Park, formerly a part of the Mount Baker National Forest. In many ways, it was a classical sociological study of community, one of the first of its kind that looked at a community in transition because of a major natural resource policy decision. I lived in the community for the better part of a year, used many of the well-known qualitative techniques, did a quantitative survey, and then tried to make sense of it all so that I could write my dissertation. Although using qualitative tools was not a high priority in my research as I moved into my career, the experience I had with fieldwork was helpful to me to this day.

At that time in natural resource programs, "social science" was almost a synonym for outdoor recreation. When one looked for a university position, this was the area in which one would work. As I came close to finishing, the several interviews I did eventually led me to take a position in the Department of Forestry and Natural Resources at Purdue University.

Getting Involved

Getting started with a university career can be challenging. I was fortunate at Purdue to have excellent colleagues and a supportive department head. But the first ideas I had about building a research program did not fare well or get funded. Finally, I was able to obtain a state-funded project to do an outdoor recreation participation survey that would contribute to the State Comprehensive Outdoor Recreation Plan required by the federal government to obtain federal funds for land acquisition. My familiarity with the

North Pacific Border Study while I was at Washington made this engagement easier and provided the first funds to support graduate students.

An important event happened during this time. First I learned that several years earlier as part of an earlier planning cycle, another university had done a statewide survey. The computer tapes with those data were sitting in a bottom desk drawer in the office of the state agency along with a copy of the last survey. But there was no codebook. Although the primary purpose of looking at this survey was to see if there were useful questions that could be employed in the new survey, this began a long drawn out drama of trying to reconstruct the former survey, examine the data for comparison, or to answer new questions through different analysis. It was my first foray into secondary analysis.

I believed that the survey could be enriched by input from questions from the nationwide surveys of outdoor recreation. These had begun in the United States just before 1960, followed by work done in 1965, 1972, and eventually 1977. Looking at these surveys for possible questions for the Indiana survey led to an effort to get the original data. Slowly but surely it became our standard operating procedure not only to get the survey and codebooks but also the original data. Because many of these studies had been done by federal agencies, personal contact with the various scientists responsible for leading these large efforts became an opportunity and special experience. Once engaged, interactions grew quickly and substantively. As students knew data were available, more began to show up at my door.

Although I had set out with a different purpose in mind, secondary analysis of recreation data became the central theme of my research program. If someone knew I had an interest in this area, suggestions about what else to look at or questions about analysis were a regular occurrence. The nationwide outdoor recreation surveys continued, but now I had also found the US Fishing, Hunting, and Wildlife-Associated Recreation Surveys begun in this country in 1955 and redone about every five years to this day. There were several pieces to these studies, but the largest file included responses from around 100,000 respondents. All of these in some way, shape, or form could be compared with the nationwide recreation survey.

In the mid-1980s, I went on sabbatical to Clemson University, USA, to work with the Cooperative Park Studies Unit located in the Department of Parks, Recreation and Tourism Management. The Cooperative Unit was funded by the National Park Service. The director of that program invited me to work on analyzing the 1982–1983 National Outdoor Recreation Survey for information useful to his agency, but also for the development of new knowledge. Being there at that time also opened up a door to be a contributor to the President's Commission on Americans Outdoors and another national outdoor recreation survey they did with the Market Opinion Research Company. Being at Clemson also gave me a chance to work closely with the US Forest Service Outdoor Recreation Research Unit located on the University of Georgia campus and specifically Ken Cordell.

Did I Find Tourism or Did It Find Me?

My entry to tourism in a formal sense begins about this time. My reputation of being a "data guy" led to a suggestion by the director of the National Park Service Cooperative Unit that I go to Atlanta and meet this Canadian with Parks Canada who was also a "data guy." He thought we might have something in common, and since he was in Atlanta for a meeting perhaps this was a chance to get acquainted. Atlanta was close; the person had data or worked with it, so why not.

I met Scott Meis one afternoon at the Atlanta Zoo. At that time, he was the assistant director of the Parks Canada Social Science research program. A "short visit" led to several hours of walking and talking about data, his experiences, projects, and opportunities, including a tourism connection. Parks Canada had been working with Tourism Canada and the US Department of Commerce on a series of studies examining international visitors to the United States and Canada and their interest in National Parks, the North American Pleasure Travel Market Studies. Both national park agencies were interested in better understanding their international tourists and the role that parks might play in the tourism experience. The first four studies had been done in the United Kingdom, France, Germany, and Japan by a private research firm. The question was posed as to whether I would be interested in a project that would bring the interests of the two park agencies together and, working with Steve Smith at the University of Waterloo, Canada, provide analyses of these surveys. It involved more survey data and sounded like a new challenge. By the time I walked out of the Atlanta Zoo, I had an interesting and different question related to travel and tourism as well as a colleague and friend that I have worked with now for almost 25 years.

The Pleasure Travel Market Studies were international studies using the same survey instrument done in a number of countries around the world and replicated in some of the aforementioned countries. On one level, the results emphasized that national parks were perceived by people around the world as true North American competitive advantages. It was a very special set of studies, because they presented a unique opportunity to compare results across countries.

Scott Meis convinced me to attend my first Travel and Tourism Research Association Conference in Montreal in 1989, and introduced me to Gordon Taylor. He was another amazing Canadian data person with whom I never could get enough time. Scott Meis emphasized the importance of industry being part of the conversation and continued to give the academic community opportunities to work with travel data of all shapes and sizes. He always said "If students work on these data and I can get one idea to act on out of 10 ideas they might suggest, then this has been an excellent investment." I did a lot of work with the Canadians, something I think was made very easy because of having gone to school there for five years and remaining in contact with many of my classmates.

I never found it difficult to move back and forth between recreation and tourism studies or data. I always believed the theory and conceptual basis for understanding these areas shared much common terrain. Activities were always the common vehicle. While there were some areas in tourism surveys that were different (hotel, trip purpose, etc.), questions dealing with activities or sociodemographic characteristics seemed to be the same the world over. It was often through these two areas that linkages to other "nonobvious" surveys that could be connected to tourism would occur. For example, the US National Endowment for the Arts conducts a regular survey in the country asking about involvement in arts, culture, and heritage activities. So do the nationwide outdoor recreation surveys and the US International Travel Survey done by the US Department of Commerce. Being able to compare the results of these independent studies is fascinating and knowledge intensive. Using data from private firms, Statistics Canada, Tourism Canada, or the Canadian Tourism Commission, the US Department of Transportation or Bureau of Labor Statistics that dealt with either transportation studies or time use surveys also contributed to a collage of knowledge development that continued to grow.

Additional Connection

Around the time I returned to Purdue from my sabbatical I began to explore opportunities to work more actively across departments and schools at the university. There was a Department of Restaurant, Hotel, Institutional and Tourism Management in the School of Consumer and Family Studies and a Department of Health, Kinesiology and Leisure Studies in the School of Liberal Arts. Faculty knew each other and some collaboration had occurred.

An interdisciplinary graduate degree in tourism was developed cooperatively across the three schools and departments that truly represented a new and exciting opportunity. Bill Theobald was a major force in making this happen from Liberal Arts and Alastair Morrison was the key collaborator in the Tourism Management program. This focus on tourism led to the growth of graduate student numbers, theses, dissertations, papers, faculty collaboration, course development, etc. Because of this developing partnership, I had a chance to learn much more from my colleagues about hospitality.

It is impossible to talk about the effort at Purdue without giving much of the credit to the amazing array of hardworking graduate students who came through the program. I was lucky to have the chance to work with many students in their graduate programs. There were two things particularly exciting about the activities under way at this time. First, I identified my responsibility as acting as an adviser, but more importantly making sure the students had the necessary resources to be successful. Eventually, the program evolved to a team of PhD, master's, and undergraduate students where the "senior" students took responsibility for helping mentor the newer ones into the program in terms of how to do research, identifying classes of particular value, and helping them understand the culture of the lab. This system gave me a chance to mentor or coach PhD students as they moved through their programs on speaking up and exerting leadership of ideas and program strengthening. We developed regular "Projects from Hell" meetings where coffee and bagels around a table served as a magnet for pulling people together from across campus. At those sessions, faculty and graduate students participated in discussions about developing papers, projects, and proposals for meetings, journals, conferences, and the like.

The dynamics of these sessions were interesting and never failed to generate multiple opportunities to be pursued. But I remember one of these in particular as an example. It was when I realized how much of a "family and community" environment had been created. There was a very talented international student in the group who had not had the opportunity to see her family back home in about five years. A conference opportunity appeared in an area very close to where her family lived. The "group" decided we would work together and do everything we could to develop a paper for the conference and make any commitment necessary to be sure she made the paper presentation. If that meant that others gave up their opportunity that was fine. The paper was prepared and accepted and the person went to the meeting and had the chance to visit her family.

During this time, this lab model of multiple students and collaborating faculty was amazingly successful and productive. It evolved from one of the students who came from an environmental and biological program where she had experienced this format. The more she spoke about it, the better it sounded; it grew and evolved based on her planting the idea.

With so many students, the fermentation of ideas, theory, analytical tools, data, and learning was exceptional. It was special and an environment I have not seen in very many places. But a complementary part of this was also to have students thinking about engagement with industry, public agencies, other universities, and departments and colleagues in our home university. I regularly tried to get students in front of public and private groups to make presentations about their work; when life got overwhelmingly busy for me, I sent them as our program emissary. I can recall very few examples where the graduate students failed to "wow" the audience.

I also found important adjunct partnerships with colleagues like Dan Fesenmaier at the University of Illinois (now at Temple University), USA, as he developed his very significant laboratory focusing on tourism and technology and with Philip Pearce and Gianna Moscardo and their work at James Cook University in Australia. I think these efforts were important because they intervened to prevent insularity in our thinking inside the program. The more stimulation we were able to receive from outside, the stronger our program would be. These were key people but also just a few of those who contributed.

Significant Others

There are some very significant people across my career who provided direction and inspiration. A few of these are people assisted me especially in graduate school and beyond, while others guided my growth and involvement in the tourism arena.

When I went to Yale University, William Burch was my first mentor who pointed me toward sociology and natural resources and gave me the opportunity to deal with an interdisciplinary reading list that changed my life. Donald Field was my PhD adviser at the University of Washington and his patience and support provided the academic foundation for my career. Scott Meis has been an amazing colleague with whom I have worked with for 25 years. His views about the "democratization of data" from the time I first met him when he worked for Parks Canada through his experiences with Tourism Canada and the Canadian Tourism Commission as a leader in their research programs have had incredible impacts on my work and thinking. He also introduced me to Gordon Taylor and at the time I did not appreciate the impact he had made on the tourism industry. But after speaking with him for only a short time, I was mesmerized by his amazing range of thinking and ideas. From that time forward, there were never enough opportunities to get my "Gordon Taylor fix." He is an incredibly talented person and generous beyond words with his thoughts and counsel. Dan Fesenmaier, now at Temple University, is a friend and colleague who has shared the hard-charging work ethic I believe in but who also has been one of the most forward and innovative thinking people I have ever met. Our working relationship was always made more exciting because I could benefit from his commitment to ideas, knowledge development, and innovation. To this day, I certainly receive much more than I ever gave back. Finally, none of what I have been able to accomplish would have not been possible without the support and patience of my wife, Joanne, and children, Joseph, John, and Jamie. My gratitude seems not enough for all that they have done for me.

First Work

The work done at the University of Washington with the North Pacific Border Study was grounded in a social action system framework complementing a social aggregate system perspective. Don Field, my adviser and principal investigator of the project, was a rural sociologist with strong demographer training. It grounded much of his thinking and he certainly engaged me with this conceptual framework. I also believe that Burch's research on social circles tied to camping participation, work done for the US Forest Service in Minnesota, was an influence. I can think of many things graduate students did with me as we moved forward over the years, but I still think my thinking was based and framed in these two earlier research and theory appreciation perspectives.

While there were many reports while I was at Washington, the first work I coauthored dealt with social groups and their participation in recreation (Field and O'Leary 1973). When people were asked about their recreation activity involvement, most of the time it was being done with others (family, friends, and the like); it was rarely done alone. Yet the data we used to measure participation almost always looked at visitors, participants, and not at the social configuration associated with participation. While there were consistencies across activities, there were also differences. Trying to understand how people became engaged with activities, how they were socialized into an opportunity, was also on the table. As an example, ideas about social groups came back around when we researched family use of hotels during pleasure travel. In my earlier survey work in Indiana, we employed the "with whom did you participate" questions as did the 1982–1983 National Outdoor Recreation Survey and found many similarities. When one looks at travel surveys, understanding behavior still requires attention to the "with whom" question.

Trying to understand the structure of participation and/or travel in its broadest sense fascinated me. When multiple sources of data allowed for comparisons, it became even more interesting. The first opportunity in tourism I had to do this was with the International Pleasure Travel Market Surveys. They had sociodemographic, travel characteristic, and motivation and preference questions that could be explored often in a cross-cultural manner. But as noted earlier, the subsequent work I did with other students and scientists evolved to include an enormous array of data sets and ideas, many of which had the same structural underpinnings to better understand and develop new knowledge about involvement.

For readers who wish to investigate a sample of this work, the following references introduce and display some of the themes and collaborations. We have undertaken work on the life span and aging (McGuire, William and O'Leary 2004; O'Leary et al 1986a); activity segmentation (Hsieh et al 1992; Jang et al 2005; Moscardo et al 1996); shopping behavior (Lehto et al 2004; Oh et al 2004); international tourism demand differences (Lehto et al 2004; O'Leary 1999; O'Leary and Meis 1999; O'Leary and Uysal 1986); expenditure patterns (Jang et al 2004); and tourist information needs (Choi Lehto and O'Leary 2006; Fesenmaier et al 1992). There are many more but for those with a specialist interest in the use of secondary data approaches, these publications provide some points of access.

In a different vein, I made two decisions in the last 10 years that took me to administrative work. First, I took on the task of being head in the Department of Recreation, Park and Tourism Sciences at Texas A&M. Building on the successes of the past and the strength of the faculty, students, staff, and stakeholders, we made many new strides together (O'Leary 2005). Perhaps most important in tourism, we developed an outstanding working relationship with the industry and with state and federal agencies that made the program a "Go To" entity in the state and nation. In addition, as a result of conversations I had with Scott Meis about practitioner and industry needs, the electronic bulletin "eRTR" (electronic Review of Tourism Research) was developed while I was at Texas A&M. This was an attempt to quickly translate research information and ideas to a broader audience of practitioners, students, and researchers. Soon after it was launched, it was identified as a significant innovation in knowledge transformation by an external publication coming out of Georgia Tech.

I followed that with a term as dean of the Warner College of Natural Resources at Colorado State University. I stepped down from that responsibility and am moving forward as a faculty member with my colleagues strengthening the tourism and hospitality program at the university.

Major Currents

As I look forward to where I am going next with my own avenues of inquiry, I see a direction that will involve sustainability, innovation, and linking these to the grand challenges of society (environment, poverty, health, and more). I continue to frame my thinking on what the synthesis might look like, but I think it represents an important step, certainly on my own journey, of moving in an exciting direction. I also believe it continues to give me a chance to immerse myself in secondary data and take it to a new level.

Although we often feel that we can make decisions based on our "gut feeling," the increasing complexity and the changes in the industry suggest that doing and understanding research will become a more important part of decision making, planning, management, modeling, and policy development. This suggests that being sure that the appropriate grounding in research, methods, and tourism statistics are being provided for persons who choose to go into research, as well as for those who opt for another focus in tourism and hospitality as a professional and practitioner must emerge as a priority.

In a recent project with the Committee on Tourism Statistics in the International Statistical Institute, we reviewed how tourism statistics were being taught in programs around the world. While there are a few bright spots, there are also many opportunities to make significant improvements. This is not simple. Many years ago, I was struck by the approach used in the tourism program at James Cook University where a core learning element of their program focused on making sure their students learned about research. The core argument was that the need to do and understand research would be a lifelong need for them regardless of what professional direction they chose. I did not appreciate that emphasis at the time, especially for undergraduate students. But as I look at the state of learning in this area in many of our tourism and hospitality programs, this core need is no different than critical thinking or problem solving. It must be addressed in a new way, especially in terms of lifelong learning programs.

Information technology is one arena that has significantly influenced behavior, knowledge, communication, decision making, marketing, and more in the area of tourism. For example, we can cite examples where survey research is being done online compared to other more "traditional" methods, including personal, telephone, and "snail mail" surveys. Arguments are very current about the legitimacy of online surveys and it is especially interesting as these data are compared with results that came from different methods. Many tourists no longer rely on printed materials like travel guides to gather information or to make decisions. Looking at opportunities and evaluating experiences are being done online in real time. When linked to a tagging system that allows the tourist to use something like a cell phone to get electronic directions to attractions and even "act smart" and make suggestions depending on which way he/she walks, it is clear that behavior is significantly impacted and will give researchers many new and important opportunities to think outside the box.

In the last 10 years, I have been fortunate to serve on several Convention and Visitors Bureau boards of directors and with industry associations in tourism. These opportunities have enabled me to work with various industry leaders and listen to their concerns, questions, and problems. The recession and economic downturn has been a major topic of conversation for at least two years, affecting every element of the industry. Combined with the changes that happened after the September 11 terrorist attack and the complementary changes under way as a result of developments in information technology, there may not be a time where more questions are being raised about behavior and marketing, as well as appropriate responses throughout the world. Most of the recent US domestic and international survey data regarding tourist behavior and decision making suggested that choices about whether and where to travel were being made later, characteristics of tourists were different, spending had changed, and duration of visit had been shifting. In short, just about every characteristic we examine to understand aspects of tourism is undergoing a change. Would we also expect motivations and attitudes to be undergoing changes?

We are moving toward a different pattern for tourism and hospitality and we are not going back to the structure of even two to three years ago. Without a broad set of longitudinal studies collaboratively developed domestically and internationally, it will be difficult to fully understand the nature of change for planning, management, and policy. In addition, tourists expect deals in almost every situation they experience. In earlier work looking at issues related to when decisions are made to travel, we discovered that times were getting shorter before booking and final decisions were made. Just in this context, the travel experience model that many researchers have considered seems to be foreshortened. Opportunities to intervene in any of the stages seem to need revisiting to assess whether there are opportunities to reconstruct this conceptual framework in this new environment. Similarly, if the tourist's response to travel is changing, then any of the postsite or destination actions may also need to be revisited. Have all market segments changed the same way or are there differences? Will some groups go back to the old patterns and some not? What does a new conversion process look like?

Human resources as they relate to hospitality and tourism are regularly identified across the world as pressing issues to be addressed as we look to the future of the industry. This typically is not one of the areas we link to marketing, but it is pivotal to the success of the experience. I can recall being at a tourism meeting in Coffs Harbor in Australia and walking back to my room at a morning break. On my way down the hall, one of the staff responsible for cleaning and making up the rooms greeted me and asked specifically how my stay was going and was everything up to my expectations. In the many years I had been traveling all over the world, this was the first time this had ever happened. I stopped, greeted the person back, thanked her for asking, and assured her things were good so far. But the impact of that interaction on my experience was enormous. In almost every setting where tourism occurs, the breadth of those involved, especially in areas where they have not been seen as part of the tourism mix, continues to grow. The impact of how they interact with the tourist can make or break an experience and often control whether someone returns or recommends to others coming to a destination.

In Texas, our extension staff did a marvelous job leading hospitality training programs throughout the state, extending those to training for fairs and festival operations. These efforts are important to the industry. Such training programs need to grow and evolve, and should be examined from a research point of view to better understand the marketing and impacts of this enormous area in tourism.

CONCLUSION

My last stints as a university administrator have underscored that the university world in which I have spent my career is changing dramatically. If for no other reason than funding, models to support the academy are very different. New ways in which we do learning, discovery, and engagement will have to develop to accommodate these shifts. This will be hard because change is not easy to achieve, especially at the scale that we are facing. These changes will occur throughout the world, not just in North America.

But there are also things that remain clear and unchanging. First, the best part of my experience across my career has been working with the students, both graduate and undergraduate. The obligation to provide them with great learning experiences is an important reason to improve our efforts at trying to achieve excellence in learning. The need for quality research remains and this has to be done well with high levels of integrity. This will become even more important. When I was working with secondary data analysis and using the many data sets that could be accessed, there were few colleagues who chose this path. In fact I used to say that I could count on one hand the number of people I knew who chose to pursue this strategy. Yet I found it helped me be successful, led to the development of new knowledge, informed primary data collection, gave multitudes of graduate students their opportunities for learning about and doing research, and was just plain fun. But since there are so many important issues that are on the horizon, the research function will continue to be important and grow.

One area where I think we have often been less successful is providing information to the public and private sectors to address the regularly posed question to academics, "What have you done for me lately?" It takes time to do that, but I have always felt working with entities outside the university is one of the most important aspects of the academic job. Years ago, one of my colleagues suggested in a meeting with public and private firms that they should implement a program of "Adopt a Scientist" to give faculty regular opportunities to get close to people, issues and problems, and insight that would likely inform their research and teaching. Sometimes this happens when people have sabbaticals, but that may only occur on a five- to seven-year rhythm and that is not enough. When students do internships, the outcomes often suggest the experience has changed their lives. The potential to have as large an impact on faculty members is also available with a similar type of program. This is one example, but there are many more. There are talented people and organizations outside of academia and working with them can only enrich our programs and their activities.

Chapter 8

A Career of Wonder

Ton van Egmond
NHTV Breda University of Applied Sciences, the Netherlands

Ton van Egmond <egmond.a@nhtv.nl> is senior lecturer and consultant in tourism at NHTV Breda University of Applied Sciences, the Netherlands. He has taught a number of courses in consumer behavior and psychology of tourism. He has been involved in the development of tourism curricula and tourism staff training all over the developing world. Currently, his educational activities focus on sustainable tourism planning and development, particularly in rural areas in developing countries. His research interests chiefly lie in the area of tourism demand. His early publications, during the 1980s and 1990s, were in Dutch. His textbook *The Tourism Phenomenon: Past, Present, Future* is a translation of the Dutch version. His most important publication in English is *Understanding Western Tourists in Developing Countries*.

INTRODUCTION

At first sight, my academic career might not seem to be very dramatic. I have worked at NHTV Breda University of Applied Sciences in the Netherlands from the very beginning in 1974 to this very day. Certainly, I have been loyal to my university, but more than that my career has benefited from being linked to an exceedingly dynamic organization. The number of students in tourism management increased from some 200 in 1974 to more than 3,000

The Study of Tourism: Foundations from Psychology
Tourism Social Science Series, Volume 15, 115–131
Copyright © 2011 by Emerald Group Publishing Limited
All rights of reproduction in any form reserved
ISSN: 1571-5043/doi:10.1108/S1571-5043(2011)0000015011

today, the courses on offer extend from an original focus on tourism and leisure management only to a more complex set of nine related programs, including hotel and facility management, urban development, logistics and mobility, international media and entertainment management, and, recently, international game architecture and design. The scope of these programs has shifted from exclusively oriented toward the Netherlands to the whole world, including the most remote corners, at least where tourism studies are concerned. It is the dynamic, ambitious, and innovative climate of this organization that has made me feel like a "fish in water." My continuing employment at one changing organization has in fact allowed me to dedicate myself to the subjects of my interests and work in all kinds of intriguing countries all over the world.

Studying Psychology

I never planned to work in tourism. During my *Gymnasium* (grammar school) years, I developed a genuine interest in understanding and explaining human behavior, in particular in the way this is influenced by outside agencies. My Roman Catholic upbringing and the process of secularization that was ongoing in the Netherlands during those school years (the early 1960s), as well as authors such as Erich Fromm, all played a role in the development of this interest. The logical consequence was the choice of one of the behavioral sciences such as sociology or psychology. I chose something in between, social psychology, at Leiden University.

In the mid-1960s, academic psychologists, on the one hand, were seeking recognition and respectability in the rigor of a scientific methodology. At least they were doing so in the United States of America and, as psychology the science in the Netherlands was increasingly modeled after American psychology, the behavioristic approach became dominant in psychology programs in Dutch universities. On the other hand, the European philosophical, particularly phenomenological, and psychiatric, particularly psychoanalytic, traditions were also still alive. These opposing movements resulted in incoherent study programs in psychology. Neither the behavioristic nor the clinical approach met my interests in understanding human behavior. I did not develop any interest in rats running a maze or studying statistics for its own sake. Scientific psychological research appeared to aim at controlling independent variables and measuring dependent ones.

Everyday life turned out to be too complicated to study, the consequence of which was that we, future researchers, were supposed to study isolated variables in laboratory settings. The more research designs met scientific qualifications and requirements, the less relevance they had for understanding everyday life. For me, that was disappointing, to say the least. The clinical approach, on the other hand, aimed at diagnosing and therapeutically treating abnormal behavior. Although that was closer to my interests, it was not really appealing, as it was focusing on disorders rather than "normal" behavior.

My master thesis clearly reflected my interests in problems of "normal" life. Assigned by a foundation that was stimulating cancer-related research, I studied (cigarette) smoking behavior of the Dutch, trying to answer questions such as "Why do people start smoking?" "Why do they generally start at an early age (12–14 years in those days)?" "Why did women start smoking later than men and are they bridging the gap currently (in the early 1970s)?" "How can we effectively prevent children from starting to smoke?" "How can we reduce cigarette smoking in our society?" It was applied science that was appealing to me. In an early stage, I decided not to aspire to a career in academia but to try to be in touch with "real" life.

During my years at Leiden University, I had a lot of holidays, all over Europe, but I had not thought of working in tourism for a single second, as I organized my trips myself and was not even aware of something like an emerging tourism industry. However, from the very moment I started working at NHTV, I realized that tourism and, to a lesser extent, leisure was a most interesting field and one to which I could dedicate myself.

WORKING IN TOURISM: THE BEGINNING

I started working at NHTV accidentally. I happened to live in Breda in 1973 and was looking for a job as a young social psychologist. Fortunately, that job was offered to me in November. The social and academic climate was still highly polarized in the Netherlands of the early 1970s, as a remnant of the turbulent late 1960s. "Recreation" had a clear connotation of being related to psychological well-being and public health, whereas "tourism" was associated with the travel industry—that is, with commercial business. In other words, recreation was something for left-wing-oriented people and tourism was much less so. At least one of my left-wing-oriented colleagues cherished an antitourist attitude until the end of his career, some 10 years ago. It was in this context that my then administrator initially suggested that "as a psychologist you'll have a left-wing political orientation and you will prefer recreation to tourism." How wrong he was in that my interests have been in international tourism rather than recreation from the very beginning.

In addition to teaching psychology of tourism and recreation, my duty was recruiting and selecting students, developing effective curricula for tourism and recreation studies, as well as teaching informatics (without computers in the mid-1970s). On the one hand, I did not have much time to develop a full-fledged program in psychology and, on the other hand, literature on psychology of tourism was almost entirely missing. From 1980 onward, Iso-Ahola's textbook *The Social Psychology of Leisure and Recreation* has been a great help.

Although members of the board, such as Theo Bodewes and, even more so, Martinus Kosters, attended many international conferences on tourism and participated in newly emerging academic networks (including hosting an annual conference of the Association *Internationale d'Experts Scientifiques de Tourisme*), tourism studies in the 1970s and 1980s were oriented primarily to the Dutch conditions. The programs were taught in Dutch; students were being prepared for the national tourism industry and recreational jobs in the public sector. My books and other publications on tourism were in Dutch as well. My first book (1987) was a social psychological analysis of the Dutch holiday market. My second book was about international tourism. It was a combination of Jafari's (2007:109) "cautionary" and "adaptancy" plat-forms, arguing that tourism was not all benefit, but on the contrary, comes with many unwanted sociocultural and economic costs, as well as advocating alternative forms of tourism. The title, *Toerisme: verbroedering of verloedering?*, which is difficult to translate into English, was inspired by Young's (1973) title *Tourism Blessing or Blight?* My book raised a lot of publicity in the Dutch media and was the start of numerous press contacts about tourism issues, including radio and TV exposure. My third book on the opportunities and threats that tourism offers to developing countries as a tool for poverty alleviation (1993) was still in Dutch, demonstrating that it took some time for me to switch to the *lingua franca* of tourism.

Going International

The first time I presented a paper at an international conference was in Warsaw 1988, in Kryzstztof Przeclawski's Institute of Tourism. This conference on Tourism and Changing Lifestyles was chaired by Jafar Jafari and Tony Travis. It turned out to be a memorable one for several reasons. One is that Travis (whom I met there for the first time) became a dear friend for life. In the concluding conference session, he shared his feeling with the participants that political change in Poland was in the air. A few months later, Poland was the first socialist country in Eastern Europe to witness a system change. For me, the fall of the Iron Curtain heralded a decade of a great many tourism projects in Eastern European countries, as both the European Union (EU) and national ministries in their funding policies prioritized market-oriented economic development in the former socialist countries.

Although neither the EU nor national Dutch ministries were tourism minded in the early 1990s, this prioritization of economic development in Eastern Europe did not exclude tourism development. During this decade, I was involved in all kinds of projects to contribute to the development of tourism curricula in universities, business schools, and hotel schools, and to train tourism staff in countries such as Hungary, Poland, Russia, and Slovakia. Some projects were funded by the EU, such as the EU Phare Program (one of the three preaccession instruments financed by the EU to assist the applicant countries of Central and Eastern Europe in their preparations for joining theEU); others were funded by the Dutch Ministries of Economic Affairs or Education. Several projects were conducted together with the Hague Hotel School. Most interventions aimed at adjusting existing tourism and hospitality curricula to the requirements of the postsocialist conditions and training the university or school staff accordingly. Generally speaking, these staff members were highly educated geographers, economists, lawyers, and language instructors, all of whom were reorienting themselves from a centrally planned economy to a market economy. One of the most striking cases was Sochi, the Black Sea resort that used to be one of the prominent holiday and spa resorts of the communist party officials in the Soviet Union. A large proportion of the staff, about 50%, was medical, ranging from doctors to masseurs. After the falling apart of the Soviet Union in 1991, bookings to Sochi dropped to almost zero. The authorities and resort staff had to thoroughly reconsider the formula of Sochi as a beach, winter sports, and treatment resort to be able to compete on the commercial holiday and treatment markets. The designation of Sochi for the Olympic Winter Games 2014 suggests that in the end it has successfully been put on the map again.

Working in these former socialist countries, I observed that young students easily adopted an entrepreneurial spirit and a market orientation, while the older generations had much more trouble in doing so. Learning the Russian language, which was compulsory during the communist times, was totally dismissed by youngsters after 1991, in favor of learning English. For me, training students, consequently, was easier than training their teachers.

A communist regime that did not change in the early 1990s was Fidel Castro's government in Cuba. In 1994, I accepted an invitation to be a keynote speaker on an international tourism conference in Havana de Cuba and in the years that followed NHTV staff trained hotel managers and public servants, both in Cuba and in Breda. My personal considerations to do so were that I expected tourism to be able to contribute to opening up this isolated island and to mitigating the rigidity of the Cuban regime. Several years later, I had to conclude that things do not work that way. Private enterprises are not allowed even in 2010 (except for a very limited extent) and the human rights conditions do not seem to have improved at all. Consequently, I stopped working in Cuba.

In 1991, I started an international course in tourism management and consultancy. In addition to the existing Dutch NHTV programs that prepare students for management positions in the tourism industry, the new course aimed at destination planning and development and site management. It appeared to be very attractive for foreign students, as a result of which many hundreds from all over Europe and, to a lesser extent, several African and Asian countries have participated since 1992.

Students of this course were (and still are) compelled to do a six-month placement abroad with a local company, a local or international nongovernmental organization, or a governmental body. Facilitated by a well-equipped placement office, thousands of students have found their way to the most remote corners of the world. To graduate, these students have to do research abroad that is related to planning and management issues in destinations, wherever in the world. Their theses have been a rich source of information on tourism development since 1992. They provide me with insights in all kinds of issues related to planning, development, and management of tourism, particularly in rural areas in developing countries.

Since tourism was not among the priorities of most donor organizations during the 1990s (some exhibited a clear antitourism attitude and others did not see any value in tourism development), the projects outside Europe I have been involved in were not referred to as "tourism" but a "human resources development," "small- and medium-sized enterprise develop-ment," or "international relations." One EU project labeled "international relations" aimed at building a bridge between China and Europe in the late 1990s via Macau, the then Portuguese colony. Together with the Hague Hotel School and the Institute for Tourism Studies, the counterpart in Macau, we developed a Macau-Europe Centre for Advanced Tourism Studies in Macau by training junior colleagues of the institute and developing a full-fledged curriculum. With my junior colleague from there,

I conducted training courses in sustainable tourism planning and development for civil servants in Macau and several times in Xi'an, China. Working
in China gave me some insight in the complicated conditions of a communist
system with a quickly emerging private sector. Macau epitomizes Chinese
pragmatism; after the handover from Portugal to China in December 1999,
it was granted a Special Administrative Region status, which allowed this
small city to plan for an almost unprecedented growth of casino facilities,
resulting in a bigger gambling turnover in the current century than in Las
Vegas.

During the late 1990s and early 2000s, the attitudes of quite a few donor
organizations, including the EU and national Dutch ministries, gradually
shifted from antitouristic to more favorable. The same holds true for
development-aid organizations, nature protection entities, and other nongovernmental agencies. A new age dawned for international tourism
consultants. Projects sponsored by donor organizations and bilateral
projects encouraged me to work in a great diversity of countries in Africa,
Latin America, and Asia.

Thinking about Tourism

In retrospect, I have to conclude that my academic development perfectly
matched Jafari's (2007:109) platforms. During the first decade, I took
tourism for granted as one of many economic activities. It was a promising
business, as it was supposed to be one of the major jobs and income
generators in both developed and developing countries and the road to
diversifying economies. My first book (1987) aimed at providing tools for
the Dutch tourism industry to better analyze their markets and use their
marketing tools more effectively. A few years later, only, my second book
(1989) reflected Jafari's "cautionary" and "adaptancy" platforms. On the
one hand, it was collecting case studies of unwanted sociocultural and
economic costs (the focus was not yet on ecological costs) all over the world;
on the other hand, it was arguing in favor of alternative forms of tourism
that do not bring along undesired impacts. My third book (1993) aimed at
specifying the road to alternative forms of tourism in Third World countries.
Based upon my experience abroad, as well as influenced by the spirit of the
times, I turned to the "knowledge-based platform" in the 1990s. In Jafari's
words, I started favoring

> a multidisciplinary, holistic treatment and understanding of
> tourism [that] seeks to discover tourism's structure and

functions, to formulate concepts or theories accounting for it, to apply research tools and methods that best reveal its nature and substance, and to articulate its dependence on, and relationships with systems outside itself, and more. (2007:110)

Actually, my academic career in tourism studies thus started only in the 1990s.

Unlike many of the contributors to Nash's book on the anthropological and sociological beginnings of tourism studies, who had to struggle against a general lack of acceptance and recognition of tourism as a serious academic subject and often felt "largely alone," I have always worked in a context that is highly supportive and conducive for studying tourism. The major historical constraint in the Dutch University of Applied Sciences system is that this used to be primarily educational institutes, not having research budgets and facilities at their disposal. Although these conditions are gradually changing, as both the Ministry of Education and the universities themselves have started to invest in research facilities, much of my tourism-related writing was done in my spare time. NHTV is currently investing a lot in facilitating research by its staff. I was happy to be the first to get my PhD (2006), with the financial support of the board.

Working at a university that started as a school for tourism studies, I did not have any reason to feel "largely alone" when studying tourism, but life is pretty lonely where the study of tourism from a psychological perspective is concerned. When any newspaper, magazine, or radio program wants to explain tourism behavior in general or holidays of the Dutch in particular, they will sooner or later ask me how come it is possible that so few academics are able to throw their light on this matter.

My "knowledge-based" career is dedicated to several lines of interest. First and foremost, it is about understanding the tourism phenomenon, or the demand side of tourism. Second, I soon found out that most tourism literature has a strong Western bias, though many publications seem to claim some universal validity. When we try to understand Western consumers, including tourists, the question will arise soon as to how they relate to non-Westerners, or what diversity can be found within Western cultures where value systems, lifestyles, and corresponding interests are concerned. My current activities are more and more focusing on cross-cultural studies.

Third, my involvement in a great number of projects in developing countries that aim to contribute to a variety of goals, such as poverty alleviation, nature preservation, rural development or revitalization, protection of indigenous cultures, and the like, increasingly led to questions as to the effectiveness of interventions by nongovernmental organization, private consultants, and local stakeholders.

Finally, in the late 1990s, NHTV established the Centre for Sustainable Tourism and Transport. Within the global discourse on sustainability, including sustainable tourism development, we have wanted to define our position. This was strengthened by the appeal of the Dutch tourism industry, the organization of tour operators in particular, which was addressed to us in terms of assistance in the development of sustainable policies and products. Fortunately, these lines of interest are not at odds with each other but, on the contrary, appear to be quite coherent and mutually reinforcing.

Understanding the Tourism Phenomenon

Although most of us will agree that tourism is a "multifaceted phenomenon" that should be the subject of multidisciplinary (Mowforth and Munt 1998; Wang 2000), interdisciplinary, or even extradisciplinary (Tribe 1997) studies, there are still few comprehensive studies that take into account the heterogeneity, complexity, and dynamics of the phenomenon. Many textbooks and articles fail to do so by reducing tourists to something simple and static and treating them as a unitary type. Textbooks easily refer to *the* cultural tourist, *the* ecotourist, *the* backpacker, *the* senior tourist, or even *the* tourist. These terms mask a plenitude of social and cultural distinctions. On the road to understanding the tourist phenomenon, Erik Cohen's publications have been among the most inspiring for me, as they tried to do justice to the great diversity of tourist motivations and practices.

Psychological studies on consumer behavior aim at explaining behavior at the individual micro level. Many (often American) textbooks on this subject devote a chapter to "consumer motivation," but motivation is about human needs, which are taken for granted as something universal, not culture bound, and are either seen as biological (innate) or learned. Learning processes are approached on individual basis, rather than collective or group processes. Understanding tourist behavior (including motivation, learning processes, and the development of tastes and preferences) in a social and cultural context requires linking up psychological and anthropological micro-level studies with historical, sociological, and economic macro-level studies. Most tourism studies, however, being disciplinary in character, are not able to link these levels. Those that explicitly attempt to show the interrelationships between the micro-level psychological and the macro-level sociological aspects of tourist behavior are almost entirely missing. I took up the challenge by relating Western tourist behavior to their social and cultural context.

Modern consumer culture is the most important keyword. Historically, a holiday was "the other life," a contrast to everyday life that offers a way to recuperate from work or to escape the mundane, routine, boredom, and paramount reality (Cohen and Taylor 1976). Present-day tourism in Western countries, however, can only be understood by including this keyword (modern consumer culture) in the explanation. One of the main characteristics of what Campbell (1987) calls a modern consumer culture is a fun morality, the search for pleasure, kicks, and interesting experiences. Our consumer behavior is motivated by the pursuit of (often sensual) enjoyment. The possession of properties, the purchase of consumer goods, having exciting experiences are not sources of satisfaction and peace of mind, but rather impulses to new purchases and more, possibly more interesting and more exciting, experiences. We are part of an experience economy. Modern man's consumption pattern does not lead to a final stage, but is rather an inseparable part of his lifestyle.

This modern consumer culture is perfectly reflected in contemporary holiday behavior, as it is in shopping and going out. A holiday is a great opportunity to spend time and money simultaneously in a hedonistic way or in search of interesting experiences. People in our modern society have learned to desire holidays and have come to think of them as essential for their psychological well-being. For many Europeans, the decision-making processes related to holidays no longer begin with the question "Are we going on holiday or not?" but rather "Where are we going for the holiday(s)?" Rather than conceiving tourism as a "departure" from the routines and practices of everyday life, tourism has become an established part of everyday life, culture, and consumption (McCabe 2002:63).

The outcomes of these decision-making processes, however, are anything but homogeneous, resulting in an ever broader range of preferences and practices, from visiting crowded beach resorts to seeking solitude in isolated landscapes, from full-moon beach partying to an ascetic stay in a monastery, from quiet hiking to adrenaline producing physical activities, from stationary to round trip holidays, and from being "mass tourists" to pioneer-like "travelers." In Western European countries, this range has grown to be immense. Tastes and preferences appear to be symptoms of the present diversity of lifestyles and are strongly related to Bourdieu's (1986) forms of economic, social, and cultural capital.

An extremely interesting issue is the notion among both academic authors and travel writers that "tourists = mass tourism = bad" and "travelers = appropriate traveling = good" (Mowforth and Munt 1998:26). They show middle class and/or elitist preoccupations with mass tourism, as opposed to traveling, and, consequently, are evaluative rather than analytical in their approaches to tourism issues. Many Western tourists demonstrate the same bias.

All respondents in my research among Western tourists who travel in developing countries want to be "travelers" rather than "tourists." Further, "authenticity" is highly valued, and the majority of respondents are eager to see "real life" and visit "unspoilt places" ("natural" and "unmarked" sites and sights not contaminated by other tourists and not staged for tourists). In practice, however, they visit "staged" and "contrived" sites, which are either created for tourists or adapted to tourists' tastes and comprehension. Most tourists (except for the pioneer-like ones) can easily cope with this paradoxical situation, as long as they are able to frame their own experiences and playfully accept "contrived" attractions as if they were real (Cohen 1995:20). In my recent publications (2007 and others), I tried to explain this search for "authenticity" in terms of the Protestant and Romantic history of the generating countries, not, or not only, in MacCannell's (1976) and Cohen's (1979) alienation terms.

Cross-Cultural Studies

Tourism literature is dominated by academics working essentially to North American, as well as Australian/New Zealand/British discourses (Prentice 2004:276). Studies of differences in motivation, interests, preferences, and behavior across cultures are only emerging recently. Most textbooks do not refer to a Northern European and North American bias in international tourism and do not account for the fact that the motivation, interests, and related concepts are culture bound and that the vast majority of the world's population does not travel, at least not for leisure purposes. The motivations of many South American, Arab, African, Indian, or non-English-speaking Europeans are hardly known (Prentice 2004). My research in the early 21st century gave an account of the motivations, interests, preferences, and behavior of British, Dutch, German, Scandinavian, Swiss, and (to a lesser extent) North American tourists, but does not explain how they relate to non-Westerners.

Asian markets that are in search of "unspoilt" pristine nature or "authentic" local life appear to be rare, if not nonexistent. According to Graburn, to most Japanese nature is boring to contemplate, dangerous to enter, and far removed from everyday life, rather than subject to romantic interest and admiration. It is only appreciated when it is strictly controlled, and when it is "naturally" represented and miniaturized (such as in *bonsai* and gardens), and socially approved for perusal (and photography) in the right seasons (1995:62). Similarly, Lindberg et al argue that Eastern cultures, including Chinese, tend to favor human manipulation of nature in order to enhance its appeal, in contrast to preservation in a pristine state. The Chinese image of natural landscapes is, according to these authors, nurtured by cultural sources, such as poems and paintings rather than the search for "unspoilt paradise" (2003:119).

According to Graburn, the Japanese nostalgic tradition resembles, at first sight, the contemporary Western interest in cultural heritage, but is itself a tradition as old as Japan. This backward-looking search reflects a millennia-old search for identity because Japan, as a peripheral island nation, has constantly had to redefine its identity *vis-à-vis* China, Korea, and the outside world. Japanese cultural and heritage tourism consequently focuses on historical creations such as shrines, temples, castles, gardens, and festivals rather than indigenous peoples (Graburn 1995:67). A study by Ryan demonstrates that interest in indigenous Maori culture in New Zealand is mainly limited to Northern Europeans and North Americans. The Asian markets—the most important markets for New Zealand in terms of arrivals and expenditures—are not seemingly interested in Maori culture. Nonetheless, they seem to appreciate the staged performances that they attend (2002:966).

Interest of Africans in "unspoiled" nature and "authentic" local life has not been the subject of any easily accessible research but, having worked in quite a few sub-Saharan countries, I never came across Africans who exhibit a romantic interest in nature (with the exception of Afrikaners in South Africa who have European roots). Hiking or camping in nature is alien to Africans rather than appealing. Local community life is something to avoid rather than visit.

In recent years, I have been working in Indonesia. In addition to spectacular monuments and photogenic culture (in Bali in particular), this country has an abundance of nature and "community life" on offer. Ecotourism and community-based tourism are among the current buzzwords. However, that ecotourism which is associated with romantic gazing at nature, conservation of nature, and contribution to the welfare of the inhabitants of nature areas is much more appealing to Europeans, Americans, and Australians than to Asians, who do make up the vast majority of arrivals to Indonesia. This also holds true for community-based tourism that has connotations of romanticizing "unspoiled" community life and participating in everyday activities that are not staged for tourists. These are non-Asian long-haul markets.

Most African countries do not have spectacular monuments or culture, but they do have nature and "local life" on offer. As Africans are not interested in visiting nature or local communities, these countries are dependent on long-haul (particularly Northern European) markets that are limited in size. The number of destinations that aim at these markets is increasing explosively, as a consequence of which competition on the ecotourism and community-based tourism markets is increasingly fierce.

For communities in developing countries that want to develop community-based tourism, an additional issue is that it is difficult to understand the interests of Western tourists. For example, in Africa, tight travel schedules of organized travelers, restless dashing around, feelings of guilt or embarrassment when confronted with poverty, interest in poor rural life, and a search for authenticity can be perceived by residents as alien to their nature. For indigenous peoples, who have been disparaged and maltreated in their home countries throughout the colonial years, European interest in their "authentic life" might be puzzling. The lifeworlds of any type of backpackers are fundamentally different from those of residents in most of the (often collectivistic) areas visited. Traveling individually, not having any social or family obligations, renouncing Western comfort, and wearing ripped clothes are among the features that can be perceived by residents as wholly alien to them. Loose sexual morality, use of drugs, and petty theft can be among the annoying features. Where volunteers are concerned, not many residents will easily understand why Europeans, Americans, or Australians from the developed world are prepared to pay handsome amounts of money to come and work with them, wanting to connect with poor rural people, and voluntarily renouncing Western comfort.

For any community in Indonesia or Africa that wants to develop community-based tourism, understanding the interests of Western tourists is a critical factor for successfully operating on this complex and diverse market, both where product development and communication with the markets are concerned.

An interesting cross-cultural issue that is challenging in its own right concerns conducting tourism-related training in countries with divergent educational systems and traditions, different stages of tourism development, and diverse political priorities. Sooner or later, this leads to the question of which educational approach is most effective in which place. Our Western systems and methodologies often cannot be simply transplanted to developing countries. While Western educational systems increasingly stress students' activities in the process of learning both academic and professional competencies (for example, by a great variety of forms of problem-based learning), non-Western systems employ more traditional top-down teaching methods. Finding a balance between those systems and identifying the most effective approach have been among the challenging aspects of working in non-Western countries.

Tourism as a "Salvation" Tool

Wherever I worked, be it Eastern Europe, Latin America, Africa, or Asia, I came across numerous tourism projects that are initiated by local authorities, communities, nongovernmental organizations, or private persons to contribute to local and regional, often rural, economic development. A growing number of development-aid organizations adopt community-based tourism as part of their strategies to reduce poverty. Many projects, however, fail to reach their economic goals. They have problems in attracting the required volume of tourists so as to pass the break-even point, or host the "wrong" (nonlucrative and/or harmful) tourists. Projects are inward-oriented rather than market-oriented; they are not set up to meet an apparent demand but rather to meet local needs (van Egmond 2007). Knowledge of potential markets is commonly lacking, as are the tools to enter and exploit these markets.

As community-based tourism projects in Africa, Latin America, or Asia are heavily dependent on the Northern/Western European markets, they all "fish from the same limited pond." Moreover, many countries where local communities or nongovernmental organizations have started this type of tourism are low in the destination hierarchy; they are among the least popular destinations. Once more, while the proportion of tourists from this part of Europe is limited, the regions and communities in developing countries that like to welcome them as a means of alleviating prevailing poverty are numerous, meaning that they are in an unfavorable competitive position. The reality is that quite a number of community-based rural projects, focused on receiving tourists thus contributing to local poverty alleviation, do not manage to earn back their investments, let alone make profits. Further, domestic and regional tourism market options in virtually every country in the "South" are ignored as a source of visits and income to local indigenous communities. "Fishing from the same pond of Europeans" requires defining which groups are best suited to the local goals and conditions and also using the scarce marketing tools effectively to reach and serve these groups.

In a similar way, nongovernmental organizations involved in nature conservation and national authorities in quite a few developing countries are increasingly aware of the potential of tourism to contribute to the protection and conservation of nature areas, of wildlife, and of biological diversity. Most conservation projects, however, are resource oriented rather than market oriented. Their managers (often conservationists) think in terms of nature protection rather than of attracting and serving specific target groups.

Theoretically, in developing countries, nature protection and poverty alleviation might go hand in hand, when local entrepreneurs or employees are involved in tourism development. Attracting both the "right" tourists and the desired number of them is one of the critical issues. Adequate understanding of tourists is an essential condition for effective marketing and management of nature.

Taking these issues into account, in the late 1990s, I started a course in local and regional rural tourism development for students in their graduation year. I developed a framework for a sustainable tourism development strategy that is based on a tourism potential assessment in rural destinations. With the help of this framework, students learn how to analyze the existing conditions in any rural destination and to develop a vision for future conditions as part of an integrated rural development perspective that is desirable for as many local stakeholders as possible and that is feasible from financial, political, physical, and market points of view. Dozens of students have done research since in all kinds of rural destinations worldwide, supplying both their commissioners with useful analyses and strategic recommendations and me with most useful on-the-spot information.

Sustainable Tourism Development

The Centre for Sustainable Tourism and Transport that NHTV initiated in the 1990s focused on a broad range of sustainability-related subjects, from emissions by tourism transport and climate change to issues related to nature protection and poverty alleviation.

In its early days, I was involved in the whole range of subjects. These included an EU project on "Multi-stakeholder European Targeted Action for Sustainable Tourism & Transport," to "increase the competitiveness and sustainable development of European Tourism and its enterprises" (Peeters et al 2004). An appreciable activity was my involvement with the Dutch Association of Tour Operators and Travel Agents. Starting in the days of the Millennium declaration, all its tour operators had to implement a sustainable tourism program, including the appointment of a sustainable tourism manager, the development of several sustainable initiatives, and the publication of these initiatives on their websites. The sustainable tourism managers had to pass an examination on related issues in order to be recognized by the association. I developed an online training course in 2001/ 2002. In those days, the association was at the forefront where thinking of sustainability in the industry was concerned. Interestingly, a few years later, the association was overtaken by the British Federation of Tour Operators, the result of which is that the federation, the association, and some Belgian and German partners jointly started Travelife <http://www.travelife.eu>, which has been set up to support an efficient and cost-effective introduction of sustainability principles within the tour operator sector in these European countries.

Whereas NHTV's Centre for Sustainable Tourism and Transport focused on emissions of tourism-related transport (aviation in particular) and the corresponding contribution to global warming and climate change (Peeters 2007), my personal interests shifted in recent years to the role of tourism in Third World destinations as a tool for economic development and nature protection. The United Nations World Tourism Organization and the United Nations Environment Program produced many publications on this subject. These are certainly valuable guidelines for planning and developing tourism in a sustainable way; but they do not discuss which types of tourism will bring along the desired rather than undesired impacts, nor do they specify how the "right" tourists should be addressed and attracted. Tourists seem to be taken for granted or "as broad a range of tourists as possible should be attracted." Good decisions by Third World governments and nongovernmental organizations as to what type of tourism is most conducive to development need to be based on a differentiated analysis. My present activities are focusing on such a differential analysis of tourism markets in and to developing countries and their economic and sociocultural effects on destination areas. Here, fortunately, the aforementioned lines of interest come together, being quite coherent and mutually reinforcing and giving me a clear focus for my tourism-related activities in the later days of my academic career, a delightful career as far as the study of tourism was concerned.

A "CAREER OF WONDER"

Why was psychology—at least in the 1960s—focusing on laboratory research rather than developing methodologies to understand "real life"?

Why do textbooks on consumer behavior take "needs" as a starting point rather than explain how and where needs originate? Why are tourists—after so many years of tourism studies—"a poorly explored part of the tourism business?" (van Egmond 2007:1). Why are cross-cultural tourism studies still in their infancy? Why do both academic authors on the tourism phenomenon and travel writers show middle class and/or elitist preoccupations with mass tourism, as opposed to traveling, and, consequently, are evaluative rather than analytical in their approaches to tourism issues? Why do Western tourists who travel in developing countries highly value "authenticity" (searching for "the real life"), while their actual behavior is often at odds with that desire? When tourism is supposed to contribute to poverty alleviation in poor countries, to nature preservation, to rural development, to empowerment of women and indigenous communities, and much more, why are differential studies that explain the economic and sociocultural impacts per type of tourism almost entirely missing?

Questions like these—but even more so the cross-cultural and differential studies that are referred to-constitute a wide field for further academic research ... I doubt if I myself will be able to contribute substantially to further exploration of these questions, as I am going to retire soon. But, I am looking forward to witnessing more and more scholars addressing these interesting issues.

Chapter 9

Career Souvenirs

Philip L. Pearce

James Cook University, Australia

Philip L. Pearce <Philip.pearce@jcu.edu.au> is foundation professor of
tourism, School of Business, James Cook University, Australia. He studied
psychology at the University of Adelaide in Australia and then at the
University of Oxford in England, where he undertook a doctorate on the
perceptions of tourists. His principal interests are in tourist behavior and
experience. He has spent his academic career principally at James Cook
University and has been involved in teaching undergraduates at all levels as
well as supervising a large number of doctoral students. He is the author of
several books about tourist behavior, the earliest being *The Social
Psychology of Tourist Behaviour,* while his latest coauthored work includes
Tourism, Tourists and Wellbeing and *Tourist Shopping Villages.* He is a
founding member of the International Academy for the Study of Tourism
and was the editor of *The Journal of Tourism Studies* for 16 years. His
personal enthusiasms include his family, sport, and Australian cattle dogs as
well as maintaining a desire to travel more.

INTRODUCTION

In early 1974, I had my first meeting with my future social psychology
supervisor at the University of Oxford. I had recently arrived from
Australia, thanks to the benefits of a valuable scholarship from the

The Study of Tourism: Foundations from Psychology
Tourism Social Science Series, Volume 15, 133–154
Copyright © 2011 by Emerald Group Publishing Limited
All rights of reproduction in any form reserved
ISSN: 1571-5043/doi:10.1108/S1571-5043(2011)0000015012

University of Adelaide. He asked me what I was interested in researching. I babbled on for a few minutes about the complexities of personality, an area where I had conducted my psychology honors thesis. Boring, he commented, what else interests you? I had taken six weeks to reach Oxford, traveling for part of the way on the cheapest of cruise ships accompanied by a cast of weird and wild compatriots. Well, I suggested, somewhat nervously, this process and experience of traveling is interesting. Yes much better, he replied, do some reading and come back with some ideas. So the interest formally began, and hopefully I am still reading and coming back with ideas.

This personal account of my early academic career tracks my early student career from Adelaide, Australia to Oxford, England. Along the way some of the formative people and events are noted. The development of my autobiography is then followed through a brief period of teaching at Flinders University of South Australia followed by my extended time at James Cook University in Northern Australia. In an application of good psychological theory, the autobiography may well contain some self-serving attribution bias—the good things I report are likely to be cast as my own achievements and the less adequate parts of my story are hidden or ascribed to outside influences. To correct this view I need and want to record the very positive influence of many other people to my ongoing work and I hope that I have mentioned most of them in these pages.

PLACES AND PEOPLE

The comment I made to my Oxford supervisor about an interest in travel was not entirely without some preparation. My parents were teachers and during the school summer holidays we usually undertook an extended road trip to see other parts of Australia. Later and during university breaks, a friend and I had also traveled a lot by hitchhiking and half-starving our way around remote parts of Australia and all over New Zealand. Our lack of planning and lack of money provided memorable encounters ranging from traveling with prison escapees to sleeping in a sewerage farm (to our defense, it was the only green grass in a remote Australian town in the parched summer landscape). I had been, in a way, slowly forming questions about the psychology of tourism. What was it good for? How did people change? How much could you remember of all the people and places? I was effectively collecting psychological questions and souvenirs for a yet-to-be-devised career.

A little more biographical detail sets these musings in a richer context. Growing up in Australia in the 1950s and 1960s was for me pleasant and comfortable, even if the country was remote from other centers of culture, intellectual ferment, and excitement. Our home city was Adelaide, South Australia, a planned settlement of English migrants which by the time I was born was growing increasingly affluent due to a successful farming hinterland. My father's family had arrived in Australia in 1851, almost at the start of South Australia's settlement, and consisted of farmers and teachers. Their roots were English, and in fact I later discovered that members of the family lived in the Cotswolds near Oxford. My mother's family was also from England, but with some Scottish heritage. They had arrived 40 years before I was born. Any residual English connections were remote and it was later to be a shock to live in England and see how much the Australia I knew was different to the United Kingdom.

Nevertheless, the education system of my high school and indeed much of the university education I experienced had firm English roots. At high school, for example, it was English literature not any modern Australian fiction or poetry that was on our curriculum. The highly streamed classes meant that if you did well at age 11, you were destined to study English literature, Latin, mathematics, and science. The competitive academic environment at school was a formative influence on my approach to study. There were social and school-supported incentives to get the highest marks one could. Even seating positions in class were altered frequently to reflect performance. It was an environment in which I was successful and it certainly encouraged ambition among those doing well. Nevertheless, the competitive theme has not always been a constructive influence on my academic life. I suspect the view that I am a competitive character has sometimes damaged cooperation and limited opportunities. The notion was perhaps reinforced by my participation in competitive sport, especially cricket. I have also been actively involved in showing and breeding dogs, which extend some of the family interests in animals (my one older brother is a successful and innovative farmer).

Adelaide: A Grounding in Psychology

The competitive jostling for class positions in high school also had the possibly unintended effect that it was better to be quite good in all of your subjects rather than outstanding in any one. As a preparation for psychology and tourism studies that has ultimately been a benefit. Not quite sure of exactly what I wanted to do after high school, I went to the University of Adelaide to undertake an arts degree. The choice of my degree was prompted by a scholarship from the state government and I was looking at a career in secondary schools, possibly teaching mathematics and English. I was one of about 400 students who took the introductory psychology class in the arts degree. The combination of numerical, analytical, and literacy skills needed in psychology, together with my solid study habits, proved to be a good match and I shared the prize for the best first year results. Despite some fuss with the government scholarship, which had been given on the basis that I would be a teacher, I was allowed to pursue the four-year honors degree in psychology.

The psychology course at Adelaide was delivered by a solid cohort of Scottish and English academics, with a couple of Australian staff. I was drawn a little more to the personality, social psychology, and developmental interests but we covered all core topics, including a fairly strenuous physiology course and experimental work on skills. I particularly remember finding Secord and Backman's textbook on *Social Psychology* initially something of a challenge; it seemed a very formal and remote way of approaching topics such as friendship and social relations. I also studied English as my other major and there was a very clear division of approaches to understanding human conduct in the two discipline areas. My psychology honors thesis was an attempt to better understand the perception of people using complexity and simplicity as a cognitive style. It was underpinned by an interest in George Kelly's personal construct theory which seemed then (and still does) to be a useful method to access the main dimensions people use to think about parts of their world.

By the time I was involved in the psychology honors year, the Vietnam War protests in Adelaide were at their height. I was certainly not a radical student, but I did participate in some demonstrations and crowd events that were both exhilarating and frightening. I also began to see the staff less as remote lecturers and more as individuals with quirks and personal struggles. We admired one of the flashy young lecturers with a red sports car and a seemingly infinite string of girlfriends. We were amused by the great enthusiasm and enjoyment of life shown by our hard-to-understand Scottish lecturer who dealt with animal behavior and we were slightly wary of the experimental researcher investigating sexual deviance. The spirit of the times also encouraged some irreverence toward the staff. We were all convinced, for example, that a certain Peter Glow had only married his attractive wife Rosie so he could always "have a Rosie Glow." It seemed amusing at the time.

On the day the final honors results were announced, 25 nervous final year students waited outside the head of department's office. We progressed one at a time into his office to learn of our marks. Finally, it was my turn. Welford, the head of department, who had spent most of his life in Cambridge, was in his third year in Australia. In a pivotal moment, he informed me that I had the top first-class honors mark and added that I should go to Oxford to study for a doctorate. It was generous advice for someone from Cambridge. In time and with his support, I won a special scholarship to embark on that more intense research career. Family, mates, and first girlfriends were all to be left behind as my life was reorganized and I chose to pursue the international opportunity.

Oxford

Apart from developing a stronger interest in certain fields of psychology rather than others, the undergraduate psychology education served essentially as a broad preparation for postgraduate study. The transition to Oxford was not an easy one, but it was the beginnings of my tourism study and a richer acquaintance with world-class scholarship. The social psychology section in the Department of Experimental Psychology at Oxford consisted of an active and quite focused group of researchers. The most senior academic was Michael Argyle. He was in the middle of a long, distinguished, and productive career of writing well-known books and supervising many PhD students. His principal interests were in social skills (a term he virtually introduced into the popular idiom), nonverbal behavior, then relationships, and later happiness. Another senior scholar, Rom Harre, the social philosopher, had a less experimental and more interpretive style to his academic work and provided a counter to Argyle's mostly positivist approach. Both Argyle and Harre respected the work of Goffman whose microsociological commentaries formed a reference point for field studies of social behavior. Desmond Morris, a zoologist who had achieved much fame and wealth with *The Naked Ape* (1968) and television appearances, was also interested in social behavior across cultures and was an infrequent but intriguing outlier of the core group. There were also several research fellows and postdoctoral staff who were dependent on research grants for their continued time at Oxford. The most senior of these, Peter Collett, became my direct supervisor, developing his own fame much later by ultimately producing a well-researched popular book on communication *The Book of Tells* (2004) and even becoming a resident television commentator on "Big Brother." Collett, like me, had come to Oxford from a "colonial country," in his case Northern Rhodesia (Zambia), and having completed his PhD in the previous five years, he was well placed to be an effective and engaged supervisor.

Collett's African roots meant that his interests were somewhat more eclectic than those of the rest of the group. Both he and Michael Argyle were keen to see a few of the PhD students attempt to expand the field of interest of social psychology inquiry and accordingly were tolerant of my interests in tourists' behavior. Over a 20-year period from 1970 to 1990, more than 40 PhD students graduated from this group, many becoming professors and departmental heads around the world. My time at Oxford coincided with the early to middle period of the flourishing of this unit; it had the financial resources for the senior staff to travel in order to conduct varied studies and the reputation to attract students from around the country and the world. At any one time there were about 6–10 graduate students attached to the group and we were frequently called upon to host visiting professors or be a part of their visits.

My supervisor was attentive to my interests and gave me a copy of Dean MacCannell's (1973) first article on authenticity. We saw some promise in it, but wondered whether people really saw the world in quite the way MacCannell described. We thought that empirical work on the topic would be insightful. Despite its interest, the paper did not directly affect my PhD work, which was emerging as studying tourism motivation and attitude change due to travel among younger budget groups. I was, though, primed to agree with Erik Cohen's revisionist appraisal of MacCannell's (1976) work, because Cohen's position was very close to the earlier supervisor–student conversations I had enjoyed (Cohen 1979b).

In some ways, the senior staff and the visitors were probably not as important as the core team of fellow graduate students with whom I shared offices and a social life. Mostly English and uniformly talented, they were intensely focused on their work while also being somewhat more sophisticated than I was in their social development and varied relationships. As an Australian and the newest member of the cohort, I was effectively no threat to any of them. My chosen topic did not overlap with theirs and my Australian background made any social class difficulties irrelevant. This had a surprising benefit. I was quite popular and able to mix with all of them as individuals as well as playing a role in the cohesion of the group. The wider Oxford environment was physically beautiful yet daunting. It had wonderful bookstores; there were always influential visitors and often public speeches by political and academic celebrities. Importantly, there were sporting opportunities that were to become important for my acceptance and social integration.

These situational benefits did not necessarily mean that my life was easy or that the PhD work went smoothly. There were several levels of difficulty. The first problem was a dearth of previous work. Despite diligent efforts to locate studies that might serve as precedents, and there were many good libraries in Oxford to make these forays, there was little work exploring the psychology of tourists. At times, this made me wonder if there was anything different about tourists and tourism at all, at least from the point of view of a psychology researcher. I did find a newish journal, *Annals of Tourism Research*, but the work it contained was that of anthropologists and sociologists and not as specifically empirical as I needed and wished to undertake. Amir's contact hypothesis in ethnic relations was useful, but still not focused on tourists' contacts.

I brought a second difficulty on myself by rather quickly taking off for a field trip to Morocco. The opportunity to join a travel group arose unexpectedly. I had only been in Oxford three months, but the chance to accompany one of the many young budget tour groups on a trip to Spain and Morocco arose through a meeting in London with an adventure travel company. It was hastily organized with my supervisor's approval, but was relatively ill-conceived in terms of what I wanted to achieve and how I would approach the fellow tourists. I know that now I would not favor my own PhD students doing what I did. I was meant to be away for 10 days, but the travel was extended to over three weeks because the 16-person trip itself was a chaotic shambles of misadventures, disorganization, passionate couplings (not mine), and failed border crossings.

We never made it into Morocco, being turned around at the border as the security guards accused the group of running guns and drugs. We detoured to Portugal without an itinerary or accommodation, an inadequate number of tents, and a rapacious driver courier who slept his way through the female company. In the long delays and under intense questioning, my student status in psychology was unearthed with the consequence that I became the counseling service for the other 15 tourists whose lives all seemed impossibly troubled. It was, however, to cite the apposite cliché "a learning experience." I felt the travel was clearly having some role in affecting attitudes, views, and life perspectives. Much overdue, I returned to the Oxford psychology department to a very amused welcoming party of fellow students and staff. For several years my supervisor sent me amusing greeting cards embellished with various images of the prodigal son returning.

On recovering from this messy adventure, I read more about the history of travel, about wayfinding and orientation, and changes in attitude. I became familiar with the work of Kevin Lynch on images of the city and adapted his coding scheme to assess tourists' knowledge of visiting locations (Pearce 1977). I pursued the Kelly construct theory as an emic (although then I did not know the concept) way to assess tourists' dominant ways of viewing the people and destinations they visited. I planned studies with a pre–post design to assess how much the intense packaged holidays changed the participants' perceptions. Slowly a pathway and a pattern of work to do a doctorate grew.

Life in the world of scholarly study was moving forward, but the rest of my existence was not yet very settled. Oxford has a system of colleges to which one belongs as a prime home base. It is a core part of the university and my college was the wealthy St. John's. The colleges are more than halls of residence and form a kind of university within the university. To an Australian, they were also full of weird rituals, status-oriented ways of behaving, and tasteless food. These views were not shared by my predominantly upper middle class and all male college companions who had been reared on similar diets and cultures in their private expensive boys' schools. Arriving in the middle of a sodden gray English winter was also not helpful in the cheerfulness stakes.

There was also the matter of a troubled and intermittent relationship with an Australian girlfriend who had come to England at the same time to travel around and who alternatively provided occasional friendship mixed with marked absences. The arrival of the spring followed by a glorious English summer and the opportunity to play cricket in a variety of beautiful settings made up for many of these challenges. My success at cricket helped my integration within the college, and the next year I became captain, which was certainly my first memorable leadership experience in dealing with talented and assertive others. I began to eat better as I learned to cater for myself and avoid college food. The wandering girlfriend became a permanent fixture as my mother, who had suffered a near fatal heart attack, came to visit and encouraged the girlfriend and me to become a more permanent couple. The years at Oxford saw me collect data for four large studies and with skilled advice from my supervisor on how to present the work, a thesis was successfully completed. I learned much from the supervision process at Oxford and hope that some of these career souvenirs are apparent to my own students as I work with them.

Flinders

Under some family pressure, low on cash, and without a definite job in England, I returned to Australia taking a junior position at Adelaide's then other university, the Flinders University of South Australia. A part of the attraction of taking that position rather than a similar one at Adelaide University was the emergence of Flinders as a more socially oriented psychology department. It boasted two of the country's leading social psychology professors, Norm Feather and Leon Mann, who were both Australians but had learned their trade in the United States. They were active researchers but followed in traditions set elsewhere exploring values and crowds, respectively.

At Flinders, I learned a lot about how to teach in the Australian context, grinding my way for 2 years through up to 12 hours of repeated practical and tutorial sessions on a regular basis. It prompted some "out-of-body experiences" as I watched myself, from afar, repeat information and instructions for the 10th, 11th, or 12th time that week. Still, I liked and understood the students and I think I was liked and did some good teaching work.

Publishing though was not an emphasis and while the two professors were active writers, the local environment was not at all about pushing out papers and I let that component of my developing career drift. The return to Australia had been rapid, and taking the Flinders job at the junior level was about earning cash. I looked around for a lectureship and settled on an offer from James Cook University, in the tropical north of Australia. This relocation was conceived by quite a few friends and southern Australians generally as an odd and remote choice. For me, it was about the potential to undertake more tourism work, since the location of James Cook was in a developing tourism region.

James Cook and Psychology

The position at James Cook was as a social psychologist in a behavioral sciences department. The department name was really a convenient label for a small regional university to group together their limited number of sociologists, anthropologists, and psychologists. While Flinders might have looked like the best place to be in Australia, its professors somehow lacked the knack of encouraging others in the right way, even though their own work was very respectable. At James Cook, Bill Scott, the senior editor of the leading US publication outlet, *The Journal of Personality and Social Psychology*, had been the founding behavioral sciences professor. His conservative values prompted him to escape the United States and seek a quieter environment for his family. He had just moved when I arrived, but his presence had attracted a set of bright young staff and his successor George Kearney was an astute department head who recognized the talent in his group and so shouldered the administrative burdens and let them build careers.

Within three or four years, James Cook was a force in the country in social psychology. International professors called by, often in preference to visiting the larger capital city universities. Michael Argyle from Oxford declared it to be the most exciting young department in Australia and showed his commitment to the words by organizing Oxford Pergamon contracts for our books, including my first tourism volume *The Social Psychology of Tourist Behaviour* (1982). Mike Smithson, a sociologist, and my first PhD student Paul Amato, both of my age, were excellent stimulating colleagues at that time. We also published a book together on *Dimensions of Helping Behaviour* (1983). I also supervised Glenn Ross, for his master's thesis and then part of his PhD in those early years, and the fact that we still write together 30 years later is a sign of friendship and mutual respect.

A feature of this 1980s' work was its controlled approach to data and the stress on theorizing about tourists and other social behaviors. In particular, much of it tried to frame the specific behaviors under study with contexts and a blueprint or map of the more general or larger phenomenon, thus partly overcoming the conundrum of approaching a big topic with picayune studies. More recently, I have termed this approach phenomenon sampling: a desire to make sure that one understands how the instances under study fit the full definitional compass of the kind of tourism or topic being considered. I did not use and remain reluctant to use simplistic paradigm labels for most of my work, but it is, I like to think, intelligently applied postpositivism, conducted hopefully with some flair. More recently, I have begun to favor more interpretive or constructivist approaches.

An Interlude to Harvard

In mid-1981, I had completed the manuscript for the book on *The Social Psychology of Tourist Behaviour* and was fortunate to win a Fulbright scholarship to be held jointly at MIT and Harvard University. I had visited Harvard briefly two years before on a quick 30-day bus tour around the United States and been impressed by a different kind of industriousness than I had experienced at Oxford and that was mostly missing in Australia at the time. The extra element was the purposeful approach to publishing and I looked forward to the time in Boston as a further plank in my academic education. I was not disappointed. Two highlights and influences remain. I was able to have conversations with the planner and architect Kevin Lynch whose work I had used in my doctorate; he was able to impress on me the notion and importance of maps and drawings as constituting another language to access memory.

Even more importantly, and toward the end of my time at Harvard, I had a number of long conversations with the very able Ellen Langer who was undertaking original work on mindfulness and cognitive processing. These meetings were enjoyable and we were close to starting a study on tour guides around Harvard University using mindfulness measures. Regrettably, my fellowship was near its end and the work was not undertaken. Nevertheless, mindfulness as a concept was very relevant to tourism and Langer's ideas returned with me to Australia. One of the impressive features in the North American Universities was a considerable willingness to share information and to be enthusiastic about people's work. This interest was more urgent and seemingly more sincere than I had experienced in Australia or the United Kingdom. Even today, my cooperative efforts with US colleagues are relatively easy; and while they are reasonably solid with other Australians, they are almost nonexistent with UK peers.

James Cook Again

On returning to James Cook from the Fulbright scholarship, I partly supervised a rather exceptional honors student with Mike Smithson. Her name was Gianna Moscardo and the next year when I had a research grant she agreed to work for me.

The crumbling of my previous relationship was under way despite the arrival of a loved daughter. Within two years, the partnership with Gianna Moscardo became personal as well as professional. Working together we produced a steady stream of publications in the mid-1980s and 1990s and we still continue to do some joint work.

In the mid-1980s, a new vice chancellor (president in North American terms) arrived at James Cook University and began an aggressive expansion of the institution. His plans, fueled largely by the growing national success of the tourism sector and associated industry lobbying, included building tourism education and research at James Cook. The attempt was not without its odd twists and turns—I was initially asked to provide much advice on whom to recruit as leader, creating something of a conflict of interest for my own ambitions. In time the first professor of tourism position in Australia was openly advertised. In late 1989, I was appointed to that position after a full and thorough competitive set of interviews.

Assuming the new professorial role ushered in a testing time, because while I had built a publication record in the psychology of tourism, I knew little about several key facets of tourism. Not unimportantly, we had a first energetic and sleep aversive son born in early 1989 and another engaging son arrived in late 1991. It was the case of a young professor with a young family in a very young new discipline. The term discipline is perhaps too grandiose a label and I prefer to view tourism work as a topic-centered special study area (Pearce 1993). Irrespective of the label, the task of devising new subjects and planning for tourism education, alongside maintaining research of an acceptable academic quality but sensitive to some industry views, was a full-time role. There is a massive and inadequately acknowledged debt that I have to Gianna Moscardo for this period and beyond, since it was her multiple roles as engaged researcher, subject designer, parent, home and finance organizer, and teacher for often marginal amounts of money, which made my position manageable. Quite remarkably in this same time period, and with Glenn Ross as supervisor, she completed her own PhD, successfully developing and applying the mindfulness ideas to museums and tourism settings.

   Unlike reports I have read from many of my tourism colleagues, some of which appear in this volume as well as in the Nash (2007) version in this same series, I was almost never troubled by snide or overly status debunking external academic remarks about being a professor of tourism. I attribute this now to a collusion of factors; the university had deliberately set about creating the first Australian chair of tourism so the role had the president's explicit approval. The regional significance of the industry was visible and my Oxford experiences and previous academic success gave me a confidence that may have stilled some direct remarks. Nevertheless, if the external scholarly approvals were in place, there were other difficulties and much work to be done.

Adjusting to Tourism

The adjustment between being at first a psychology researcher and then a tourism researcher characterized some of the stresses at this time. My 1988 book *The Ulysses Factor*, like Krippendorf's volume *The Holiday Makers* (1987), published a year earlier, but which at that time I had not read, asserted the centrality of tourists' experiences to any tourism study. This was sufficiently understandable to tourism marketing personnel, since they could translate some of the research into justifications or links to their actions. The harder people to convince that I had something to say were the key tourism business interests whose worlds were about building lobbying arguments to government. They were predominantly concerned with topics such as investment, taxation, union issues, financial regulations, association memberships, and policies. To them, the psychology of the tourist was a marginal issue, a backstreet going nowhere in their pursuit of more profit.

Quite fortunately, I was also reading about and developing a working competence relating to sustainability, tourism, and the environment. An opportunity arose to be a little more public in my communication efforts. The industry lobbyists used what they thought of as their new professor (they had made contributions to James Cook University to help set up the chair) to provide some speeches and rebuttals directed against some antitourism publications that had presented simplistic views about tourism's environmental destructiveness. I enjoyed undertaking such performances, some in front of key government review panels and political power brokers. Speaking in Canberra in Australia's Parliament House was a highlight at one of these tourism summit meetings and I was fortunate to spend some time on the Federal Minister's Advisory Panel. I am not sure I was much more than a token appointee, but my actual speeches and documents were built on good evidence and, I think sound logic, and stood up well against less well-researched and often modest subjective opposing arguments. These efforts won some industry acceptance. An in-house publication on budget youth travel *The Backpacker Phenomenon* (Pearce 1990) also helped lower some of the doubting voices about academics and their value to the world of tourism.

Despite these efforts, I sometimes found myself in serious trouble with the university's most senior personnel and the national industry leaders by not being sufficiently political and placing teaching, student needs, and research duties above attending industry meetings and working groups. It was also easy to cause offense with people who were rich and powerful and more used to willing subordinates than willing discussants. The criticisms were unpleasant and usually directed at the practical value of what we were doing. In time I built a picture of what other people thought of as relevant. I also learned a little in the way of changing my language to suit different audiences. Much later I explained some of this in my article in the final issue of *The Journal of Tourism Studies* entitled "Professing Tourism" (Pearce 2005b), but I wish I had known more of these points at the time.

Some of the subjects we constructed within the first tourism degree were undoubtedly creative, certainly idiosyncratic, and possibly eccentric. I like to think many were actually quite scholarly. In an era before plentiful tourism textbooks and Internet access, we built subjects around journal articles and contributions from multiple disciplines. We were also of course doing this in an Australian and Asian context and, as is undoubtedly apparent from other biographies in this series, the formation of tourism analysis and research in this part of the world is distinctively different from the recreation roots of North America and the hospitality and social science traditions prevailing in Europe and the United Kingdom. As well as Gianna Moscardo's considerable contributions, Laurie Murphy and Alastair Birtles were key staff, as was Trevor Sofield for some time. James Cook University graduates Neil Black, Joy Rutledge, and Glenn Ross were great contributors until retirement. We had very able and supportive administrative and secretarial staff in Anne Sharp and Robyn Yesberg who jointly bore the workload of bringing Australia's first refereed tourism journal *The Journal of Tourism Studies* (1990–2005) through its twice yearly publication deadlines.

As well as editing the journal, I taught quite a few subjects, including introduction to tourism, research methods, regional planning, and tourist behavior. I supervised tourism honors and PhD students in a much wider variety of topics than I had when working in behavioral sciences. I felt this was necessary to allow students to study types of tourism and infrastructure issues, as well as the more specialist tourist behavior themes. Quite quickly, the PhD students became increasingly important as Australia opened up its educational doors to international applicants. Edward Kim, a Korean, and Chiemi Yagi, who was Japanese but who had studied for her masters with Jafar Jafari in Wisconsin, were I believe the first international students from their countries to complete PhD studies in tourism in Australia.

Sabbaticals

A sabbatical break away from James Cook University occurred in 1994. The choice of location for the study leave was Kangaroo Island, a scenic farming community off the southern coast of the Australian mainland. We packed our utility tray—the back of the truck for American readers—with papers and books as well as clothes and necessities for ourselves and two small boys and drove across the country. We spent five months in a basic, isolated farmhouse perched on a windswept hill near the island's spectacular beaches. It was an escape from the world of universities and administration and its principal goal was to write the book *Tourism and Community Relationships* (Pearce Moscardo and Ross 1996).

Glenn Ross had contributed some of the initial ideas, I wrote some of the chapters, but Gianna Moscardo wrote the heart of the book. In our style of trying to be new and innovative in tourism studies, it advocated the value of seeing tourism's impacts as a result of the views and social representations about tourism that subgroups in communities already held, thus inverting most researchers' views of impacts and attitudes. I believe the main ideas are still powerful and it has been the basis for more work building an understanding of tourism development attitudes. There were also other tourism research-linked benefits. Kangaroo Island was popular with international tourists because wildlife was everywhere. The long stay enabled us to see new facets of tourism management more in the roles of observant residents rather than as researchers. I gave some talks about tourism in unlikely places to audiences as varied as sheep farmers and national parks staff, and we laid the foundation to return and study wildlife tourism and visitor center planning (Moscardo 1998; Pearce 2004; Pearce and Moscardo 2007).

The development of tourism studies around Australia was expanding in the mid-1990s, and a part of that expansion was generated by the Federal Government's Cooperative Research Centre program where teams of researchers tackled topics. As tourism researchers, we were the first to be involved in this program establishing studies and receiving funding for work on Australia's Great Barrier Reef and tropical rain forest environments. In time, a Cooperative Research Centre on tourism would be established with other universities more centrally involved, but we benefited from the reef and rain forest research studies and teams we established. Again Gianna Moscardo's role here as organizer and project leader was pivotal; we wrote both joint and independent papers on markets and management issues that pushed the effort forward.

From a broad perspective, the Cooperative Research Centre world that lasted in total from 1993 to mid-2010 generated solid opportunities for many Australian tourism researchers and graduate students. Slightly less positively, there were consequences in terms of limiting the research agenda, which was seen as acceptable for funding. As the programs wore on the industry control issues become more powerful. From an individual perspective, I had participated in the earliest and probably the best phases of Cooperative Research Centre work, but later I became wary and troubled by the orthodoxy and hegemonic industry influence of the organizations during their latter stages.

For the next sabbatical in 1997, the United States beckoned. We had been to some conferences in North America and enjoyed the experience. We had hosted Alastair Morrison and Donald Getz as visitors to James Cook University, and we chose Purdue University in Indiana where Morrison was stationed to spend our time. Importantly at Purdue, we met and greatly appreciated the friendship of Joe O'Leary with whom Alastair Morrison worked, and we physically set up office amid O'Leary's graduate students in the forestry department. Together, we had some excellent times and formed a productive and supportive publishing team with different individuals adding complementary skills and resources to the process. The large data sets to which Joe O'Leary had access enabled some of our ideas to be tested; and we used these resources to prepare special issue and key papers on topics such as the visiting friends and relatives market, specialist accommodation, cruise tourism, and wildlife tourism. Just after this visit, I worked with Alastair Morrison and a James Cook University staff member Joy Rutledge to produce a tourism textbook, *Tourism Bridges across Continents* (1998), which was successful for a while in Australia and had some innovative features.

A Career Choice

While I was at Purdue, James Cook University reorganized its departmental structures and the Department of Tourism was folded into a larger School of Business, which included management, marketing, accounting, and economics. Tourism was undoubtedly the most prominent research group among these units; for three years I became the head of the new School of Business. I continued to teach quite a lot and supervise graduate students. I also tried to write research papers as well as be the kind of miserly manager of the school's financial resources which the university needed. The larger group was more divisive, less focused, and probably less talented on average than had been the case for our Department of Tourism. At times, the administrative job was tough going, and on other occasions achievements were tangible and somewhat satisfying. There were days when I was pleased to be in charge of decisions and directions that maintained the value of tourism study and education, but on occasions I had the nagging feeling that some matters were really wasting my time.

At the start of the new century, a career choice presented itself—should I seek further administrative jobs such as dean or pro-vice chancellor or should I pursue more of a research and educator role. There were no specific offers I turned down, no moments of epiphany about the issue, just a view that while I could possibly do this work, it was not a style of employment where I was distinctively skilled. At that time, Gianna Moscardo wisely provided advice that I should not go in the senior administrator direction. She pointed out that I complained frequently about the difficult people and the frustrations (she was probably right).

If there was an additional element to this emerging decision, it was the fascination I felt after a first major trip to Xi'an, China in 2001. I had been traveling more and more each year with academic visits to Indonesia, Korea, Thailand, and Malaysia. Much of this travel was prompted by James Cook University being recognized as one of the UNWTO's leading tourism education centers. I participated in the international tourism education program "Educating the Educators" in Malaysia in 1994, China in 1996, and Thailand in 1998. The demise of this program was regrettable, as it was a tangible benefit of being linked to UNWTO since the simple physical distance between Australia and Spain tended to limit our involvement in other politically motivated intrigues and activities. In particular, the rapidity of change in China's ancient culture and the scale of the country and its population have left deep impressions. Together these forces created an enthusiasm for seeing more of the world and less of local university politics.

The New Millennium

The first decade of the 21st century has been one of trying to fulfill my decision to see more of the world, to work with graduate students, to concentrate on teaching well, and to have the capacity to write more. In the last few years, I have been fortunate to be invited to teach short, weeklong intensive courses in Sardinia, then in Milan, and also in Bangkok and Singapore. These have been enjoyable and have been assessed by others as successful, so I have continued to pursue opportunities of this kind. In 2005, I completed a new and up-to-date overview of some of my and other scholars' work on tourism. It was published as *Tourist Behaviour Themes and Conceptual Schemes* (2005a). I have been very saddened in the same period by the deaths from cancer of two PhD students, Lui Lee and Diya Ernawati. Lee, in particular, contributed work reshaping the travel career approach to motivation.

Also in 2005, I made an executive decision to discontinue *The Journal of Tourism Studies* and we published a final special issue on tourism scholarship. It seemed to me that the time of university departments publishing journals was at an end, our key publication editor was retiring, and the university support for this sort of activity was shrinking. Unless one has been the chief editor of a journal for a long time (in this case it was 16 years), it is hard to understand the constancy of the effort and the hidden work of correspondence for both the articles that are published as well as the many that never appear. Possibly I did not use associate editors wisely, taking on too much of the coordination of reviewers' work personally in an attempt to control the overall quality. Rankings of journals for some years suggested that it was generally perceived as a successful quality journal. Lacking the support of a publishing house and its services, the editorial role involved everything from the cerebral to the physical, including packaging the issues for subscribers. It has been suggested to me that the journal effort was equivalent to editing 16 books consisting of 14 articles, and I tend to agree. I express admiration for those who have undertaken or who now occupy such roles for the major journals. There were offers for other people to take up the journal, but we wanted to keep open a James Cook University possibility of resuscitation, just in case we realized the decision had been faulty. That realization has never arrived.

For over 20 years, my founding membership of the International Academy for the Study of Tourism has played a role in linking me to people whose work I have read and respect. I have particularly enjoyed time with Erik Cohen and Chris Ryan. Visits to Cohen in Thailand, inherently stimulating in themselves, also facilitated my meeting Darya Maoz who has helped me travel through Israel twice. Both times the experiences have been powerful and intense. Chris Ryan has visited James Cook University and we share a lot of similar thoughts and experiences about the development of tourism scholarship particularly in Asia. I have had a long-standing positive relationship with Jafar Jafari developed by my contributions to *Annals of Tourism Research*, shared students and personal contact.

Select attendance at the Travel and Tourism Research Association conference, the Asia Pacific Tourism Association conference, and the Australian tourism research conference event (CAUTHE) has helped me maintain good links with diverse people. I have been back to China and Xi'an several times and benefited from being escorted through a different world by my charming Mandarin-speaking honors students, at first Harriet Vogt and then recently Lu Huan. The work has produced a limited trickle of publications and may be an arena for more cooperative study. In Thailand, Pim Rocharungsat, one of my former PhD students, remains one of my closest international contacts. I have participated in tourism research development workshops in Thailand several times in the last five years and it remains a favored destination. A brilliant part of this work has been the emerging opportunity to have my sons occasionally accompany me on such travel, and I am confident they are beginning to enjoy it as much as I do. Two trips to Africa have been intriguing and very memorable and former James Cook University PhD student, Haretsebe Manwa who is now in Botswana, is the kind of hospitable international colleague everyone should have. South America and much of Europe still beckon and I have hopes of eventually visiting more countries on those continents in a professional role.

Current publishing activities involve work with doctoral students as well as with long-standing colleagues Laurie Murphy, Pierre Benckendorff, and less frequently these days, Gianna Moscardo. Pierre, one of my former and successful doctoral students, has been a key figure in our tourism group; his role in tourism curriculum design has been much appreciated. More generally, the style of undertaking some pioneering work in various topic areas, underpinned wherever possible by mini-theories or conceptual schemes, has paid several dividends. One of these benefits has been the ability to return to areas of work we started. Some of these study topics can now be monitored for progress. Laurie Murphy, a key academic tourism colleague, has worked with me on backpacker studies, as we see further prospects to maintain our successful partnership in this area. Other topics where it has been possible to develop a sequence of studies with a continuity of publications include tourism motivation, tourists' relationships, the visiting friends and relatives market, visitor centers, tourism and community effects, and the benefits of travel.

The ideas that form the basis of much of the thinking and theorizing include the travel career pattern model of tourist motivation, attitude change, mindfulness, and social representations. We have used a rich variety of methods with phases of preferring purpose-built questions, as well as secondary data. Archival studies, interviews, mapping studies, and netnography have been employed. A strong emphasis has been placed on analysis at the right level. Some work uses multivariate analysis, predominantly multidimensional scaling, factor-cluster approaches, and analysis of variance. There are also papers colleagues and I have constructed using only qualitative data or in the style of innovative perspectives and schemes for reorganizing existing work. The advances in psychology, most notably the consolidation of a positive psychology approach that emphasizes human happiness and well-being, have been closely monitored. Some of the recently published work, including a book with Sebastian Filep and Glenn Ross, views these developments as making a fresh contribution to tourism studies (Pearce 2009a; Pearce et al 2011).

CONCLUSION

In concluding this biographical account, it is tempting to try to offer advice and career planning directives to younger colleagues. I will try to resist simple recipes, since the world we all now work in is a very different place to that in which my career was formed. For example, my doctoral thesis and early publications were written, at least for the early drafts, in longhand and certainly without access to the resources of the Internet. I believe, therefore, that in general terms it is simply best to see this biography as an account, hopefully not too self-aggrandizing, of one researcher's efforts through previous decades.

Despite my hesitation to dispense broad advice, I feel there are at least some specific enduring themes that do have a potential longevity for all tourism scholars. Seeing the scope of any phenomenon is an important principle for a researcher. The challenge here lies in seeing beyond local situations and realizing how context matters, while still tracking specific situations. This is the phenomenon sampling point mentioned earlier and is assisted by developing well-structured definitions and providing systematic descriptions of how contexts differ. This approach is illustrated well by our work on the visiting friends and relatives markets and the components of that market (Moscardo Pearce et al 2000). The ideas can also be traced to the early work on helping behavior where we empirically differentiated between helping situations, thus potentially resolving differences among explanations that were shown to be context dependent (Smithson et al 1983).

Developing an emic international perspective usefully complements or assists in seeing the range of a phenomenon. International tourism experiences and teaching international students can be a means of facilitating this nonlocal view. My own international educational experiences mattered very much to me, but it is possible that they are less relevant with 21st-century communication tools. A close familiarity with the discipline of psychology provided a foundation for many of my tourist behavior studies, and this resource has continued to provide a background of methods and approaches across the years. Nevertheless, as an individual who selected a pioneering role in tourism leadership (an alternate route was probably that in time I could have become a more conventional professor of psychology), it has been particularly important to be bold enough to tackle new topics and undiscovered fields. The contexts of tourism are diverse from remote natural locations to the most contrived and sophisticated, and human behavior within these settings can be surprisingly adaptable. As mentioned elsewhere in this volume (Nisbett 2003), psychology the discipline could benefit from a little more emphasis on cross-cultural and context-dependent behavior, and tourism is one of the richest of these contexts.

It is good to work with others, but I have found it important to work alone as well. From a pragmatic career advice point of view, a demonstration of individual achievement sits well alongside cooperative efforts with peers, senior scholars, and students. The pace at which work is completed, the level of compromise that is involved in writing together depends of course on what level and social links you have with these coresearchers. I think a test of truly integrative work is when one cannot remember who wrote what sections or who had what ideas. If these contributions can be identified, then possibly the cooperative effort was still effective and different skills usefully employed.

Individual scholarly efforts though are perhaps the clearest statements of one's intellectual functioning and hopefully one's growth. Certainly the effortful construction of solo papers and books can involve revisiting one's previous academic travels, and like inspecting old photo albums can provoke detailed memories of people, places, paths not taken, and problems yet to be resolved. In thinking about career advice, I also display in my office and treasure a large Korean parchment given to me by an elderly Korean professor. It translates as "Do Research but do not forget to teach well." The advice is sound and I like to think I am a better researcher because I have tried to be an effective educator.

Do I regret anything? Of course, but mostly work left undone rather than thwarted or failed career issues. Do I have a sense of what is next? Yes, but only vaguely, as I will try and be adaptable to new directions. I have ambitions to undertake more work on motivation across countries and plans to assess tourist behavior and cultural interaction experiences in China and other locations outside Australia. I expect to continue to have a group of PhD students and see our joint work as having an elastic quality, stretching and extending into new and curious pockets of the tourist and local transaction process. David Lodge, one of the most astute fiction writers about academic life, highlights the relationship complexities of this mentor role as he muses on the thoughts of an older academic contemplating resuming a role as supervisor:

> the idea of applying my knowledge and expertise ... and meeting with this obviously intelligent and articulate and let us be very honest, very personable young woman on a regular a basis to discuss it, was not unattractive. But experience has taught me that postgraduate supervision can be a very complex and worrying business: you easily find yourself being somehow responsible for the students' achievement, self-esteem, destiny and it goes on for years. (Lodge 2008:95)

I am somewhat more positive about the supervision role, but I do experience the responsibility issues Lodge raises on a regular basis. As my former PhD students are now assuming more senior roles across Australia, in North America, and Asia, I also find that the James Cook University diaspora provide positive personal connections as well as responsibilities for further travel and research.

Does tourism as a study field have a strong future? Possibly, but only if the interconnections with other study fields and people's life choices and aspirations are better appreciated. If I had to recommend just one item I have written what would it be? Perhaps a recent paper I have written for *Annals of Tourism Research* on humor (Pearce 2009b), because it reminds me that that tourism is fun and readers might at least find it amusing and rich in possibilities. It is, I hope, representative of the kind of work I have done and will continue to do: reading, researching, and coming up with ideas. In a sense my publications are my career souvenirs but I like to think that the people I have worked with value the time we have spent together as least as much as the work we have done.

Chapter 10

Choosing Tourism

Chris Ryan
University of Waikato, New Zealand

Chris Ryan <caryan@mngt.waikato.ac.nz> is professor of tourism at the University of Waikato. Well known for his publications and for his role as editor of *Tourism Management*, he began his academic career in the United Kingdom. His social science background is in economics and psychology having degrees from London, Nottingham, Nottingham Trent, and Aston Universities, United Kingdom. His interests and major publications have always tended to have a strong emphasis on the tourist experience. He has worked at a number of universities, including those now known as Nottingham Trent University and Charles Darwin University (Australia), as well as the University of Saskatchewan (Canada). Over the last 17 years, he has spent most of his academic career in New Zealand and has developed multiple research partnerships with colleagues in China and the Middle East. His books include *Recreational Tourism, Tourist Satisfaction*, and *Tourism in China*. He has varied and rich research interests and has contributed to both tourist satisfaction and behavior studies, as well as a range of topics on tourism planning and development.

INTRODUCTION

This chapter can begin by asking why embark upon such an undertaking. In 2000, I was fortunate enough to be invited to attend the First APEC

The Study of Tourism: Foundations from Psychology
Tourism Social Science Series, Volume 15, 155–169
Copyright © 2011 by Emerald Group Publishing Limited
All rights of reproduction in any form reserved
ISSN: 1571-5043/doi:10.1108/S1571-5043(2011)0000015013

Tourism Ministers' Meeting in Seoul, South Korea, to speak at various meetings and also to prepare various papers. At the same meeting, Jafar Jafari was also present, and one morning we sat down together at breakfast. We reminisced about past colleagues, and how tourism as an academic venture had progressed. We both realized that a number of those who had been the original pioneers in developing tourism as a subject for research were retiring, and indeed some were no longer with us. He commented that our subject was at a stage where a doctoral student should really be developing a history of thought in our subject area and catching the memories of these early pioneers while they were alive, so as to develop a history of our field, its development, its concepts, and the thoughts of our leading exponents.

This made sense to me. As an economics undergraduate in the 1960s, I had to read Mark Blaug's *Economic Theory in Retrospect*, and now, as I write in my office, my bookshelves contain collections written by various thinkers in sociology and psychology (Blaug 1962). Each of the social sciences has its histories and collections of key writings, and such collections are a sign of maturation of any given arena of academic endeavor. Today, tourism as an academic subject has its encyclopedias, and again on my bookshelves I see collections of the work of writers such as Erik Cohen, Bill Faulkner, and various past published papers. Thus, the present volume and the companion collections edited by Dennison Nash, another by Stephen Smith, and still another (forthcoming) by Larry Dwyer are not forms of vanity publishing, but recognition of the growing maturation of a field of academic work that has dominated my own life for almost 30 years. They become collective stores of memories that may have some interest for future scholars as the field develops its own history of thought. Additionally, as the numbers of books and papers published about tourism increase, how might we best guide future students as to their reading if we lack such "signposts" for their own journeys? In another work on the ethics of research (Ryan 2005), I also argued that a key to good ethical research is reflexivity, where the researcher continually questions the data, the nature of the inquiry, the mode of data collection, and the implications they have for all involved. As I continually tell my own students, the act of asking a question is never a neutral act. So now, at the editor's request, I have a responsibility to be reflective about my own work: past, present, and hopefully future. To be otherwise would indeed mean this chapter would be little more than a vanity.

THE BEGINNING

In the introduction to my work on *Battlefield Tourism* (Ryan 2007), I noted how, as a small boy, I enjoyed play around the then weed-infested grounds of Oystermouth Castle in Mumbles on the Gower Peninsular, United Kingdom. I can remember how my uncle Frank would arrive on Sunday afternoons to take my sister and me to different parts of the Gower, and I would sit in our lounge waiting to see along a deserted street, the sign of his Jaguar SS Saloon turn the corner into our road. Today, that same road outside my mother's house is jam-packed with cars as tourists arrive, seemingly continuously, to the Mumbles and the Gower. Without knowing of Butler's (1980) "tourist area lifecycle," I experienced it then, as what had been a weekend summer resort for the miners of the Welsh Valleys and the steel workers of Port Talbot became a summer holiday destination for the populations of London and Birmingham with the building of the motorways. I saw houses turned into bed and breakfast accommodation with parts of Caswell Valley disappearing under tarmac to provide car parking for those visiting the bay and its beach. Even as I write, I can recall in the early 1960s my grandmother having a conversation with a stallholder. She bemoaned the fact that there were fewer visitors, because the Gower could not compete in price or sunshine with the emerging destinations of the Spanish *costas* being offered by the packaged holidays touted in every travel agent's window.

Each year I still visit my mother in the Mumbles, and I have seen for some time now that the Knab Rock, which I once climbed and became in my imagination a fort that I defended against various attackers, has become but a minor pimple on the extended promenade. In the 1980s, I also recall, coal mines closed to open as mining museums, while the then-modest hotels are now refurbished to become spa resorts, and the old industrial declining areas have become educational centers for South Wales' industrial heritage. So in many respects, I would say that I became aware of tourism at an early stage in my life by spending, after my parents moved to Croydon, every summer as a tourist in my birthplace, and so observing the changes that I have just described. That pattern of summer holidays on the Gower Peninsula with my grandparents continued until I was about 16 or 17 years, when the arrival of girlfriends and other interests meant my trips became shorter in duration and more of a duty than an enjoyment.

On completion of my economics degree, I stayed in London and commenced work with Facit-Addo, a company making and installing data capture equipment for the mainframe computers that businesses had started to use by the late 1960s and early 1970s. As a grandly entitled "systems analyst," my job was to sell, set up, and program equipment to produce managerial reports on, at that time, normally payroll and stock control systems. It was also a time when the London-based hotel groups were starting to install computerized systems that involved paper tape and punch cards, and one of the clients that Facit-Addo had was a company that no longer exists, but which then had nine properties in London. Little did I realize at the time how that tenuous link with hotels was to subsequently help shape my career. After two years of this, and applications for other jobs, I decided to go to Leicester University to complete a postgraduate certificate of education, and during that period I undertook teaching practice at what later was to become Nottingham Trent University. On the basis of that limited teaching experience, I gained a job at Clarendon College, also in Nottingham. At the interview, I was informed that as the college had a large Hospitality Management Department, it would be advantageous if I could teach business management to hotel and catering students, especially as I had some experience of hotel systems. I naturally agreed (as one does at job interviews), and so in due course, I came to write my first book, *An Introduction to Hotel and Catering Economics* (Ryan 1980), born out of that teaching experience.

To cut a long story short, on the basis of that book and by that time possessing two master's degrees that I had studied part-time, I was offered a senior lecturer's post in 1979 at the Nottingham Business School in what, within a short time soon after, became the Nottingham Trent University. It was there that I commenced my career as a tourism academic in company with Brian Wheeller. Not that this occurred immediately, as first I taught a mix of different topics, but the then Dean Peter Franklin was sympathetic to my plight when I argued that it was difficult to cover both retailing and tourism within a service marketing curriculum, given that both industries were so rapidly developing. "Choose" was his request, and I selected tourism, and my world has never quite been the same since.

Getting Involved

In the mid-1980s, two key turning points in my career occurred. I cannot fully remember the chronology, but they occurred close in time. The first was that Allan Williams and Gareth Shaw had obtained funding to develop a tourism research center at Exeter University, and they organized what must have been one of the first tourism conferences to have taken place in the

United Kingdom. Brian Wheeller and I duly drove to Exeter. I can clearly remember our conversation as we drove back along the motorway to Nottingham. It was one of those "why are we wasting our time?" conversations, where we concluded that while we had done some research (such as, in my case, for the East Midlands Tourism Board), we had really been concentrating on teaching and thus letting others gain advantages in terms of attracting research monies.

The second key event was that my wife, Anca, had started an MBA at Sheffield University and the course supervisor informed her of a conference hosted by the US Academy of Marketing Science in Ohio, on tourism services marketing. This was in 1986, and I went there to present a paper on weekend break holidays that had been initiated by British Rail and some of the national hotel chains. At the same conference, papers were presented by colleagues, such as Bonnie Guy, Ed Mayo, Arch Woodside, Laurel Reid, Joe O'Leary, Muzzafer Uysal, while Pauline Sheldon and Turgut Var with Juanita Liu presented one of their early findings on resident attitudes in North Wales. For me, a significant meeting at that conference was with Professor Farouk Saleh from the University of Saskatchewan, who came to visit Brian Wheeller and me at Nottingham Trent (and who also attended a Notts County football match as an introduction to British culture). So it came to pass that in 1990 I took up a yearlong visiting position at the University of Saskatchewan, after which my career came to be based in New Zealand. Indeed, the immediate result was that my wife and son, over the next few years, became suffering members of an itinerant family—within eight years, we moved from Canada to the United Kingdom, to New Zealand, to Australia, and then back to New Zealand. Therefore, I want to publicly say much of what it is that I have achieved would not have been but for the love of my long-suffering wife. I was recently interviewed by a serious doctoral candidate from an American University and was asked, what was required to become a "top scholar." One necessity is undoubtedly to have a loving, supportive spouse, or the other alternatives are simply not to marry (or to become divorced).

In Saskatchewan, I became involved in research projects relating to the Meewasin Valley Authority and the establishment of the World Heritage Site at Wanuskewin, which exists at a former buffalo kill site and is still used by local North American Indian peoples as a site for sweat lodges. This was my first experience of coming to grips with alternative ways of seeing the world. This was to later serve me well as I came to research and write about tourism and the Maori of New Zealand and Australian Aboriginal peoples, and those experiences have become very important to me in my research of the last seven years in seeking to understand tourism and its development in China and the United Arab Emirates. I truly believe that the heart of tourism lies in the tourist's experience of place and the personal connections made at that place—and the consequences of those interactions for tourists, the residents, and the social and natural environments.

My research has been driven by these interests, but I do not believe that it is possible to fully capture the multiple truths that underlie these interactions without immersion in the place, and in the realities of the lives of respondents. At the very least, it is important that researchers visit and experience the places about which they write, and that those stays should involve more than simply observation based on a day-trip. I worry that some of the published research is written by those who collect data by postal surveys, use students to collect information, or work from secondary data sets to produce statistical analyses that are not informed by personal experiences of the places being surveyed. The "publish or perish" message produces stress on researchers that diminishes the quality of much of their works. Here I digress from the story line set by the volume editor, but the rubric permits me to muse on these matters later. Suffice it to say that involvement by the researcher with place and people's lives is essential to my mind for good research in tourism which, by its very nature, is about people and their experiences.

My time in Saskatchewan was also fruitful as it was there that I wrote my third book, *Recreational Tourism* (Ryan 1991), which was to sell successfully and which was largely rewritten much later in 2001. It was also in Saskatoon that I wrote with Farouk Saleh our papers critical of the ServQual model, thereby gaining many future citations if only because the paper was one of the first to critique ServQual. At that time, and every time since, I have not been able to replicate the five dimensions. By 2008, at a conference in Taipei, I was able to give a paper entitled "Whither ServQual?" although my original title was "ServQual is Dead: It is Time to Bury It." In practice, many of my criticisms were not new and were an appraisal of arguments I had rehearsed in Abe Pizam's and Yoel Mansfeld's book, *Consumer Behaviour in Travel and Tourism* (Ryan 1999).

My Present Location

The rubric provided by the editor of this publication asks one to state "where are you now, and have you progressed?" In a geographical sense since 1993, my family and I have been located in New Zealand with a stay of almost two years in Australia (1997–1998). The geographical move has proven vitally important to me in my own progression as a researcher, and, I think, has made me a better researcher than if I had stayed in the United Kingdom. As I have already noted, being located in these countries with a colonial history and indigenous peoples forced me to consider more the role of travel, tourism, and culture. Neither New Zealand nor Australia is a simple replica of the United Kingdom with a better climate. Some of these influences appear in the book *Researching Tourist Satisfaction* (Ryan 1995b).

While English is the common language, the outlooks are subtly different, perhaps based on a colonial history which meant that, to survive, one had to simply do things and be self-sufficient. Both societies are also smaller in population than the United Kingdom, and here one can actually talk to a government minister or official far more easily than in the "mother country." Equally one's reputation is an important asset. Failure to perform is duly noted, and one can then find that monies and help can dry up. But if one does provide good-quality work, then government and industry will be supportive and accessible in ways that I had not really experienced in the United Kingdom. A combination of facing cultural change, different governmental attitudes, and generally friendly industry provided rich resources and opportunities for research, even if, particularly in New Zealand, the financial resources are often inadequate. In New Zealand, we have looked with mixed views at Australia's Cooperative Research Centre for Sustainable Tourism in terms of the financial support that it provides for our trans-Tasman colleagues. But not being financially bound to a single source of funds provides greater freedom to pursue research interests that are of personal interest.

The need to face cultural issues in tourism meant a significant shift in the research paradigms that I employed, and I was faced with the challenge to learn new skills. With my undergraduate training in economics and my master's degree and subsequently doctoral thesis that employed psychometrics, much of my early publications were based on statistical methods and were located in a postpositivistic paradigm. I still continue to learn new statistical tools, including the use of Statistica, Stata, and AMOS as well as SPSS and seek to develop technical skills that go beyond the mere manipulation of drop-down menus on Windows-based operating systems. Sometimes graduate researchers giving presentations at conferences have learned this as I innocently ask "I see your coefficient of determination was 0.11; do you think this is a 'good result'?" This question, asked at an APTA Conference in Bangkok in 2008, gave rise to a stimulating discussion between me, Dan Fesenmaier, and Philip Pearce in and after the session. I hope the student learned something from it.

Another question in this mold is "Why did you use... .?" (Here one can insert a statistical test.) Increasingly, I conclude that statistical testing is just as much an evaluative (and subjective) process on the part of the researcher as any interpretation of qualitative data. Often this did not get to the "why?" of things even if it answered "what?" and "how?" questions, no matter how one sought quantitative relationships between variables. Often statistical models are abstractions from reality, parsimonious by design, whereas I wanted the richness of thought that I found among tourists as they described experiences, or the stories of residents' experiences with those tourists.

I had already commenced on this path back in the United Kingdom with a paper published in *Tourism Management* on conversations in Majorca with the over-55-year-olds (Ryan 1995a). Given my geographical location, I explored these forms of research more as I delved into the world of Maoridom. One of my greatest satisfactions is when Maori sometimes see me and congratulate me on work done, which now is very much a decade or so ago. In Maori and other societies, certain forms of knowledge are exclusive, and thus the sharing of it is a gift, and as such is to be used with the purpose intended by the gift giver. As a recipient of that knowledge, I assume responsibilities to use it well, and, where possible, to provide benefit to the community from whence that knowledge came. I am afraid this perspective makes me intolerant of some papers I read on indigenous peoples and tourism, where I suspect a lack of immersion in a society and the use of knowledge for career advancement, with little given back to the community who initially provided that knowledge.

Therefore, as a researcher, and as I become a repository of stories, it seems to me that among one's responsibilities there is a need to take care in the interpretations of conversation, text, and interview material that is collected. I have become a fan of textual analysis software, not in the belief that it provides easy answers (it does not), but because it imposes a discipline upon the researcher with the provision of evidence of how one moved from the original text to a final explanation. However, quite often I find that referees are not always aware of these techniques and thus require explanations that would not be needed if, for example, one was using a statistics package.

Hence, in terms of technical skills, I feel that I have progressed significantly while I also feel that in recent years I have been challenged as a researcher by some remarkable colleagues and students. I am indeed very fortunate in that my department has developed a significant doctoral and postgraduate program that also permits me to teach research methods and a directed study paper entitled "Epistemologies in Tourism Research."

My colleagues Alison McIntosh and Jenny Cave are both creative thinkers and generate new ways of viewing tourist experiences, and indeed in my view Jenny Cave's work on the Pacific Island peoples in Auckland and their involvement in small businesses and tourism has successfully interwoven this unique perspective and mutual reciprocal action research into new ways of community-based research.

Both colleagues share my conviction that, even while they use quantitative methods, we have to be more imaginative in our approaches to eliciting the richness and potentially cathartic experiences present in tourism. My colleague, Asad Mohsin, was a former doctoral student and has brought me his knowledge and generosity along with his enthusiasm. I met him while I was professor at what was then Northern Territory University, and this was a rich professional period of my life. The Territory is truly remarkable, peopled with strong characters as befits its "outback" image. In the "Top End," there is a true tropical climate, which can be immediately experienced away from the city of Darwin and its air-conditioning. Here I would like to acknowledge the support that Jeremy Huyton gave me, and to also acknowledge his enthusiasm and willingness to drive the many miles into central Australia.

One of the first postgraduate students I had when appointed to a professorial position at Waikato University was Birgit Trauer. Her background was in leisure studies and she subsequently went on to complete her doctoral studies at the University of Queensland. It was she who reintroduced me to the theories of serious leisure and involvement (she possesses an almost encyclopedic knowledge about that literature). In some of our papers, I felt we created some new concepts and ways of examining tourist experiences, while also adding to the adventure tourism literature by inserting the role of the media in making familiar to the tourists the roles they wished to play, even if they had not directly experienced the activity previously (Ryan and Trauer 2005). She influenced my analytical approaches and I thus began to incorporate more open-ended, discursive techniques into my research, while her own enthusiasm and love of life made me less cautious when considering areas for research. Birgit Trauer is someone to whom I owe a debt. Equally, another significant colleague was Steve Pan. I first taught him as a master's student, and he subsequently completed his doctoral degree at Waikato, and currently teaches at Hong Kong Polytechnic University. He required only a light touch from me as a supervisor, but I have come to depend on him significantly in my role as editor of *Tourism Management*, as he and his wife, Ruby, configure the 600 or so manuscripts each year into the formats required by the Elsevier electronic submission system.

For much of the last decade, my research has been dominated by two geographical areas: the United Arab Emirates and China. The former commenced after I had initially met Morag Stewart at a conference. After September 11, I began flying to the United Kingdom via Dubai rather than Los Angeles. I hence stayed at the Emirates Academy as a stopover, and then began teaching a paper there as a visiting professor. This is a time I always enjoy if only because it permits me three weeks away from educational administration and offers an opportunity to engage in writing. Over time, as I got to know the Emirates better, I commenced research there, first with Morag Stewart's support and then later with the help of Ivan Ninov. Dubai is, of course, a wonderful place for any tourism researcher. The glitz of its high-rise buildings, the opulence of the Burj Dubai, the contrasts between Emirati "high society," migrant workers, the "ex pat" professional workers, and Arabic trading traditions of the Creek and the Bedouin lifestyle of the desert cannot fail but generate questions. In turn, these are combined with futuristic visions of a 21st-century megacity based on finance, tourism, and construction. As the oil runs dry, these combine to a fusion, a hybridity that can only be fascinating, well at least to me.

Ivan presented one of our papers on perceptions of Dubai at the 2009 EuroCHRIE Conference (Ryan and Ninov 2009) in which we examined how people perceive the contrast of tourism attractions based on an Arabic heritage with the skyline of modern Dubai. In particular, we explored how destination image is formed when such contrasts exist between old and new, rich and poor, and a modern artifice that seemingly ignores a recent historic tradition other than being used for touristic purposes. Further how people make sense of something that many regard as "unreal" yet which continues to grow in spite of the recent recession is of interest.

In many ways though, my research career and continuing development as an investigator seem to have been preparing me for making sense of China. What can be said of China: a vast country, far from homogenous, teetering on a narrow path between lifting literally millions from poverty and potential social, political, and environmental harm, seeking growth based on tenets of "Socialism with Chinese Characteristics" and "Social Harmony with Science" (to use the statements of Hu Jintao), and producing divisions between the new and the old, the rural and the urban, the prosperous East and the still poor West (and income divisions within the major cities too), between a better educated, Internet savvy younger generation and an older generation whose youth was formed by Maoist traditions, and a country that increasingly engages with tourism as a sign of modernity, a quest to better know the world, and as a deliberate component of economic and political policies?

To research China and its tourism requires sensitivity toward the role of ancient Taoist, Buddhist, and Confucian traditions. There is too a scientific rationalism born of the 19th century as distilled through Maoism and the Chinese Communist Party, a youthful exuberance of consumerism and IT proficiencies, and a sense of *"real politick"* as to what is, and what is not acceptable, possible, desirable, and permissible. Parenthetically, I am tempted to add that any training in university politics in the West would also be of help here. Kissinger is reputed to have asked, "Why are university politics so vicious?" Perhaps it is because there is so little to fight over.

I am convinced that research based on questionnaires alone does little to really advance our understanding, other than to prove that the writer is competent in sophisticated numerical manipulation. A mixed methods approach—pragmatic possibly in that it is driven by a carefully considered research question, but flexible in that as data become available, the nature of the research process can reflect changing research agendas—is a requirement. For example, work I am currently undertaking with Cui Xiaoming at Ankang University in Shaanxi Province started as a conventional resident-based survey as to the perceived impacts of tourism, but has become more nuanced for several reasons (Ryan and Cui 2009). These include the realization that responses are as much to the perceived processes of modernization as to tourism alone (in rural areas of China, tourism is a representation of a growing modernity). There are issues too in collecting data from those who may be illiterate and not used to expression of opinion. Even more daunting perhaps is the further recognition that our role as researchers was empowering the respondents by making them aware of the potential future impacts of tourism when they had no knowledge of what, in the long term, could eventuate. These forces draw one very much into the tourism planning processes.

Much of my early research in China was undertaken with Gu Huimin from Beijing International Studies University. If there is serendipity in personal patterns of life, then this liaison was truly of that nature. I first spoke to her when sitting on a coach that was conveying conference delegates to the demilitarized zone in Korea for a field trip. I was already seated on the bus, the place next to me was spare, and she asked if she could sit next to me. We chatted, and then a few months later I received an e-mail to say that she was on a delegation from China coming to New Zealand, and might she visit Waikato University.

From these meetings, and at the time I had no idea of how influential a figure she was, and is, in Chinese and Beijing academic and industry circles, we identified joint research projects that have led to a number of research papers and our edited book *Tourism in China*. That meeting on the coach has also led to a memorandum of understanding between our two universities, doctoral students coming to Waikato, master's degree students in Beijing helping and publishing in various projects, and colleagues from Waikato going to teach in Beijing. Professor Gu Huimin continues to be a source of help, and without her contacts and insights, little of my research in China would have eventuated. She is another to whom I owe a large debt. It is through her goodwill and introductions that I have gone on to publish with other Chinese coauthors, but all the time acquiring new experiences in my travels, new understandings, and being continually challenged in my understandings of a different country and culture. This is perhaps illustrated by the paper undertaken on tourist motives and perceptions of Grand View Gardens in Beijing. In the analysis of the data, it seemed to me that a key data source was in the novel that gave rise to the attraction, namely Cáo Xuĕqin's *Dream of the Red Mansion*. Sometimes ignorance is a blessing. If I had known that the novel is over 1,720 pages in length, which I would have to read in two translations plus commentaries on the novel, I may well have not started the project. Written with Gu Huimin, Zhang Yanning, and Ling Song, it is one of my more challenging works as I sought to incorporate the Buddhist and Taoist understandings of the novel that motivated visitation by many tourists with the empirical data. Of course I was pleased when the paper was accepted for publication in *Journal of Travel Research*.

Similar challenges underlay the final publication of our interpretation of the opening events at the 4th Buddhist Festival at Wutaishan (Ryan and Gu 2010). As we describe in the paper, in our view the event brought together a hybrid pattern of economics, politics, and faith that represents the complexity of tourism development in China at this moment in that country's history, and we welcomed Robert Shepherd's (in press) critique of that paper for several reasons. First, it was nice to know that one's work is read and taken seriously; second, because it permitted further examination of the research paradigms needed to analyze such situations; and third, because it provided an opportunity to update the developments that had taken place since the time of our visit.

CONCLUSION

As a researcher, my journey has taken me far, both geographically and conceptually. Starting in the United Kingdom as a quantitatively-based researcher, I now live on the other side of the world, espousing research that uses qualitative means, aware of the way in which social truths are constructed and filtered through cultural and social understandings, and grappling with different countries and emergent tourism patterns that now seem very far away from the package holiday to the south of Spain. Within the wider remit of university-based research and the "publish or perish" syndrome, I can proudly admit to being a "grumpy old man" or a "whinging pom." RAEs, PBRFs, SSCIs, and ERAs and the other acronyms that are found in the English-speaking world all seem to me to be an anathema that undermines what it is they purport to support: good research. I am realistic enough to know that if I was starting my research career today, I would have to study for a PhD almost at the outset of my journey, even though I would know little about research processes. In order to build my curriculum vitae, I would have to analyze secondary sets of data and use fancy statistical methods, or alternatively use postal questionnaires to get three articles a year. Today, for the emerging researcher, there is no luxury of being able to visit and immerse oneself in a location or a community for 12 or more months before even considering setting pen to paper or fingers to keyboard. Nor is it sufficient to say, produce two good articles from 24 or more months of ethnographic research. That is simply not seen as productive for the KPIs (key performance indicators) of the above-mentioned research assessments or the tenure process of an American university. The result today is that there are many more articles, but not necessarily more seminal papers.

For me, the early influences were people like Erik Cohen and Philip Pearce. The work of the former on backpackers in Thailand and the latter's *The Social Psychology of Tourist Behaviour*, in spite of their very different approaches, share a common trait. They place the tourist as an individual experiencing places and interactions to the forefront of the experience. Today, as editor of *Tourism Management*, I think we sometimes lose that in our statistical and mathematical analyses. Not that I am blind to the values of empiricist methodologies and the capability of such methods to permit prediction, but sometimes I think we forget the basics that by their nature such methods are abstractions from reality. They are simplifications that permit a quantification of what are thought to be key variables, and the relationships between those variables, to produce a parsimonious statement that allows generalization.

Therefore, there is a continuing tension between that which is statistical in nature and the individual experiences and stories of place that lie at the basis of tourism. I also wonder whether, in an espousal of mixed methods research, there is not at times a reinforcement of the postpositivistic as the qualitative data are subjected to tests of credibility. At times, tourist behaviors are irrational and based on fantasy (irrational in the sense that people take risks they would not normally take, or engage in behaviors that are irresponsible and potentially harmful in the long term), simply because they are on holiday: that period of socially condoned escapes from daily responsibilities. Such behaviors may be "rational" in terms of meeting a temporary want. But the desires themselves may not always be easily explained by reference to longer term self-interest. Holidays are escapes, and are sometimes hidden periods in the sense that the tourist returns from the liminal status of a nonworker (but not an unemployed person, and thereby possesses a sanctioned, privileged position) in a place where they are not known, having engaged (perhaps) in activities they might not wish others to know about, to return to their everyday world, but in some way now psychologically healthier.

Yet we need to recognize that social attitudes change. In April 2009, at Richard Sharpley's conference at the University of Central Lancashire, I was invited to be the keynote speaker. There I commented that 40 years earlier smoking was common, but after the release of the Surgeon General's report in the United States, attitudes began to harden against smoking, which today is often perceived as being antisocial. Today, we are living in a time when concerns are beginning to be expressed about carbon emissions resulting from aircraft travel. Are we seeing the initiation of a time when flying may become to be seen as antisocial? This is something that airlines are taking seriously as they search for the new generation of biofuels such as the *jatropha* nut. Additionally, I see so many trends that will affect tourism in the future and a far-from-homogenous world is emerging. In the Western world, Generation Y may have global patterns of work. Thus, their holiday patterns might involve less travel as they explore the places where they work before they move elsewhere, while the new middle-aged, middle-class Chinese and Indians may wish to replicate the current patterns of holidaying taken by their counterparts in the West.

Today the latter population ages, but the 60-year-olds of today have different life experiences and expectancies to those who were 60 but only 20 years ago. Soft adventure products may become more important, while the young seek thrills from computer-based adventure. What are the implications of the social challenges of such a discrepancy in incomes around the world? Over all of this lies the challenge of environmental change (degradation?), which appears to be accelerating as we wonder whether the Arctic ice caps will survive future summers. Holidaymaking will continue, but the forms, constructs, motives, and products will evolve in different ways. Some of these we might, at least with the use of hindsight, have easily foretold, while others may be very new indeed.

Tourism is a continually fascinating social phenomenon. We can displace spatially so many places (there are, I seem to remember being told, some 40 replica Eifel towers in the world today. If one is visited, then are all seen? We render history asunder from the places of its origin and make myths that come to have importance to modern generations of tourists, and create new fusions of culture as modern technologies and needs merge with old traditions. Given these new hybrids it is indeed a privilege to be a researcher into tourism. Being a tourism professor is, as I told an immigration official at Auckland International Airport on a recent return to New Zealand, the second best job in the world after being a presenter on *BBC TV*'s "Top Gear." He thought I was joking, but I was not. Perhaps one day I might change places with Jeremy Clarkson; however, for the moment, tourism continues to perplex me (why do people spend so much money doing such strange things?), challenge me (how does one make sense of this?), and engages me in trying to inform people of the consequences of travel. That fun is important, and also serious, but seriously, one must have fun.

So, where do I stand today? I believe we must undertake research with integrity by which, at least in part, I mean with continuing self-questioning as to whether we are true to our informants, our readers, and our peers. We must endeavor to fully understand the techniques we use, but equally understand they are techniques that are manipulated and do not, of themselves, provide easy answers. We must display empathy born out of an understanding of circumstance, but that does not mean we do not evaluate and judge. We must recognize the power of asking a question, and appreciate that responses are made articulate by that which is absent as well as that which is said. We need to hone our sensitivities to listen to the silence, which requires a disciplined imagination. We need to be humble enough to realize that at times we may be wrong, and brave enough to admit it. We must learn from our students when appropriate. Often as supervisors we are not inherently cleverer (just more experienced). We seek to shorten the learning curves of our students so that they can surpass us. Therefore, we need to point out errors to them. Perhaps, just possibly, when we get asked to write about what influenced us and motivated us, we should not decline, but be honest in the hope that somewhere, at sometime, someone may find something that will be of help to them.

Chapter 11

Serendipitous Gleanings

John C. Crotts

College of Charleston, USA

John C. Crotts <crottsj@cofc.edu> is professor of hospitality and tourism management at the College of Charleston, USA. His research encompasses the areas of economic psychology, tourism marketing and sales strategies, and the management of cooperative alliances. Most of his career has been at undergraduate teaching universities, demonstrating that the lack of graduate students and university research support does not in and of itself preclude someone from research. He received his PhD degree in Leisure Studies and Services from the University of Oregon in 1989. He also holds a bachelor's degree in sociology from Appalachian State University, an MS degree in experiential education from Minnesota State University, and an EdS degree in adult education/higher education administration from Appalachian State University, all located in the United States.

INTRODUCTION

Writing this chapter has given me the time to reflect on my journey to and within academia. This journey had its fair share of climbs, obstacles, and forks in the road that we all must face in some form. More importantly, it also contains many chance encounters with others that have made all the difference. I hope it both informs and inspires readers who have set upon

The Study of Tourism: Foundations from Psychology
Tourism Social Science Series, Volume 15, 171–185
Copyright © 2011 by Emerald Group Publishing Limited
All rights of reproduction in any form reserved
ISSN: 1571-5043/doi:10.1108/S1571-5043(2011)0000015014

such a path for themselves. A career in academia focused in hospitality and tourism management has been a choice I have never regretted.

Way Back When

Most who have followed my work would be surprised to learn that my early career was relatively far removed from academic research and tourism. In my formative years, I had a passion for the outdoors, focused on what today would be called relatively extreme sports related to cliffs, white water, caves, and the backcountry. Looking back, I see that those years conditioned me to seek out challenges and find joy in the ascent (or descent) with others. Similar to academia, reaching a particular summit is anti-climatic, as the excitement is in the journey itself.

These avocations eventually afforded me an opportunity to return to my undergraduate alma mater—Appalachian State University—to head a program that is basically a guide and outfitting program, focused on adding adventure-based experiential components to student life and academic programs. Success in offering various levels of programs in white water, rock climbing, spelunking, equestrian, cross-country skiing, and even mountain biking morphed over the years into also assuming management of the university's large alpine skiing instruction program as well as teaching responsibilities in their undergraduate recreation major. The areas of alpine skiing and white-water rafting centered me in the heart of the region's tourism attractions.

Years later, with a wonderful wife and a first child on the way, I sensed I had gone as far as I could go along that particular path, and began looking for my next challenge that would allow me more time at home. Buying into an outfitters business was a desirable option that never materialized. I then considered graduate school, applied, and was accepted into a recreation program at the University of Oregon, USA. Though my graduate assistantship consisted of working in its outdoor recreation program, my future mentor Dennis Howard influenced me to track my PhD in tourism for which I remain indebted.

The Transition

At the start of studies for my PhD, intellectually I was more attuned to theories of sociology and educational psychology than marketing and consumer behavior. That all quickly changed with weekly tutorials lead by Dennis Howard, who would later chair my dissertation. I was further influenced by taking a course in consumer behavior with Lynn Kahle of "The nine nations of North America" fame (Kahle 1986).

Looking back, it is illuminating how a few relatively obscure learning opportunities made such a profound impression on me. In a seminar with Kahle, I recall that a graduate student in marketing was asked why he, a social psychologist from the University of North Carolina at Chapel Hill, chose to transition to a then consumer behavior-dominated marketing department at the University of Oregon. His response still echoes with me, as he stated that it all boiled down to the freedom of choice the disciplines gave its researchers in their choice of variables. In social psychology, a researcher's career will evolve around a host of dependent (outcome) variables, but only one, perhaps two, independent variables. On the other hand, consumer behavior researchers can be wide ranging in their choice of independent variables, but limited in their choice of dependent variables (such as consumer choice). What he meant by this is that academic research is much more interesting over the long haul when one can cross disciplines for explanations to fundamental problems/issues.

During that time at Oregon, I was afforded the opportunity to correspond with Fred van Raaij who then was at Erasmus University (the Netherlands). During this time, he was the editor of the *Journal of Economic Psychology*. Though my initial correspondence was related to my dissertation, he pointed me to the economic psychology literature, which at the time framed much of the European thought concerning consumer behavior. Two basic principles of economic psychology have always resonated well with me. First, a purchase requires a consumer who has both the ability and willingness to make a purchase. Once you can prequalify the consumer as to their ability to pay, the question then becomes one that is social-psychological in nature. The second principle comes from the European tradition where researchers focus on consumer behavior at various levels of aggregates, from the individual consumer to the collective behavior found in organizations, industries, and even entire nations. The point here is that sociology can contribute as much as psychology to our understanding of economic behavior. In addition, the dependent variables of economic psychology can be unique, ranging from purchase decisions to willingness adopt conservation practices to tax compliance (such as collection and reporting of accommodation taxes). Years later, Fred van Raaij collaborated with me in coediting my first book, *The Economic Psychology of Travel and Tourism* (Crotts and van Raaij 1994).

Two years later, with PhD in hand, it was time to move away from my outdoor recreation career into the teaching/research world at the University of Florida at Gainesville (USA), where I founded the Center for Tourism Research and Development in their Department of Recreation, Parks and Tourism. This workplace environment at the time was less than ideal with large classes, little research support, and a tyrannical chair. Nevertheless, my time there afforded me opportunities to further develop my independent research agenda and begin working in an interdisciplinary manner on a number of other worthwhile topics.

A chance experience led me to what was my first major contribution to the tourism literature and practice. One weekend, my wife, two small children, and I escaped to an area of the state to canoe and snorkel with the manatees. Manatees are incredibly gentle giants who swim up the freshwater rivers in the winter to warm and nurture themselves in the many freshwater springs of central Florida. Living on a modest budget, we checked into a simple motel/marina at the edge of a rural stretch of the river. Dropping off our bags in the room we ventured off to the marina's restaurant, only to discover after dinner that our room had been burgled and credit cards stolen. Informing our front desk clerk of the crime only evoked a reaction of surprise on his part. Later, the investigating police officer showed me where the room lock had been repeatedly picked. The thought came to me that what was the probability that a tourism researcher would be criminally victimized when traveling, if indeed the incidence rate was minimal.

The following week I began exploring the possibility, only to discover a wealth of available secondary data in the United States. "The uniform crime report" is a compilation of crime data for every US state and county that can break out reported criminal victimization by residents and nonresidents for specific times and places. Later that same year, a series of disturbing crimes against international tourists occurred in Florida that captured wide media attention. My familiarity with the available data, along with the advice of Ron Erdmann (US Tourism Industries), allowed us to help frame the response of the state's destination marketing organization to what they initially conceived of as a media relations crisis. This effort yielded a book chapter, which involved collaboration between University of Florida sociologist Richard Hollinger, my graduate student Susan Schiebler, and me. The publication introduced both "hot spot theory" and "routine activity theory" (Schiebler et al 1995). Both theories provide a good foundation for understanding why tourists make ideal targets for criminals, why some communities are more prone to criminal victimization than others, and what can be done about it. The point is that opportunities can come to you by chance, and an effort to be open to the possibilities is likely to be very valuable, even if this requires that you must learn new subjects and areas of the literature.

A happier aspect of my time at the university was my involvement with a group of engineers and extension specialists who, in the early 1990s, had developed a statewide program targeting Florida's hospitality and tourism industry with energy efficiency, recycling, and water conservation programs. For the better part of a year, I served as the program evaluation specialist, assessing the impact of their programs in terms of energy and resource savings, and return on investments. State funding for the program was eventually diverted to other purposes, drawing to a close this wonderful team. In light of today's high energy costs and concerns over global warming, I wonder where we would have been if the program could have retained its funding and appropriate incentives been given to encourage industry adoption of these energy saving programs.

Geoff Kearsly of the University of Otago (New Zealand) recruited me to join him in his one-person tourism program in the university's business school. This was in 1994, when the United States was in the throes of a double-dip recession where university jobs in tourism were few and far between. My wife, with much anxiety, allowed me to give Geoff Kearsly a two-year commitment for which he blessedly agreed. Our time in New Zealand was a wonderful experience for the family and a productive time for me. In addition, it was the time I had the great fortune of working with David Wilson of Penn State University (USA), who, while serving as a visiting scholar, exposed me to the field of business-to-business marketing and strategic alliances. This is one of the most neglected and important fields in hospitality and tourism management, and encompasses such sociological-economic variables as trust, commitment, social bonding, comparison level of the alternatives and value, that ultimately determine the level of success of buyer–supplier relations (Crotts et al 1998, 2001; Crotts and Turner 1999; Crotts and Wilson 1996; Pearce 2008).

Two years later, it was time to come home, and the College of Charleston provided me the opportunity to build, from scratch, an undergraduate business concentration in hospitality and tourism management (HTM) in a city I saw as having much untapped tourism potential. In 12 years, I was able to build it to a major, employing six faculty serving 200 students, with the Office of Tourism Analysis that conducts all the regional research for the region under contract with the region's Convention and Visitors Bureau.

I am now a full professor—stepping down from all administrative duties—which is, arguably, the best job in the world. It took a fair share of risks, setbacks, and more than a few anxious times to get where I am; I could not have accomplished it all without my wife, who no doubt at times felt abandoned as the mother of our children. It was not all that bad though, since we have truly enjoyed the travel and experiences our industry affords its members. Moreover, my career is not over yet, and I always have more areas I would like to pursue than my time and resources permit.

Significant Persons Who Have Impacted Me

I have not often had the opportunity to thank individuals publicly for what they have meant to me. In my personal journey, they are

- Dennis Howard (University of Oregon), my mentor, who through countless rewrites taught me how to write for academic research journals.
- Muzzo Uysal (Virginia Tech University) who taught me in word and deed that it is the responsibility of all members of academia to continually grow, stretch, and challenge us through our research and publications.
- Lynn Kahle (University of Oregon) who opened the doors for me into consumer behavior research.
- W. Fred van Raaij (Erasmus University) who broadened my perspectives of the research possibilities in economic psychology.
- David T. Wilson (Penn State University) who exposed me to the other one half of the economy involving business-to-business marketing and buyer–supplier relationships.
- Bruce Money (Brigham Young University) who helped me develop my curiosities in cross-culture research.
- Arch Woodside (Boston College) who demonstrates that there is a privilege and joy inherent in following one's intellectual curiosity.

ROAD TRAVELLED, ROAD AHEAD

My research agendas are spread out across a variety of tourism topics. Some derive from areas for which I have had a sustained passion, dating back to my earlier studies in sociology, anthropology, and educational psychology. Others are reactions to the realities that confronted our industry or me at some point in time.

Customer Diversity

Customers, not producers, decide what sells in the competitive marketplace, and it is the task of researchers to identify those who have not only the ability to purchase but also a willingness to do so (Hsu and Crotts 2006). Over the years, we have experimented with a wide range of segmentation strategies. Chief among them is the form of collective behavior, which I call national cultural differences. National culture as a segmentation strategy should be thought in terms of geography and its psychographic perspectives. It is this approach to segmentation that we believe provides researchers interesting and useful research agendas.

National culture has been shown to influence tourist choice (Reisinger et al 2009), risk taking (Kozak et al 2007), novelty seeking (Kivela and Crotts 2006; Tse and Crotts 2005), buying behavior (Crotts 2004; Money and Crotts 2000), and satisfaction with purchase decisions (Crotts and Erdmann 2000; Crotts and McKercher 2005; Crotts and Pizam 2003). It has also been shown to be an effective tool for target marketing (Mykletun et al 2001). Given that international tourism is by definition cross cultural in nature, there is much to be done either in replicating or extending the above research agenda.

National culture has been defined numerous ways (Erez and Early 1993), but the one that I often reference is Kluckhohn's description of "patterned ways of thinking, feeling, and reacting, acquired and transmitted; ... the essential core of culture consists of traditional (i.e., historically derived and selected) ideas and especially their attached values" (1954:86). The dimensions of culture most widely utilized by researchers are the five presented by Hofstede (1980) and his colleagues (Hofstede and Bond 1988; Hofstede and Hofstede 2001) from their instruments called the "values survey module." Briefly, they are power distance (a tolerance for class differentials in society), individualism (the degree to which welfare of the individualism is valued more than the group), masculinity (achievement orientation, competition, and materialism), uncertainty avoidance (intolerance of risk), and later, the Confucian dynamic, or long-term orientation (stability, thrift, respect for tradition, and the future). Applying these values to a tourist's country of birth (Crotts and Litvin 2003) has been a useful means to explore national and regional differences germane to market segments.

A relatively neglected area that begs for research is that which focuses on cultural differences within as opposed to between nations. Most of the world's developed countries are experiencing increased ethnic diversity due to immigration for both short- and long-term durations. For example, ethnic minorities in the United States in 2008 represented one quarter of its population and are expected to become the majority by 2042. Though the economies of host countries benefit from the skills and expertise these individuals bring with them, such diversity has implications to the practice of tourism marketing and management. In an effort to reach, motivate, and engage in commerce with an increasingly diverse domestic population, it is important, for marketing purpose, to gauge if and for how long an immigrant and their descendents should be considered to be a member of an ethnic minority with unique needs and values, and when the immigrant can be considered to be an integrated part of the mainstream culture. Correctly or not, countries like the United States have long been considered to be a racial melting pot for the ability to absorb immigrants into a single national identity. However, evidence suggests a salad bowl or tapestry may be a better characterization.

Acculturation is "a long-term process in which individuals modify or abandon certain aspects of their original culture as they adopt patterns of the new (adopted) culture" (Park et al 2003:142). Although within-group diversity has been shown to exist (Reisinger and Crotts 2009) as immigrants become immersed in their dominant host culture, the values and modes of behavior of their host culture are, over time, incorporated into their own norms and lifestyles (Sasidharan et al 2005). Numerous studies have looked at the degree of assimilation on recreation preferences and behaviors (see Sasidharan et al 2005 for a literature review). However, few have addressed the issue from a tourism perspective. Hence, when marketers focus on their domestic tourism markets, it is often based on research findings from samples of a country's dominant culture—those who, by definition, were born in that country, and overlooking immigrant populations who also reside in that country, representing significant populations with large purchasing power.

Given that all immigrants experience acculturation in numerous ways, there are competing theoretical models describing the process. The unidimensional model of acculturation posits that an individual can be placed along a continuum from low to high assimilation with the dominant host culture (Meridith et al 2000). Migration status, length of residency, social affiliations, language preferences, language proficiency, cultural identity/pride, and a combination of the above are often scaled as measurement constructs (Magnini 2003). The bidimensional model assumes that individuals can maintain multiple cultural identities that may differ in strength (Ryder et al 2000). Given that acculturation involves the interaction of two or more cultural legacies, the process can, at times, be characterized as a process of assimilation, while at others a high need to maintain a cultural tradition. As a result, the immigrant assimilates on certain levels, but at the same time holds onto other cultural traits, gradually transforming the host culture itself into a multicultural society. Thus, acculturation has an influence not only on the immigrant but also on the host culture itself, explaining why in a survey of British citizens the two most popular dishes are spaghetti Bolognese and curry and rice (Mitchell 2006).

Magnini (2003) and Gentry et al (1995) extend the bidimensional model into a four-mode conceptualization that, arguably, captures more fully the nature of multiculturalism. The four modes are integration—the individual adopts some aspects of the host culture while holding onto to aspects of his/her own native culture; separation—the individual avoids interaction with the host culture, resisting acculturation; assimilation—through acculturation the individual gradually adopts the host culture, thereby forgetting his/her culture of birth; and marginalization—the individual feels rejected by the host culture while at the same time has no desire to maintain an identification with their culture of birth. All this portrays a society better described as a salad bowl, where immigrants identify themselves as Korean Americans, Mexican Americans, Irish Americans, and the like, as opposed to a melting pot of fully assimilated new citizens of the host culture. Though the multidimensional models are conceptually appealing, they nevertheless rely on the same-scaled measurement constructs of the unidimensional model. Differences lie in the analysis, where clusters are looked for in the measurement constructs.

The models of acculturation have similarities with the concept of cultural convergence. Convergence theory claims that an immigrant will be under pressure to adapt to the dominant host culture, where over time they will become increasingly similar in their needs, tastes, lifestyles, values, and behavior patterns to that of their host. Not unlike the concept of acculturation, the immigrant's attitudes and values over time will converge culturally with their host as the immigrant embraces their adopted home (Kelley et al 2006). The process may accelerate when education in the host culture is involved. However, this is conjecture and may not hold. Some immigrants might be resistant to a change and disapprove of many of their host's cultural norms and values.

There are many cross-cultural questions yet to be addressed from a tourism context. Research clearly shows that each of us has our own unique personality, but overlaid on top of personality are tendencies and assumptions and reflexes handed down to us by the history of the community in which we were born and nurtured. It is these differences that can have an extraordinarily specific influence on us for the rest of our lives (Gladwell 2008). It is central to consumer behavior research to understand the role cultural legacy plays on the benefits sought by consumers.

Motivations as a Needs Satisfaction Process

What motivates a person to travel for leisure purposes? What specific needs are they attempting to satisfy? What specific amenities or services help satisfy those needs? These are fundamental questions, given that in order for a tourism enterprise (or destination) to be successful, the image and information it projects through its advertising and the product/service it delivers to its guests need to be based upon an understanding of customer needs and motivations.

In the early days, we often employed fixed response surveys to identify such trip purposes as to see and experience a new environment, escape, self-education, relax, and spend time with friends and family. Though efficient, such survey methods did not afford us an ability to probe for a true understanding of more detailed tourist motives that lie behind these generic motivations. Furthermore, questions go unanswered as to the specific amenities (existing or not) that can satisfy the tourist's needs.

The study of what motivates tourists is reasonably well researched utilizing various qualitative and quantitative methods (Baloglu and Uysal 1996; Crompton 1979; Fondness 1994; Oh et al 1995; Pearce and Caltabiano 1983). Much of this research is based upon Maslow's (1954) hierarchy of needs that purports that basic needs (such as physiological, safety, and security) must be met before the next levels in the needs hierarchy can be met (sense of belonging, self-actualization). Development of this theory has evolved to the point where tourist motivation should be seen as a combination of push/pull factors. Push factors—such as self-expression, self-development, relaxation, and prestige—internally motivate a person to travel. Pull factors are external to the individual and are illustrated in the attributes of a destination (Crompton 1979).

Sirgy and Su (2000) purport that tourism behavior is influenced by both self-congruity (match between self-concept and destination image) and functional congruity (match between a destination's attributes and a tourist's ideal expectations). Moscardo et al (1996) put forward a model that explains why a consumer chooses one destination over another (the tourist is motivated by what a destination offers); in other words, there is a link between the benefits sought and the activities pursued. Another proposition is that the former are a more direct and useful means to segment markets (Frochet and Morrison 2000). Since needs motivate behavior, the fundamental research question is to discover what those needs are and how they can be fulfilled (Hudson 1999). We all know that tourists purchase expectations, and the degree to which these expectations are met will ultimately determine the level of their satisfaction and repeat purchase intent (Kotler et al 1998; Pearson and Sullivan 1995).

One underutilized methodology designed to yield a better understanding of customer needs and motives is the "means-end or hierarchical value method." This technique is designed to gain insights into the underlying psychological motivations of tourists and why a particular site over another is visited. This provides deeper understanding of customer motives as opposed to that which can be achieved from surveys, only offering respondents fixed lists of generic motivations, since it captures motives and feelings in one's "own words" that can later be analyzed quantitatively.

The method is based upon the proposition that motives of tourists are deeply rooted in their network of expectations, goals, and values (van Rekom 1994). The "hierarchical value method" (HVM) or "laddering" technique is designed to identify both higher and lower values and their connections via a series of probing questions. There are three different approaches that have been developed to date: the classic approach of Reynolds and Gutman (1984), the hard laddering approach illustrated by Jewell and Crotts (2001), and the soft pattern technique (Bagozzi and Dabholkar 2000; Bagozzi and Dholakia 1999; Hofstede et al 1998; Jewell and Crotts 2009).

The HVM pioneered by Reynolds and Gutman (1984) has evolved as a methodology that allows researchers a deeper understanding of individual's needs and motives that they are consciously and subconsciously attempting to satisfy (Bagozzi and Dabholkar 2000; Bagozzi and Dholakia 1999; Jewell and Crotts 2009). This means-end framework of the laddering technique attempts to discover not only the key motives and values the consumer is seeking to satisfy but also the linkages between these motives and values that form the individual's overall cognitive network (Crotts and van Rekom 1998).

We recommend the HVM technique purported by Bagozzi and Dabholkar (2000) and Bagozzi and Dholakia (1999), where the respondent makes a series of claims and then is asked to justify and defend those claims. The process can begin by asking respondents to indicate whether their overall evaluation of a consumed (purchase) experience is positive, negative, or neutral and to what degree ("strongly" or "somewhat"). This creates a basis for communication between interviewer and respondent by allowing the respondent to express their definite stance on an issue of importance (Bagozzi and Dabholkar 2000). Once expressed, the respondent is then asked to provide their own personal reasons for such an evaluation. Beginning with the first reason given, the interviewer then asks the respondent to explain in regard to their own personal significance. They are then asked to justify their explanation in terms of personal relevance. This explanation and justification process is continued until the respondent is no longer able to give any further justification. The procedure is then continued for each of the remaining reasons originally stated in the respondent's evaluation (Bagozzi and Dabholkar 2000). It is argued that data generated from this HVM method represents interconnected, ordered sets of reasoning in terms of how individuals actually reflect their own self-concept and social presentation to others (Bagozzi and Dabholkar 2000; Bagozzi and Dholakia 1999).

The HVM technique has been applied to determining means-end chains or motives for attending a fine arts museum (Crotts and van Rekom 1998; Jansen-Verbeke and van Rekom 1996), selecting a ski destination (Klenosky et al 1993), use of a state park's interpretive services (Klenosky et al 1998), corporate values (van Rekom 1994, 1997), and how people felt about a US president while he was in office (Bagozzi and Dabholkar 2000; Bagozzi and Dholakia 1999). In reviewing this literature, we found that most end states sought to contribute to the customer's quality of life in positive ways (learn, reflect, and escape). Understanding what are the desired end states tourists seek and working back from the HVM maps provides managers with the means to help their guests achieve them (Jewell and Crotts 2001).

Optimizing the Marketing Mix

The marketing mix is the most fundamental concept of marketing. Coined in the late 1950s, the term conceptualizes the marketer as a mixer of ingredients, who creates and executes an experiment involving the product, price, promotion, and place distribution as the primary ingredients of a marketing strategy. An expanded list of marketing mix variables classifies the ingredients into two categories: the "offering" that consists of the product, service, packaging, brand, and price; and the "process" or "method" that includes such variables as advertising, promotion, sales, publicity, distribution channels, and new product development (Frey 1961). Booms and Bitner (1981) added people (employees) to the model, recognizing the importance of relationship development skills in marketing.

Marketing represents one of the largest line item expenses in the hospitality sector and has attracted our attention over the years on a somewhat piecemeal basis. To illustrate, the intent of our work in consumer information searches was to inject a degree of accountability into determining where and how much advertising dollars should be directed toward specific media to maximize commercial benefit. Aided recall surveys and various strategies of tracking consumer responses to specific advertising efforts are all methods we have tried in the past at various levels of success.

Today, I find great promise in a relatively obscure but emerging method called "marketing mix modeling." It is an analytical approach that uses historical sales data to quantify the impact of specific marketing activities on sales. The method accomplishes this by setting up a model where sales volume becomes the dependent variable and the independent variables are derived from various marketing efforts. Once the data set is assembled, multiple iterations are carried out to create a model that best accounts for the changes in the sales volume. Issues related to reliability and validity of the model are addressed by running the final model on a separate set of data. Once the final model is deemed acceptable, it can be used to simulate marketing scenarios. In these scenarios, the marketing manager can experiment with reallocating the marketing budget and see the direct impact on forecasted sales, allowing one to optimize spending on specific marketing efforts that provide the greatest potential return on investment. Once adopted, the results provide two necessary ingredients of all formalized marketing plans: sales volume goals and the marketing tactics effort to reach these sales goals.

Proctor and Gamble, Kraft, Coca Cola, and Pepsi are examples of firms that today make optimization modeling as a fundamental part of their marketing planning. The method to date is as much an art as a science due, in part, to the lack of transparency and peer review given the proprietary nature of the data and results. Hence, much of my current efforts are focused not only on learning how to employ the method but also on making further refinements to it as currently applied before it is more broadly adopted in hospitality and tourism. To illustrate, consumer demand in our industry is more variable when compared to other goods and services and, not accounting for such variations brought about by seasonal patterns, holidays, and weather, can serve to bias results on marketing effectiveness and its return on investment.

The net effect of this research agenda is twofold. First, if successful, it will provide marketing managers a new tool designed for the hospitality industry that they can use to optimize their marketing dollars in such a way that provides the greatest likelihood of producing the strongest return on investment. Second, it is an effort to essentially operationalize and analyze all elements of the marketing mix as to their abilities to optimize desired benefits. To date, the dependent variables have been exclusively financial (sales, sales volume). I believe the methods can be applied to blog narratives that can isolate the effects of changes in the product offering and marketing processes on brand image, customer satisfaction, and perhaps changes to the customer's quality of life.

LOOKING AHEAD

The theories and methodologies that guide our research are constantly being advanced, challenged, and refined, and will no doubt continue to do so indefinitely. Therefore, I encourage the young scholar to read broadly and be open to the possibilities of finding new ways to frame and approach the issues of today.

Tourism marketing is inherently an interdisciplinary field of research and continues to benefit from researchers from a broad spectrum of disciplines. In particular, I am convinced that the field of neuroscience is poised to transform our understanding of consumer behavior and marketing practice in the not so distant future. The emerging fields of neuroeconomics and neuromarketing employ brain-imaging devices (fMRI, CAT scans, etc.) that identify areas of the brain, which control distinct processes of consumer decision making. Early efforts suggest that marketing is not confined to social psychology, but draws from deep biological functions organisms possess that have evolutionary roots (Montague 2006).

Though most tourism researchers will never have access to fMRI and CAT scans for their research, we can learn and benefit from those who do. Today, among neuroscientists, it is broadly understood that the human brain is a highly inquisitive and efficient organ that at times governs itself through memory (reinforced learning), but at the same time can be willfully controlled and capable of learning. In other words, there is neurobiological evidence that indicates that the human brain is always moving from deliberative (explicit) to automatic (implicit) control in its decision making (Cialdini 2009; Cialdini and Goldstein 2002; Crotts 2008). In today's world of being stressed and overstimulated environments, consumers could not function if they deliberated on every decision. What all this means to marketers is that there are two simple questions that frame consumer decision making: what the choices that are worth making are and how much they cost. Rewards that the brain evaluates positively are paired with the emotion of trust and stored in memory to guide future decisions. Conversely, rewards that are evaluated negatively are paired with the emotion of regret to be evoked from memory when confronted with the same choice decision. Learning takes place but only in those settings where the consumer willfully makes the choice to deliberate, and which, according to "mindfulness theory," can be influenced. All this has enormous implications to our research on consumer information search, novelty seeking, satisfaction, and loyalty.

As final thoughts and recommendations, choosing academia as a career requires a commitment to a journey that is costly and time consuming, requiring considerable tenacity and a fair share of good luck. It is a giant leap of faith to pursue a PhD in hopes that you can obtain one of the 25 or so academic posts in one's specialized field that historically will be available worldwide each year. Moreover, the journey does not end there, since faculty must survive a tenure and promotion process that grows more rigorous each year by increasingly constrained universities.

My advice to those who make this commitment is to read widely (within and beyond hospitality and tourism journals); condition oneself to write one to two pages per day for research publications; enjoy and serve the students (be their gateway to the middle class and beyond); get involved with the local industry (think globally but act locally); and continue to learn, grow, and have fun. University life is far from perfect, and it is typical to encounter both the best and worst of individuals in academe. I encourage you to seek out and surround yourself with good people and good things will happen. Know it is not always possible to find colleagues in the department or school motivated to engage in research, let alone share the same research interests. It is important to work with those one can and be respectful of those not accommodating, but also seeking out others to collaborate with from related departments and institutions. However, one can go alone to pursue intellectually appealing areas of research. The quality and quantity of research will determine mobility and opportunities for advancement along professional journeys. All academia requires is to be productive, and the individual alone has the privilege of choice as to where research efforts are focused. No other profession affords its ranks such freedom.

SECTION 3

REFLECTIONS AND DIRECTIONS

Chapter 12

Reflections and Directions

Philip L. Pearce
James Cook University, Australia

All readers who have considered the autobiographies presented in the preceding pages are likely to have formed impressions of the researchers and their careers. The final section of this monograph provides my personal synthesis of some themes arising in these accounts. The views offered here are those of a participant observer rather than an outsider. Of course, as Simmel (1950) observed, the outsider can view any community through fresh eyes. If the themes I explore in the following remarks are not entirely the same as those identified by some readers, then that can be taken as a healthy sign that this monograph has at least prompted some unique engagement. First, the chapter draws together select observations from the autobiographies and provides links to the works of others who could not participate in this endeavor. Second, the discussion considers the more immediate future for the kinds of studies and interest areas pioneered by the representative authors.

CONSIDERING CASE STUDIES

As a preliminary observation on the value of synthesizing themes from the case studies, it is possible to note some key points about the number and variability of the cases considered. Questions that can be asked of this kind of approach include: How many cases are enough to provide value in

The Study of Tourism: Foundations from Psychology
Tourism Social Science Series, Volume 15, 189–202
Copyright © 2011 by Emerald Group Publishing Limited
All rights of reproduction in any form reserved
ISSN: 1571-5043/doi:10.1108/S1571-5043(2011)0000015015

drawing out general themes (Yin 2009)? Along the same line, what kinds of previous work may be seen as analogous or supportive of the sampling employed?

Krueger and Casey (2000), describing the issue of how many focus groups should be selected by researchers, suggest the concept of saturation can be used. In this view, the number of units (in their case focus groups) to be sampled should continue until no more fresh ideas or insights are provided. In a sense, the meaning and value of the research effort are saturated by the information drawn from previous instances. In focus group work in commercial settings researching tightly constrained product choices, an adequate number of cases may lie between three and six. A wider number of sampling units are suggested by other procedures and practices. Eisenhardt (1989), in a key publication on integrating case studies, chose to look at six similar cases and extracted the commonalities and crossover factors from these select instances. Other allied research methods and statistical procedures suggest that a slightly greater number of instances might be valuable. In marketing research, the task of comparing products and competitors is frequently an issue and the statistical procedure of multidimensional scaling is sometimes employed to provide product comparison maps (Pearce and Fenton 1994). A rule of thumb for making such comparisons and producing stable product maps is to use at least eight cases.

Other kinds of social science inquiry also use multiple case studies. Becher (1989), for example, sampled 12 academic disciplines in his book on academic tribes and territories. In his work on the collapse of preindustrial societies, Diamond (2005) used data from 11 societies. Gardner (1995), in analyzing leadership, drew implications from the lives and experiences of 11 notable figures. Getz, Carlsen and Morrison (2004), examining small family tourism businesses across three continents, considered 15 case studies. Their work raises the specific matter of the internal variability of the cases. In the case of our present authors, we have a mix of nationalities and some variation in their ages and subareas of interest. The evidence from the kinds of parallel case study work suggests that if there is a lot of coherence and similarity in the material with little need for stratification, five to eight cases might be tentatively recommended, with a slightly higher number suggested when very diverse units for analysis are under review. Given that we have 10 cases from multiple settings, we can now proceed with some confidence to assert that it is worthwhile to attempt to build a comprehensive overview of the beginning of tourism study in this area of interest.

Early Forces

As might be expected with a new topic area in academic research, the participating authors often report circuitous paths to their tourism research destination. The study of psychology itself was undertaken by several of the participants, while others forged their approach to the study of people's behavior with undergraduate courses in forestry, economics, marketing, leisure, and recreation. Such beginnings were usually advanced by theses and research investigations built on these ideas. Individuals in their case histories report the prominent role played by doctoral-level supervisors and many undoubtedly have been influenced by these mentors beyond the duration of their theses.

Some of the prominent names from the career histories that coincide with the evolution of psychology itself include supervision and contact with notable identities, such as Gordon Allport, Jerome Bruner, Michael Argyle, and Martin Fishbein. For others, their supervisors at the graduate level were specialists in recreation and social behavior; they included William Burch, Donald Field, and Dennis Howard. A common thread among all these mentors appears to have been a tolerance and indeed encouragement for novel and innovative topics, which makes one speculate that possibly other graduate students elsewhere thought of studying tourist markets and behaviors in the 1960s and 1970s, but were dissuaded by more conservative supervisors.

Another force with considerable influence on the early careers of the researchers was the institutional support that allowed tourism-related research. These priorities were delivered through the attitudes of deans, heads of department, and the funding they provided. In the early part of the careers, it can be noted that the institutional acceptance of tourism-linked studies seems to have been strongly influenced by locational issues. This is not, as one might expect, necessarily due to an institution's location within a prominent tourism region. In the United States, in particular, the emergence of recreation and tourism programs has been tied in part to the state-funded universities and notably those universities where national parks and recreation programs were developed to deal with domestic visitors and leisure.

In earlier accounts of the development of tourism study in the United States, Robert McIntosh (1992) noted that it was the universities in the Midwest that had started under Abraham Lincoln's Land Grant programs which eventually developed tourism interests. The trajectory of influence here was that those universities with an agricultural emphasis built forestry, parks, and recreation programs. These slowly evolved to a consideration of the multiple uses of forestry lands and public spaces, and hence in time to the behavior of visitors and tourists. Sometimes, the study of agriculture led to programs in hospitality and food services. At other times, natural environment planning became an additional or separate pathway of study (Gunn 2004). Extension specialists from these programs formed an important role in supplying practical information to communities from the research and teaching efforts. Harvard, Yale, Princeton, and Stanford universities, for example, were not a part of this history, and the absence of tourism scholars from these institutions is in some ways explained by the predominance of recreation interests in the Land Grant Universities and their ties to the US parks and recreation system. Aspects of these roots persist in the United States today and are reflected in several scholars' career histories. There are though, some locations with a tourism prominence, including George Washington University, the University of Hawaii, and the University of Central Florida, which have a more purpose-built tourism story.

By way of contrast, the scholars whose doctoral study was outside of the United States—Josef Mazanec, Ton van Egmond, Chris A. Ryan, and Philip L. Pearce—were more likely to have undertaken a mainstream psychology education or learned their core skills from programs arising from linkages to marketing and hospitality. Arguably, this set of international scholars did not discover tourists and tourism in quite the same way as their US counterparts. Since all of these non-American scholars studied in the United Kingdom/Europe in the 1970s, the international tourism phenomenon was already highly visible.

The career histories document some distinctive, even idiosyncratic psychodemographic factors that assisted the scholars' career choice to study tourists and their worlds. It will have been apparent to many already that all of the career histories are from men. It is important to note that some significant female contributors to tourism study were invited, but either they declined or felt they were not quite in the first cohort of founding figures. Pauline Sheldon (USA), Gianna Moscardo (Australia), Cathy Hsu (China), Regina Schluter (Argentina), Alison Morrison (Scotland), Darya Maoz (Israel), Gu Huimin (China), and many others have all made notable contributions in their respective countries and contexts to studies of tourist markets, behavior, and experience. Future autobiographical records may possibly incorporate their perspectives and those of many emerging and productive female scholars. The gender perspective is important here, because an appreciation of wives and partners is a commonly expressed theme in the career stories. Perhaps the scholars' current appreciation of wives, partners, and children should also be read at times as apologies for career-related absences.

Some researchers note that participation in sports added to their mobility or assisted their social integration. Not surprisingly, for scholars linked to recreation and natural environment programs, there is also some common appreciation of outdoor and adventurous activities, both as pastimes and as personal insights into tourism and leisure experiences. Involvement in arts and music as well as much enthusiasm for other cultures and travel itself are further themes in select autobiographies. It can be suggested that these personal influences and interests have both fostered the professional study and maintained the scholar's interests, particularly during those times when being a tourism student and scholar was more about office work than fieldwork.

The interplay between locational stability and mobility is an interesting dimension of career development in these autobiographies. It is noteworthy that there is a fairly common pattern. For many scholars, there was often relocation from place to place, which persisted during the early career years. Then, in many cases, this mobility was followed by a relatively long period of stability in one location, so much so that the citing of many of the scholars' names in this set of authors will evoke an immediate association with a university. For many, there were, and are, family-linked pressures fostering settling in one setting. Undoubtedly, the institutional tolerance and support for the kind of work being conducted were also important. Of course, the particular case reported by Seppo E. Iso-Ahola, which describes the demise of tourism courses at the University of Maryland, is a counter to this trend. In its own way, it provides instruction to all about the ways in which university priorities can shape individual careers. In terms of overall mobility, undoubtedly Chris A. Ryan has shifted continents and countries the most, while Joseph Mazanec and Ton van Egmond have each been located at one institution in their own country for nearly all of their careers.

Additionally, it is important to note that few of the scholars have worked in isolation. Instead, they have been engaged widely in local and broader academic communities. Some have formed long-term collaborations with a small number of scholars, while others have worked closely with their leading students, hence assisting their mutual careers. Peers too have mattered, notably in terms of support, collaboration, and direct coopera-tion. An implication of some significance for those building careers lies in these patterns. It would seem to be valuable to cultivate some strong and continuing partnerships, as well as being prepared to experiment with new colleagues. This approach is consistent with the view that the career histories reveal individuals who might be said to have inquiring minds with multiple interests. The autobiographies suggest that many of the authors have been ready to take advantage of chance encounters and events. Nevertheless, the success of the scholars reinforces the view that detailed hard work and the desire to complete a project through to publication are healthy attributes that usefully accompany the recognition of opportunities to work with others.

Career Development: Communities and Industry

A strong theme in the autobiographies is the usefulness of tourist behavior studies to tourism business communities and to the managers of tourism and recreation settings. This functional and utilitarian approach to research is expressed strongly by nearly all authors, although the specific way in which these links are managed appears to be somewhat different. In some career histories, the effectiveness and usefulness of hospitality, tourism, and tourist behavior research is expressed through direct consultancy work or in response to well-defined industry needs as expressed through grants for specific work. The work of some scholars portrayed in the autobiographies was shaped by direct contracts with government or industry association agencies, thus creating close and continuing relationships. On other occasions, the academic work explores possibilities from large data sets and primary studies and offers perspectives to decision makers rather meeting direct targeted needs.

If all the contributors were confined to one room and asked to discuss this usefulness or relevance issue, there would be some clear differences in the approaches and perceived responsibilities. There are rich veins of debate here about the proper role of universities, and about how individuals can survive and better create opportunities as tourism researchers. If the hypothetical meeting of all the participants in this book were to take place, there would probably be agreement that, at least at times, being useful to business communities is important. Disagreements would be more likely in the arena of how much time should be allocated to being useful versus seeking a better understanding of phenomenon. In brief, the debates would most likely center on how important is scholarly curiosity and/or assisting stakeholders other than those managing and profiting from tourism. One of the contentious issues here is how to define relevance and usefulness.

The ways in which relevance in tourism studies has been interpreted has often been problematic (Jafari 2005; Pearce 2005b). Too often relevance has only been applied to work that is short term, local, sector biased, unit oriented, and then economic and action inspiring. These are not inherently bad criteria; it is simply that they are not the only criteria. Work in other styles can be relevant and valuable. As the sophistication of the research community and its users grow, it can be anticipated that these wider frames of relevance will be better appreciated. I have discussed this topic previously (Pearce 2005b:27–28), arguing that relevance may also derive from longer term studies, work concerned with policy as well as business issues, studies addressing sociocultural and environmental topics—not simply profit-ability—and work embracing a diversity of sectors linked to, but sometimes beyond tourism. There is also the perspective that being located in the business world's view of relevance is often comparable to dealing with Einsteinian relativity. Just as one produces findings for a past problem, the nature of space and time has shifted, with yesterday's problem being overtaken by the urgency of today's concerns.

It can be added that the limited way in which relevance has been viewed is also connected to a simplistic view of knowledge transfer and knowledge management. This is a large discussion in contemporary tourism studies (Cooper 2006). Again, if our scholars were locked into a room and asked to debate this issue, the conversations could take some time. One key to understanding the use of tourism research is to recognize that the pathways to its deployment are varied. Occasionally, a direct application can be seen from one study. More often, an iterative and then cumulative program of work is required; this program should give solid and reliable findings, rather than scattered and idiosyncratic information (Crompton 2005). Even then, there may be circuitous pathways to the adoption of the research with multiple intermediaries between the researcher and the user.

In this context, an insightful guide is provided by the work of Flyvbjerg (2001) in his *Making Social Science Matter*. The argument he employs, and of use to tourism study, is that researchers who want to make a difference have to develop public voices. This view suggests that the way to significant influence lies in engagement in the media, participation in public debates, submissions to hearings and policy processes, as well as active membership of organizations. Many of the authors in this monograph are skilled at these conversational styles and the autobiographies reveal that they have learned to move quite easily among audiences with different agendas. As Crompton (2005) reports, it is arrogant for academics to simply believe that busy professionals will be able to find, read, and sort through the implications of the necessarily formal and refereed academic work.

More broadly, three key concepts from the expanding knowledge management literature have the potential to alter the adoption of tourism research. Cooper, among others, considers the transfer of tourism research to be a long-standing challenge "with few advances so far" (2006:48). The concepts that may provide a new way forward supplement Flyvbjerg's views and include knowledge capture, codification, and diffusion. Knowledge capture involves a formative stage of mapping what people already know. There are two sources of information here: first, there is the information available in the form of documents and reports and, second, the information that is implicit or tacit (the latter being the information in the minds of the potential research users). An awareness of what is known and thought by research users can provide a first useful frame for the collection of further information.

Importantly, if researchers seek to have local, sector-specific, and short-term relevance, then a key second step in the knowledge management and capture process is the alignment of researcher and user objectives at the earliest stages of research planning. Once the work is done, the form or code in which it is expressed is critical. Codification means a translation of research work into a language and a medium (such as decision rule systems or illustrative cases) that heighten the accessibility of the material. Finally, knowledge transfer is a multifaceted concept invoking Flyvbjerg's point about the styles of delivery, as well as the roles of intermediaries and the capacities of organizations to absorb information. Even the most elegant speeches and the best writing need to be delivered at the right time to mindful and receptive audiences. In all of this literature, there is a guiding view that different solutions prevail for different research goals, and the simple charge that academic research is irrelevant or not well accepted will be answered by tailored solutions and a broad appreciation of relevance.

There remains, though, an argument that there should be space for tourism and tourist behavior researchers to be independently intellectually curious; that is, somewhat free to contemplate the quirks of tourism and its distinctive phenomenon without the press of always being mindful of being useful. It is this kind of thinking that Dann (2007) reports in his autobiographical contribution to Nash's book when he describes his attempt to restrict *Annals of Tourism* research publishing to disinterested academic inquiry. His view involved preventing *Annals* from publishing any business-relevant or marketing studies. The editorial consensus rejecting Dann's appeal does not imply that the style of study he recommended is not important. There are traces of support for such curiosity-driven inquiry and the benefits it confers for more applied work in several of the autobiographies, including ideas expressed by Ryan, Pearce, and Crotts.

Dealing with the Status of Tourism Study

As Becher (1989) and others have reported, issues of status and intellectual snobbery are attached to study areas. Tourism research rarely fares well in these kinds of rankings. Status concerns are pervasive and penetrate many universities through their schools, departments, and divisions, especially when researchers compete for resources (Page 2005). In many fields, the meaning of citation rates and the prestige of journals are neatly linked to their value. As most tourism scholars know, journal rankings and citation rates are only rough and approximate guides to the quality of individual tourism contributions (Benckendorff 2010). How then did status issues affect our select group of tourism researchers and, assuming they managed to master any difficulties, what mechanisms did they employ to negotiate this issue?

The answers appear to depend partly on the researcher's institutional base. Innovative institutions that were prepared to tolerate work that moved outside the frame of the psychology and related social science journals have clearly been the best academic homes in which to reside (Nash 2007:258). Status or tolerance by institutions and deans and department heads was also assisted if practitioners showed support, especially funding. This theme is demonstrated in most of the autobiographies with contracts and grants solidifying their positions in the 1980s and 1990s.

The status issue also relates to our previous discussion about perceived relevance. As Fuchs (1992) has noted, newly developing fields are very much influenced by what practitioners see as important with a consequential emphasis on operational and instrumental work. At least engaging in some kinds of locally significant work or working with students to forge these links appears to have been a practical and successful strategy to build status. Some of the scholars had built credibility in their base disciplines—such as marketing, recreation, and psychology—which boosted their wider colleague acceptance when they focused more on writing about tourism. The new publication outlets, which included tourism conferences, journals, and book series, also conferred status on the work being done. They offered some international validation of the scholar's local activities (Goeldner 2005). This was a little slower for our authors writing in Dutch (van Egmond) and German (Mazanec), but their recent publications in English rapidly achieved awareness of much of their research.

In those academic systems that rely heavily on student numbers as funding sources, the viability of tourism and leisure programs, in particular, was and is never far from the surface. Again Iso-Ahola's experience of closing down an area of activity and leaving the tourism study field suggests that some vigilance about the funding issue is important even among those who are not departmental leaders. Finally, but not unimportantly, some protection against hostile forces can be afforded by the individual's personality. It would seem from the autobiographies that the ability to report confidently the tourism/recreation/hospitality/marketing story within and across institutions is a skill worth cultivating. The character strengths of many of the authors arguably shine through the preceding career histories. Their personality styles seem very consistent with those noted by Rushton et al (1983) and Smart et al (2000) in Chapter 1 of this volume: confident, assertive, sociable, and not easily dissuaded from achievement.

Topics Explored and Undeveloped

A review of the intersections between psychology as a major investigative social science and the development of the tourism field was initiated in Chapter 1, but the discussion traced developments only until the early 1980s in order to allow the authors to present their own contributions and career histories. It is timely now to assess some of the dominant parts of the landscape that have been developed in the last 30 years. Additionally, by taking note of regions yet to be explored, some assistance may be provided to those who wish to go boldly forth.

Key books and special issues of journals are convenient ways to highlight the growth and content of fields of inquiry. This information will be employed here, but it is important to observe that for many North American researchers priority is given to individual journal articles and textbooks rather than research monographs. To illustrate this trend, two of the very productive researchers in tourism and recreation in North America, Joe O'Leary who has contributed to this volume and John Crompton who has provided earlier autobiographical reflections, are researchers whose names are not linked to defining research monographs or books, but rather their influence lies in the cumulative power of numerous coauthored articles.

A conception of tourist behavior and experience as a sequence of activities and human reactions usefully pinpoints some areas of strong activity in this field. There is plenty of work on destination selection and consumer choice behavior. These topics, along with a line of work on tourist motivation, may be considered to be key considerations at the front end of the tourists' phases of experience. Models and examples of this work are shown in the early studies by Woodside, Crompton, Plog, Pearce, and others. They are also evident by the continued interest in motivation and destination selection topics illustrated in the series of CABI-published books, *Consumer Psychology of Tourism, Hospitality and Leisure*. March and Woodside (2005) present a creative summary of these interests in destination selection and Hsu and Huang (2008) report on the progress of motivation research.

An even more popular set of topics in tourist behavior studies is that of market segmentation. This kind of work is approached in several ways. The detailed empirical studies and classifications represented in this monograph by the research of Mazanec and O'Leary have been on the largest scale and with the most innovative and technically sophisticated analyses. There are, however, numerous other researchers with a specialist interest in a component part of tourism who have also conducted market assessment studies. While they may not necessarily think of themselves as fitting into the core disciplinary traditions described in this book, much of the work they do is possible because of the fundamental ways in which attitudes and values have been studied by earlier scholars. This identification of topic interested tourism researchers thus draws all those who provide classifications and profiles of special tourist groups into the ambit of tourist behavior and experience work. The studies include plentiful papers on such groups as wildlife, urban, and adventure tourists, the visiting-friends-and-family market, cruise tourists, casino visitors, ski tourists, short break visitors, sports tourists, volunteer tourists, sex tourists, and many more.

While the initial decisions made by tourists and attempts to categorize all kinds of tourists are important topics, much work has also been conducted on the outcomes of their holidays. In particular, the field of study here is dominated by two kinds of outcomes: assessing satisfaction and monitoring impacts. Leading volumes in demonstrating these interests include further articles in the *Consumer Psychology of Tourism, Hospitality and Leisure Series*. Pioneering contributions to these topics can also be noted in the formative volume by Noe (1999) and the edited books by Pizam and Mansfield (2000) *Consumer Behaviour in Travel and Tourism*, as well as Kozak and Decrop's (2009) *Handbook of Tourist Behaviour*. The impacts of tourists are also a prominent topic in the wide-ranging field addressing sustainability issues (Bramwell and Lane 2005). Special issues of journals, such as *Tourism Recreation Research* and *Journal of Sustainable Tourism*, have provided contributions highlighting the international variability in sustainable practices and the need for tourists to be aware of their role in this type of development. Some of this work is linked to efforts to improve tourist education and interpretive services. This forms a link to the growing interest in ethical and responsible tourist behavior (Pearce et al 2011: Chapter 4).

These two major interests (destination selection and tourist satisfaction/ impacts) can be seen as the bookends of the psychology of studying tourists. There are other possible outcomes of the tourists' holidays that are slowly being appreciated, and these understudied consequences of traveling include attention to tourist health and learning. There is also the topic of the nature of on-site experiences and how tourists react to the settings and the people they encounter, both as a process and as a microscale of analysis that is not fully served by overall holiday satisfaction appraisals. The studies of scholars such as Moscardo (1999) on mindfulness, Bitgood (2002 2006 2009) on visitor movement patterns, Reisinger and Turner (2003) on cross-cultural interaction, Baerenholdt et al (2004) on activity practices, Uriely (2005) on experience analysis, and Noy (2007) on group communication, as well as Ryan's (1997) overview of experience, have made some contributions to on-site studies. Much other work is now developing detailed assessments of the meaning and the sociocultural interaction processes that exist when tourists are at the places they visit. Such studies include some of the work of our autobiographers, Crotts on crime awareness and van Egmond on cross-national contact.

A synopsis of the major currents of tourist behavior, and related recreation and marketing studies applied to tourism, almost inevitably prompts questions about what has not been covered and indeed the more subtle question of the ways in which the existing and future topics might be approached. In the arena of topics that might be understudied, an expansive list can be generated by referring to the observable behaviors of tourists and the scope of the larger founding discipline of psychology. From these plentiful examples a few illustrations may be of interest. There is little work on motion sickness (or sickness generally), nor much about the physiology of travel within tourism studies. More could be made of the psychology research understanding human memory processes. The sensations of tourism are beginning to be researched, but the distinctions between the sensual and the sensuous are worth further effort as new ways to enhance tourist experiences are constructed. There are dominant tourist behaviors and their derivatives that some might find interesting; shopping and shoplifting, watching and being watched, bargain hunting and being scammed, photographing and being framed, accessing technology and being pursued by it, providing quality to the quality service providers, and perhaps above all treating other people and places ethically.

New activities and new places demand attention if only because of the ways technology is altering the on-site communities and blending the experience of being away with live reporting to those whom one has recently left behind. Then there are the cognitive geographies of the new markets— the non-Western tourists who are bringing Confucian, Hindu, Buddhist, and Islamic ideas to their interactions and destinations. The study of tourist behavior and experience might have begun slowly but its reach and importance are very likely to gather pace in the coming decades.

Jafari (2005), in an important article challenging tourism researchers, argued that mounting respect for the study area would be built by publishing studies about tourism in the core parent disciplinary journals of social science. In the case of authors for this volume and researchers who follow in their footsteps, it means principally psychology, social psychology, marketing, and consumer behavior outlets. It would be a candid assessment at this stage in the evolution of the tourism–parent discipline conversation to suggest that there is little of this feedback to parent sources. There is some, but the likelihood of having an influence from a scattered distribution of individual articles is not very great. It might be a future activity to have a group of tourism researchers approach editors of major journals in the psychology and marketing world and propose special issues and major subconference themes showcasing tourism and recreation behavior studies. It has taken a while to get to this point, but the documentation of what people do and how they behave in the globally important industry of tourism arguably add to the understanding of human behavior patterns and interests. At the very least, many tourism studies reveal the broader applicability of foundation ideas from conceptual schemes in psychology, while the most significant studies offer modifications to those ideas. Such claims, however, do need to be tested through the review process from the broader social science community.

It is appropriate at this near-to-closing point of this monograph to at least provide some succinct comments on the epistemological and ontological styles of early tourist behavior work and to foreshadow change in the approaches that Generation T researchers might adopt. It was documented in Chapter 1 of this monograph that the construction of experimental laboratories to assess sensation and perception was pivotal to the very foundation of psychology. Positivism was at the very heart of this approach. It was noted further that fluctuations of interest across countries and continents introduced different emphases. In a methodological and epistemological sense, there was a slightly aberrant dalliance with psycho-analysis and some enthusiasm for third-force views about human capacity, but postpositivist approaches to research have been the disciplinary standard. It is worth repeating a comment made earlier in Chapter 1 about psychology in the 1970s that reinforces this view:

The broad conversation might have been about topics of public interest, but the in-house conversations were centered on clever research designs, sample selection, statistical assumptions, and probability values.

Change, though, is under way. The arrival of positive psychology as a significant interest area, at first in the United States and then globally, is arguably a part of the incorporation of new topics and ways of researching topics in the field (Diener and Biswas-Diener 2008; Seligman 2002). Positive psychologists seek to understand happiness and well-being, and in particular consider the development of human character strengths and abilities as a part of their defining interest area. Such a focus is an addition, not a replacement, for the previous half century of attention to the study of individuals perceived to have problems or frustrations in their lives. Narratives and Web logs, autobiographies, and public talk are now seen as legitimate sources of information and publications discussing well-being may be approached with interpretive and constructivist paradigms, as well as through the more traditional positivist frameworks.

Researchers in tourism marketing and recreation need to be aware of these changes in psychology and not be trapped by standards of positivist science that are now no longer always current (Tribe 2009). Of course, many tourism researchers are knowledgeable about these areas of change since the digital access to source materials offers opportunities for benchmarking study styles and assessing paradigmatic approaches. Clever experimentation, well-structured questionnaire and observational data and appropriate statistical analysis, will continue to offer powerful tools for postpositivist appraisal. It is though heartening to think that coming decades will see these tried and tested tools supplemented by the rich treatment of naturalistic modes of behavior skillfully interpreted by researcher keen to understand the mental life of the globe's traveling citizens.

References

Albert, H.
  1967 Marktsoziologie und Entscheidungslogik. Neuwied: Luchterhands.
Association of American Medical Colleges
  1999 Assessment of Professionalism Project. <http://www.aamc.org/members/gea/
  professionalism.pdf#search = %22definition%20of%20professionalism%22>
  (Accessed October 8, 2006).
Baerenholdt, J., M. Haldrup, J. Larsen, and J. Urry
  2004 Performing Tourist Places. Aldershot: Ashgate.
Bagozzi, R.
  1980 Causal Models in Marketing. New York, NY: Wiley.
Bagozzi, R., and P. Dabholkar
  2000 Discursive Psychology: An Alternative Conceptual Foundation to Means-
  End Chain Theory. Psychology & Marketing 17:535–586.
Bagozzi, R., and U. Dholakia
  1999 Goal Setting and Goal Striving in Consumer Behavior. Journal of Marketing
  63(Special Issue):19–32.
Baloglu, S., and M. Uysal
  1996 Market Segments of Push and Pull Motivations: A Canonical Correlation
  Approach. International Journal of Contemporary Hospitality Management
  8(3):32–38.
Baumeister, R., and B. Bushman
  2008 Social Psychology and Human Nature. Belmont, CA: Thomson Higher
  Education.
Becher, T.
  1989 Academic Tribes and Territories: Intellectual Enquiry and the Culture of
  Disciplines. Milton Keynes: Open University Press.
Bell, P., J. Fisher, and R. Loomis
  1978 Environmental Psychology. Philadelphia, PA: W.B. Saunders.
Benckendorff, P.
  2010 Exploring the Limits of Tourism Research Collaboration: A Social Network
  Analysis of Co-Authorship Patterns in Australian and New Zealand Tourism
  Research. In Proceedings of the 20th Annual CAUTHE Conference. Hobart,
  Australia.
Biswas-Diener, R.
  2008 Material Wealth and Subjective Well-Being. In The Science of
  Subjective Well-Being, M. Eid, and R.J. Larsen, eds. New York, NY: Guilford
  Press.

Bitgood, S.
   2002 Environmental Psychology in Museums, Zoos, and Other Exhibition Centers. *In* Handbook of Environmental Psychology, R.R. Bechtel, and A. Churchman, eds., pp. 461–480. New York, NY: Wiley.
   2006 An Analysis of Visitor Circulation: Movement Patterns and the General Value Principle. Curator 49:463–475.
   2009 Museum Fatigue: A Critical Review. Visitor Studies 12(2):1–19.
Blaug, M.
   1962 Economic Theory in Retrospect. Cambridge: Cambridge University Press.
Bochner, S. ed.
   1982 Cultures in Contact. Oxford: Pergamon.
Booms, B., and M. Bitner
   1981 Marketing Services by Managing the Environment. Cornell Hotel and Restaurant Administration Quarterly 23(1):35–40.
Boring, E.
   1950 A History of Experimental Psychology (2nd edition). New York, NY: Appleton-Century-Crofts.
Bourdieu, P.
   1986 The Forms of Capital. *In* Handbook of Theory and Research for the Sociology of Education, J. Richardson, ed., pp. 241–258. New York, NY: Greenwood Press.
Bowen, D., and J. Clarke
   2009 Contemporary Tourist Behaviour. Wallingford: CABI.
Bramwell, B., and B. Lane
   2005 From Niche to General Relevance? The Journal of Tourism Studies 16(2):52–62.
Braun, K., R. Ellis, and E. Loftus
   2002 Make My Memory: How Advertising Can Change Our Memories of the Past. Psychology and Marketing 19:1–23.
Brückner, P.
   1967 Die Informierende Funktion der Wirtschaftswerbung. Berlin: Duncker & Humblot.
Butler, R.
   1980 The Concept of a Tourism Area Life Cycle of Evolution. Canadian Geographer 24(1):5–12.
Campbell, C.
   1987 The Romantic Ethic and the Spirit of Modern Consumerism. Basil: Blackwell.
Choi, S., X. Lehto, and J. O'Leary
   2006 What Does the Consumer Want from a DMO Website? A Study of US and Canadian Tourists' Perspectives. International Journal of Tourism Research 9:59–72.
Cialdini, R.
   2009 Persuasion: The Science and Practice. Needham, MA: Pearson Education.

Cialdini, R., and N. Goldstein
    2002 The Science and Practice of Persuasion. Cornell Hotel and Restaurant Administration Quarterly 43(2):40–51.
Cohen, E.
    1972 Towards Sociology of International Tourism. Social Research 39: 164–182.
    1979a A Phenomenology of Tourist Experiences. Sociology 13:179–201.
    1979b Rethinking the Sociology of Tourism. Annals of Tourism Research 6:18–35.
    1995 Contemporary Tourism – Trends and Challenges: Sustainable Authenticity or Contrived Post-Modernity? *In* Change in Tourism: People, Places Progresses, R. Butler, and D. Pearce, eds., pp. 12–29. London: Routledge.
Cohen, S., and L. Taylor
    1976 Escape Attempts. The Theory and Practice of Resistance to Everyday Life. London: Routledge.
Collett, P.
    2004 The Book of Tells. Australia: Doubleday.
Cooper, C.
    2006 Knowledge Management and Tourism. Annals of Tourism Research 33:45–58.
Cosgrove, I., and R. Jackson
    1972 The Geography of Recreation and Leisure. London: Hutchinson University Library.
Crompton, J.
    1979 Motivations for Pleasure Vacation. Annals of Tourism Research 6:408–424.
    1981 Dimensions of the Social Group Role in Pleasure Vacations. Annals of Tourism Research 8:550–568.
    2005 Issues Related to Sustaining a Long Term Research Interest in Tourism. The Journal of Tourism Studies 16(2):34–43.
Crotts, J.
    2004 The Affect of Cultural Distance on Overseas Travel Behavior. Journal of Travel Research 42:186–190.
    2008 Book Review: Why Choose This Book? How We Make Decision. Tourism Analysis 13:345–346.
Crotts, J., A. Aziz, and A. Raschid
    1998 Antecedents of Supplier's Commitment to Wholesale Buyers in the International Travel Trade. Tourism Management 19:127–134.
Crotts, J., and A. Pizam
    2003 The Effect of National Culture on Consumers' Evaluation of Travel Services. Journal of Tourism, Culture and Communications 4(1):17–28.
Crotts, J., and B. McKercher
    2005 Visitor Adaptation to Cultural Distance on Visitor Satisfaction: The Case of First Time Visitors to Hong Kong. Tourism Analysis 10:385–391.

Crotts, J., and D. Wilson
  1996 An Integrated Model of Buyer-Seller Relationships in the International Travel Trade. Progress in Tourism and Hospitality Research 1(2):1–15.
Crotts, J., and G. Turner
  1999 Determinants of Intra-Firm Trust in Buyer-Seller Relationships in the International Travel Trade. International Journal of Contemporary Hospitality Management 11(2–3):116–123.
Crotts, J., and J. van Rekom
  1998 Exploring and Enhancing the Psychological Value of a Fine Arts Museum. Tourism Recreation Research Journal 23(1):31–38.
Crotts, J., and R. Erdmann
  2000 Does National Culture Influence Consumers Evaluation of Travel Services? A Test of Hofstede's Model of Cross Cultural Differences. Managing Service Quality 10:410–419.
Crotts, J., and S. Litvin
  2003 Cross-Cultural Research: Are Researchers Better Served by Knowing Respondents' Country of Birth, Residence, or Citizenship? Journal of Travel Research 42:186–190.
Crotts, J., and W. van Raaij, eds.
  1994 The Economic Psychology of Travel and Tourism. Binghamton, NY: Haworth Press.
Crotts, J., C. Coppage, and A. Andibo
  2001 Trust-Commitment Model of Buyer-Seller Relationships. Journal of Hospitality and Tourism Research 25:195–208.
Csikszentmihalyi, M.
  1975 Beyond Boredom and Anxiety. San Francisco, CA: Jossey Bass.
  1990 Flow: The Psychology of Optimal Experience. New York, NY: Harper Perennial.
Dann, G.
  2007 The Life and Times of a Wandering Tourism Researcher. *In* The Study of Tourism Anthropological and Sociological Beginnings, D. Nash, ed., pp. 76–92. Amsterdam: Elsevier.
Dann, G., D. Nash, and P. Pearce
  1988 Methodology in Tourism Research. Annals of Tourism Research 15:1–28.
de Botton, A.
  2004 Status Anxiety. London: Penguin.
Deci, E.
  1975 Intrinsic Motivation. New York, NY: Plenum Press.
Diamond, J.
  2005 Collapse: How Societies Choose to Fail of Survive. London: Penguin.
Diener, E., and R. Biswas-Diener
  2008 Happiness: Unlocking the Mysteries of Psychological Wealth. Oxford: Blackwell.

Dolnicar, S., and B. Grün
2007 How Constrained a Response: A Comparison of Binary, Ordinal and Metric Answer Formats. Journal of Retailing and Consumer Services 14:108–122.

Dunn-Ross, E., and S. Iso-Ahola
1991 Sightseeing Tourists' Motivation and Satisfaction. Annals of Tourism Research 18:226–237.

Eisenhardt, K.
1989 Building Theories from Case Study Research. Academy of Management Review 14:532–550.

Elrod, T., G. Russell, A. Shocker, R. Andrews, B. Bayus, J. Carroll, R. Johnson, W. Kamakura, P. Lenk, J. Mazanec, V. Rao, and V. Shankar
2002 Inferring Market Structure from Customer Response to Competing and Complementary Products. Marketing Letters 13:219–230.

Erez, M., and P. Early
1993 Culture, Self-Identity, and Work. New York, NY: Oxford University Press.

Evans, R.
1980 The Making of Social Psychology. New York, NY: Gardner Press.

Fesenmaier, D., C. Pena, and J. O'Leary
1992 Assessing the Information Needs of Indiana Convention and Visitor Bureaus. Annals of Tourism Research 19:571–573.

Fesenmaier, D., H. Werthner, and K. Wöber, eds.
2006 Destination Recommendation Systems: Behavioral Foundations and Applications. Wallingford: CABI.

Field, D., and J. O'Leary
1973 Social Groups as a Basis for Assessing Participation in Selected Water Activities. Journal of Leisure Research 5(Spring):16–25.

Fischer, G.
1974 Einführung in die Theorie Psychologischer Tests. Bern: Huber.

Flyvbjerg, B.
2001 Making Social Science Matter. Cambridge: Cambridge University Press.

Fondness, D.
1994 Measuring Tourist Motivations. Annals of Tourism Research 21:555–581.

Franke, N., and J. Mazanec
2006 The Six Scientific Identities of Marketing: A Vector Quantization of Research Approaches. European Journal of Marketing 40:634–661.

Fredrickson, B.
2001 The Role of Positive Emotions in Positive Psychology: The Broaden-and-Build Theory of Positive Emotions. American Psychologist 56:218–226.

Frey, A.
1961 Advertising (3rd edition). New York, NY: Ronald Press.

Frochet, I., and A. Morrison
2000 Benefit Segmentation: A Review of Its Applications to Travel and Tourism Research. Journal of Travel and Tourism 9(4):21–45.

Fuchs, S.
  1992 The Professional Quest for Truth: A Social Theory of Science and Knowledge. Albany, NY: State University of New York.
Furnham, A.
  1984 Tourism and Culture Shock. Annals of Tourism Research 11:41–57.
  2008 50 Psychology Ideas You Really Need to Know. London: Quercus.
Gentry, J., S. Jun, and P. Tansuhaj
  1995 Consumer Acculturation Processes and Cultural Conflict: How Generalizable Is a North American Model for Marketing Globally. Journal of Business Research 32:129–139.
Gardner, H.
  1995 Leading Minds and Anatomy of Leadership. New York, NY: Basic Books.
Getz, D., J. Carlsen, and A. Morrison
  2004 The Family Business in Tourism and Hospitality. Wallingford: CABI.
Gladwell, M.
  2008 Outliers: The Story of Success. New York, NY: Little, Brown and Company.
Goeldner, C.
  2005 Reflections of the Historical Role of Journals in Shaping Tourism Knowledge. Journal of Tourism Studies 16(2):44–51.
Grabler, K., G. Maier, and J. Mazanec, eds.
  1996 International City Tourism, Analysis and Strategy. London: Pinter.
Graburn, N.
  1995 The Past in the Present in Japan: Nostalgia and Neo-traditionalism in Contemporary Japanese Domestic Tourism. *In* Change in Tourism: People, Places, Progresses, R. Butler, and D. Pearce, eds., pp. 47–70. London: Routledge.
Gunn, C.
  2004 Prospects for Tourism Planning: Issues and Concerns. Journal of Tourism Studies 15(1):3–7.
Hartvig-Larsen, H. ed.
  1998 Cases in Marketing. London: Sage.
Hatzinger, R., and J. Mazanec
  2007 Measuring the Part-Worth of the Mode of Transport in a Trip Package: An Extended Bradley-Terry Model for Paired-Comparison Conjoint Data. Journal of Business Research 60(12):1290–1302.
Hawking, St.
  1993 Black Holes and Baby Universes and Other Essays. London: Bantam.
  1997 The Objections of an Unashamed Reductionist. *In* The Large, the Small and the Human Mind, R. Penrose, ed., pp. 169–172. Cambridge: Cambridge University Press.
Hofstede, G.
  1980 Culture's Consequences: International Differences in Work-Related Values. Beverly Hills, CA: Sage.
Hofstede, G., and J. Hofstede
  2001 Culture's Consequences (2nd edition). Thousand Oaks, CA: Sage.

Hofstede, G., and M. Bond
1988 The Confucius Connection: From Cultural Roots to Economic Growth. Amsterdam: Elsevier.
Hofstede, J., A. Audenaert, J. Steenkamp, and M. Wedel
1998 An Investigation into the Association Pattern Technique as a Quantitative Approach to Measuring Means-End Chains. International Journal of Research in Marketing 15(February):37–50.
Howard, J.A., and J.N. Sheth
1969 The Theory of Buyer Behavior. New York, NY: Wiley.
Hruschka, H., and J.A. Mazanec
1990 Computer-Assisted Travel Counseling. Annals of Tourism Research 7(2): 208–227.
Hsieh, S., J.T. O'Leary, and A.M. Morrison
1992 Segmenting the International Travel Market Using Activities as a Segmentation Base. Tourism Management 13(2):209–223.
Hsu, C.H.C., and S. Huang
2008 Travel Motivation: A Critical Review of the Concept's Development. *In* Tourism Management Analysis, Behaviour and Strategy, A. Woodside, and D. Martin, eds., pp. 14–27. Wallingford: CABI.
Hsu, C., and J. Crotts
2006 Segmenting Mainland Chinese Residents Based on Experience, Intention and Desire to Visit Hong Kong. International Journal of Tourism Research 8:279–287.
Hudson, S.
1999 Consumer Behaviour Related to Tourism. *In* Consumer Behaviour in Travel and Tourism, A. Pizam, and Y. Mansfield, eds. New York, NY: Haworth Press.
Hunt, J.D.
1968 Tourist Vacations – Planning and Patterns. Logan: Utah Agricultural Experiment Station, Bulletin 474.
1975 Image as a Factor in Tourism Development. Journal of Travel Research 13(3):1–7.
1988 State Tourism Offices and Their Impact on Tourist Expenditures. Journal of Travel Research 26(3):10–13.
Hunt, J.D., and D. Layne
1991 Evolution of Travel and Tourism Terminology and Definitions. Journal of Travel Research 29(4):7–11.
Hwang, C.L., and K. Yoon
1981 Multiple Attribute Decision Making: Methods and Applications: A State-of-the-Art Survey. Berlin: Springer.
Iso-Ahola, S.E.
1980 The Social Psychology of Leisure and Recreation. Dubuque, IA: W.C. Brown Co. Publishers.
1982 Toward a Social Psychological Theory of Tourism Motivation: A Rejoinder. Annals of Tourism Research 9(2):256–262.

210   *The Study of Tourism: Foundations from Psychology*

1983 Toward a Social Psychology of Recreational Travel. Leisure Studies 2(1):45–46.
1989 Motivational Foundations of Leisure. *In* Understanding Leisure and Recreation: Mapping the Past, Charting the Future, E.L. Jackson, and T.L. Burton, eds., pp. 35–51. State College, PA: Venture Publishing.
Iso-Ahola, S.E., and J. Allen
1982 The Dynamics of Leisure Motivation: The Effects of Outcome on Leisure Needs. Research Quarterly for Exercise & Sport 53:141–149.
Jafari, J.
2005 Bridging Out Nesting Afield Powering a New Platform. Journal of Tourism Studies 16(2):1–5.
2007 Entry into a New Field of Study: Leaving a Footprint. *In* The Study of Tourism: Anthropological and Sociological Beginnings, D. Nash, ed., pp. 108–121. Amsterdam: Elsevier.
Jang, S., B. Bai, G. Hong, and J.T. O'Leary
2004 Understanding Travel Expenditure Patterns: A Study of Japanese Pleasure Travelers to the United States by Income Level. Tourism Management 25:331–341.
Jang, S., L.A. Cai, A.M. Morrison, and J.T. O'Leary
2005 The Effects of Travel Activities and Seasons on Expenditure. International Journal of Tourism Research 7(6):335–346.
Jansen-Verbeke, M., and J. van Rekom
1996 Scanning Museum Visitors: Urban Tourism Marketing. Annals of Tourism Research 23(2):364–375.
Jewell, B., and J. Crotts
2001 Adding Psychological Value to Heritage Tourism Experiences. Journal of Travel and Tourism Marketing 11(4):13–28.
2009 Adding Psychological Value to Heritage Tourism Experiences Revisited. Journal of Travel and Tourism Marketing 16(3):244–263.
Kahle, L.
1986 The Nine Nations of North America and the Values Basis for Geographic Segmentation. Journal of Marketing 50(April):37–47.
Kelley, L., B. MacNab, and R. Worthley
2006 Crossvergence and Cultural Tendencies: A Longitudinal Test of the Hong Kong, Taiwan and United States Banking Sectors. Journal of International Management 12(1):67–84.
Kivela, J., and J. Crotts
2006 Tourism and Gastronomy: Gastronomy's Influence on How Tourists Experience a Destination. Journal of Hospitality and Tourism Research 30(3):354–377.
Klenosky, D.B., C.E. Gengler, and M.S. Mulvey
1993 Understanding the Factors Influencing Ski Destination Choice: A Means-End Analytic Approach. Journal of Leisure Research 25(4):362–379.

Klenosky, D., E. Frauman, W. Norman, and C. Gengler
1998 Nature-Based Tourists Use of Interpretive Services: A Means-End Investigation. Journal of Tourism Studies 9(2):26–36.

Kluckhohn, C.
1954 Culture and Behavior. New York, NY: Free Press.

Kluckhohn, C., and H.A. Murray
1967 Personality in Nature, Society and Culture (2nd edition). New York, NY: Knopf.

Kotler, P., J. Bowen, and J. Makens
1998 Marketing for Hospitality and Tourism. Uppersaddle River, NJ: Prentice-Hall.

Kozak, K., J. Crotts, and R. Law
2007 The Impact of the Perception of Risk on International Travelers. International Journal of Tourism Research 9:233–242.

Kozak, M., and A. Decrop
2009 Handbook of Tourist Behaviour. New York, NY: Routledge.

Krippendorf, J.
1987 The Holiday Makers: Understanding the Impact of Leisure and Travel. London: William Heinemann.

Kroeber-Riel, W.
1975 Konsumentenverhalten. Munich: Vahlen.

Krueger, R., and M. Casey
2000 Focus Groups—A Practical Guide for Applied Research (3rd edition). London: Sage.

Langer, E.
1989 Mindfulness. Reading, MA: Addison-Wesley.

Lashley, C.
2000 In Search of Hospitality: Towards a Theoretical Framework. International Journal of Hospitality Management 19(1):3–15.

Lashley, C., and A. Morrison, eds.
2000 In Search of Hospitality: Theoretical Perspectives and Debates. Oxford: Butterworth Heinemann.

Lehto, X.Y., L. Cai, J. O'Leary, and T.C. Huan
2004 Tourist Shopping Preferences and Expenditure Behaviors: The Case of Taiwanese Outbound Market. Journal of Vacation Marketing 10(4):320–332.

Lindberg, K., C. Tisdell, and D. Xue
2003 Ecotourism in China's Nature Reserves. In Tourism in China, A. Lew, L. Yu, J. Ap, and G. Zhang, eds., pp. 103–122. The Haworth Hospitality Press.

Little, J.D.C.
1970 Models and Managers: The Concept of a Decision Calculus. Management Science 16(8):466–485.

Lodge, D.
2008 Deaf Sentence. London: Penguin.

MacCannell, D.
   1973 Staged Authenticity: Arrangements of Social Space in Tourist Settings.
      American Journal of Sociology 79(3):589–603.
   1976 The Tourist: A New Theory of the Leisure Class. New York, NY:
      Schoecken.
Magnini, V.
   2003 A Look at Changing Acculturation Patterns in the United States and
      Implications for the Hospitality Industry. Journal of Human Resources in
      Hospitality and Tourism 2(2):57–74.
Mannell, R., and S.E. Iso-Ahola
   1987 Psychological Nature of Leisure and Tourism Experience. Annals of
      Tourism Research 14(3):314–331.
March, R., and A. Woodside
   2005 Tourism Behaviour: Travellers' Decisions and Actions. Wallingford: CABI.
Martin, G.N., N.R. Carlson, and W. Buskist
   2007 Psychology (3rd edition). Harlow: Pearson.
Martinetz, T., and K.J. Schulten
   1994 Topology Representing Networks. Neural Networks 7(5):507–522.
Martinetz, T.M., S.G. Berkovich, and K.J. Schulten
   1993 "Neural Gas" Network for Vector Quantization and Its Application to Time-
      Series Prediction. IEEE Transactions on Neural Networks 4(4):558–569.
Maslow, A.
   1954 Motivation and Personality. New York, NY: Harper.
Mazanec, J.A.
   1972 Über den Wissenschaftslogischen Standort der Werbelehre. Jahrbuch der
      Absatz- und Verbrauchsforschung 12(1):63–72.
   1978 Strukturmodelle des Konsumverhaltens. Vienna: Orac.
   1979a Probabilistische Messverfahren in der Marketingforschung: Ein empiri-
      scher Anwendungsversuch zur Planung Absatzwirtschaftlicher Strategien des
      Imagetransfers. Marketing ZFP 2(3):174–186.
   1979b Sortierprobleme des Marketingforschers in 'großen' Stichproben: Ein
      Praktikables Clusteranalytisches Verfahren mit Empirischem Demonstrations-
      beispiel. Der Markt 68 + 69(4 + 1):140–150.
   1979c Zielgruppenplanung im Fremdenverkehrsmarketing: Empirische Ergeb-
      nisse einer Segmentierungsanalyse der Österreichischen Urlaubsreisenden.
      Journal für Betriebswirtschaft 29(3):176–193.
   1979d Voraussetzungen Rationaler Entscheidungsvorbereitung im Fremdenver-
      kehrsmarketing unter Rücksicht auf Neuere Analysemethoden. Der Markt
      71(3):190–204.
   1981a The Tourism/Leisure Ratio: Anticipating the Limits to Growth. Revue de
      Tourisme 38(4):2–12.
   1981b Über den Einsatz der Verbundmessung zur indirekten Erfassung der
      Präferenzwirksamkeit einzelner Produkteigenschaften. Zeitschrift für Markt-
      und Meinungsforschung 23 + 24:5261–5289.

1982 Practicing the Causal Approach to Consumer Behavior Model Building: An Example from Tourism Research. Der Markt 84(4):127–138.

1983 Tourist Behavior Model Building: A Causal Approach. Revue de Tourisme 38(1):9–18.

1984 How to Detect Travel Market Segments: A Clustering Approach. Journal of Travel Research 23(1):17–21.

1986a A Decision Support System for Optimizing Advertising Policy of a National Tourist Office: Model Outline and Case Study. International Journal of Research in Marketing 3(2):63–77.

1986b Allocating an Advertising Budget to International Travel Markets. Annals of Tourism Research 13(4):609–634.

1990 An Expert System Approach to Travel Counseling. *In* The Tourism Connection: Linking Research and Marketing, 21st Annual Conference, pp. 81–87. Salt Lake City, UT: Travel & Tourism Research Association.

1992 Classifying Tourists into Market Segments: A Neural Network Approach. Journal of Travel and Tourism Marketing 1(1):39–59.

1993 European Lifestyles and Tourism: 'Exporting' the EUROSTYLES to the USA. International Journal of Contemporary Hospitality Management 5(4):3–9.

1995 Positioning Analysis with Self-Organizing Maps: An Exploratory Study on Luxury Hotels. Cornell Hotel and Restaurant Administration Quarterly 36(6):80–96.

2000 Mastering Unobserved Heterogeneity in Tourist Behavior Research. Tourism Analysis 5(2–4):171–176.

2001 Neural Market Structure Analysis: Novel Topology-Sensitive Methodology. European Journal of Marketing 35(7–8):894–914.

2002a Tourists' Acceptance of Euro Pricing: Conjoint Measurement with Random Coefficients. Tourism Management 23(3):245–253.

2002b Introducing Learning and Adaptivity into Web-Based Recommender Systems for Tourism and Leisure Services. Tourism Review 57(4):8–14.

2005 New Methodology for Analyzing Competitive Positions: A Demonstration Study of Travelers' Attitudes Toward Their Modes of Transport. Tourism Analysis 9(4):231–240.

2006 Evaluating Perceptions-Based Marketing Strategies: An Agent-Based Model and Simulation Experiments. Journal of Modelling in Management 1(1):52–74.

2007a New Frontiers in Tourist Behavior Research: Steps Toward Causal Inference from Non-Experimental Data. Asia Pacific Journal of Tourism Research 12(3):223–235.

2007b Exploring Tourist Satisfaction with Nonlinear Structural Equation Modeling and Inferred Causation Analysis. Journal of Travel and Tourism Marketing 21(4):73–90.

2009 Tourism-Receiving Countries in Connotative Google Space (available online). Journal of Travel Research.

Mazanec, J.A., and A. Ring
  Tourism Destination Competitiveness: Second Thoughts on the World Economic
  Forum Reports 2008 and 2009. Tourism Economics.
Mazanec, J.A., and H. Strasser
  2000 A Nonparametric Approach to Perceptions-Based Market Segmentation:
  Foundations. Vienna: Springer.
  2007 Perceptions-Based Analysis of Tourism Products and Service Providers.
  Journal of Travel Research 45(4):387–401.
Mazanec, J.A., and K. Wöber, eds.
  2009 Analysing International City Tourism. (2nd edition). Vienna: Springer.
Mazanec, J.A., A. Ring, B. Stangl, and K. Teichmann
  2010 Usage Patterns of Advanced Analytical Tools in Tourism Research
  1988–2008: A Six Journal Survey. Journal of Information Technology and
  Tourism. 12(1):17–46
Mazanec, J.A., G.I. Crouch, J.R. Brent-Ritchie, and A.G. Woodside, eds.
  2001 Consumer Psychology of Tourism, Hospitality, and Leisure, Vol. 2.
  Wallingford: CABI.
Mazanec, J.A., K. Wöber, and A.H. Zins
  2007 Tourism Destination Competitiveness: From Definition to Explanation?
  Journal of Travel Research 46(1):86–95.
McCabe, S.
  2002 The Tourist Experience and Everyday Life. In The Tourist as a Metaphor of
  the Social World, G.M.S. Dann, ed., pp. 61–75. CABI.
McGuire, F.A., C.N. William, and J.T. O'Leary
  2004 Constraints to Participation in the Arts by the Young Old, Old and Oldest
  Old. Advances in Hospitality and Leisure 1:43–58.
McIntosh, R.W.
  1992 Early Tourism Education in the United States. Journal of Tourism Studies
  3(1):2–7.
Mehrabian, A., and J.A. Russell
  1974 An Approach to Environmental Psychology. Cambridge, MA: MIT Press.
Melton, A.W.
  1933 Studies of Installation at the Pennsylvania Museum of Art. Museum News
  12:5–8.
  1936 Distribution of Attention in Galleries in a Museum of Science and Industry.
  Museum News 14:5–8.
  1972 Visitor Behavior in Museums: Some Early Research in Environmental
  Design. Human Factors 14:393–403.
Meridith, S., N. Wenger, H. Liu, N. Harada, and K. Khan
  2000 Development of a Brief Scale to Measure Acculturation among Japanese
  Americans. Journal of Community Psychology 28(2):103–113.
Mitchell, J.
  2006 Food Acceptance and Acculturation. Journal of Foodservice 17(1):77–83.

Money, B., and J. Crotts
   2000 Buyer Behavior in the Japanese Travel Trade: Advancements in Theoretical Frameworks. Journal of Travel and Tourism Marketing 9(1–2):1–19.
Montague, R.
   2006 Why Buy This Book? How We Make Decisions. London: Penguin Books.
Montana, J. ed.
   1994 Marketing in Europe: Case Studies. London: Sage.
Morris, D.
   1968 The Naked Ape. London: Pan.
Morrison, A., and G.B. O'Mahony
   2003 The Liberation of Hospitality Management Education. International Journal of Contemporary Hospitality Management 15(1):38–44.
Moscardo, G.
   1998 Interpretation and Sustainable Tourism: Functions, Examples and Principles. Journal of Tourism Studies 9(1):2–13.
   1999 Making Visitors Mindful: Principles for Creating Quality Sustainable Visitor Experiences through Effective Communication. Champaign, IL: Sagamore Publishing.
Moscardo, G., A. Morrison, P. Pearce, C. Long, and J. O'Leary
   1996 Understanding Vacation Destination Choice through Travel Motivation and Activities. Journal of Vacation Marketing 2(2):109–122.
Moscardo, G., P. Pearce, A. Morrison, D. Green, and J.T. O'Leary
   2000 Developing a Typology for Understanding Visiting Friends and Relatives Markets. Journal of Travel Research 38(3):251–259.
Mowforth, M., and I. Munt
   1998 Tourism and Sustainability: Development and New Tourism in the Third World (2nd edition). London: Routledge.
Mykletun, R., J. Crotts, and A. Mykletun
   2001 Positioning an Island Destination in the Peripheral Areas of the Baltics: A Flexible Approach to Market Segmentation. Tourism Management 22(5): 493–500.
Nash, D.
   1981 Tourism as an Anthropological Subject. Current Anthropology 22(5):461–481.
Nash, D. ed.
   2007 The Study of Tourism Anthropological and Sociological Beginnings. Amsterdam: Elsevier.
New Mexico Commission on Professionalism
   1999 <http://www.nnmcle.org/rules/prof.guidelines.asp> (Accessed October 8, 2006).
Nisbett, R.E.
   2003 The Geography of Thought. London: Brearley.
Noe, F.P.
   1999 Tourism Service Satisfaction. Champaign, IL: Sagamore.

Noy, C.
2007 A Narrative Community. Detroit, MI: Wayne State University Press.
O'Leary, J.T.
1999 International Travel and Resource Management. *In* Outdoor Recreation in American Life, K. Cordell, ed., pp. 294–298. Champaign, IL: Sagamore Publishing.
2005 Thoughts on Building Academic Staff Careers and a Successful Department. Journal of Tourism Studies 16(2):14–20.
O'Leary, J.T., and M. Uysal
1986 A Canonical Analysis of International Tourism Demand. Annals of Tourism Research 13(4):651–656.
O'Leary, J.T., and S.M. Meis
1999 International Tourism: Current Trends and Market Research with Implications for Managing Public Attractions. *In* Ecosystem Management: Adaptive Strategies for Natural Resource Organizations in the 21st Century. J. Aley, W.R. Burch, B. Conover, and D. Field, eds., pp. 17–24. Philadelphia, PA: Taylor & Francis.
O'Leary, J.T., F.A. McGuire, and F.D. Dottavio
1986a Outdoor Recreation and the Third Age: Results of the United States Nationwide Recreation Survey. Leisure and Recreation 28(2):18–21.
O'Leary, J.T., F.D. Dottavio, and F.A. McGuire
1986b Constraints to Participation in Outdoor Recreation across the Life Span. The Gerontologist 26(5):538–544.
Oh, H., M. Uysal, and P. Weaver
1995 Product Bundles and Market Segmentation Based on Travel Motivations: A Canonical Correlation Approach. International Journal of Hospitality Management 14(2):123–137.
Oh, Y.J., C.K. Cheng, X.Y. Lehto, and J.T. O'Leary
2004 Predictors of Tourists' Shopping Behaviour: Examination of Socio-Demographic Characteristics and Trip Typologies. Journal of Vacation Marketing 10(4):308–319.
Page, S.J.
2005 Academic Ranking Exercises – Do They Achieve Anything Meaningful? – A Personal View. Tourism Management 26(5):663–666.
Park, S., H. Park, J. Skinner, S. Ok, and A. Spindler
2003 Mother's Acculturation and Eating Behaviors of Korean American Families in California. Journal of Nutritional Education Behavior 35(May–June):142–147.
Pearce, D.
2008 Channel Performance in Multichannel Tourism Distribution Systems. Journal of Travel Research 46(3):256–267.
Pearce, P.L.
1977 Mental Souvenirs: A Study of Tourist and Their City Maps. Australian Journal of Psychology 29:203–210.

1982 The Social Psychology of Tourist Behaviour. Oxford: Pergamon.

1988 The Ulysses Factor: Evaluating Visitors in Tourist Settings. New York, NY: Springer-Verlag.

1990 The Backpacker Phenomenon: Preliminary Answers to Basic Questions. Townsville: James Cook University of North Queensland.

1991 Travel Stories: An Analysis of Self-Disclosure in Terms of Story Structure. Valence, and Audience Characteristics. Australian Psychologist 26(3): 172–174.

1993 Defining Tourism as a Specialism: A Justification and Implications. Teoros International 1(1):25–32.

2004 The Functions and Planning of Visitor Centres in Regional Tourism. Journal of Tourism Studies 15(1):8–17.

2005a Tourist Behaviour: Themes and Conceptual Schemes. Clevedon: Channel View.

2005b Professing Tourism: Tourism Academics as Educators, Researchers and Change Leaders. Journal of Tourism Studies 16(2):21–33.

2009a The Relationship between Positive Psychology and Tourist Behavior Studies. Tourism Analysis 14:37–48.

2009b Now That Is Funny Humour in Tourism Settings. Annals of Tourism Research 36(4):627–644.

Pearce, P.L., and G. Moscardo
2007 An Action Research Appraisal of Visitor Centre Interpretation and Change. Journal of Interpretation Research 12(2):29–50.

Pearce, P.L., and M. Caltabiano
1983 Inferring Travel Motivations from Travelers' Experiences. Journal of Travel Research 22(2):16–20.

Pearce, P.L., and M. Fenton
1994 Multidimensional Scaling and Tourism Research. In Travel, Tourism, and Hospitality Research: A Handbook for Managers and Researchers, J.R.B. Richie, and C.R. Goeldner, eds., pp. 523–532. New York, NY: Wiley.

Pearce, P.L., A.M. Morrison, and J.L. Rutledge
1998 Tourism: Bridges across Continents. Sydney: McGraw-Hill.

Pearce, P.L., G.M. Moscardo, and G.F. Ross
1996 Tourism Community Relationships. Oxford: Pergamon.

Pearce, P.L., S. Filep, and G. Ross
2011 Tourists, Tourism and the Good Life. New York, NY: Routledge.

Pearl, J.
2001 Causality: Models, Reasoning, and Inference (2nd Printing). Cambridge: Cambridge University Press.

Pearson, M., and S. Sullivan
1995 Looking After Heritage Places – The Basics of Heritage Planning for Managers, Landowners and Administrators. Melbourne: Melbourne University Press.

Peeters, P.M. ed.
  2007 Tourism and Climate Change Mitigation: Methods, Greenhouse Gas Reductions and Policies. Breda: NHTV.
Peeters, P.M., T. van Egmond, and N. Visser
  2004 European Tourism, Transport and Environment (Final Version). Breda: NHTV CSTT.
Pizam, A.
  2003 What Should Be Our Field of Study? International Journal of Hospitality Management 22(4):339.
  2006 Are We Talking and Listening to Each Other? International Journal of Hospitality Management 25(3):345–347.
  2007 Educating the Next Generation of Hospitality Professionals. International Journal of Hospitality Management 26(1):1–3.
  2008a Green Hotels: A Fad, Ploy or Fact of Life? International Journal of Hospitality Management 28(1):1.
  2008b What Is the Hospitality Industry and How Does It Differ from the Tourism and Travel Industries? International Journal of Hospitality Management 28(2):183–184.
  2008c Advances in Hospitality Research: From Rodney Dangerfield to Aretha Franklin. Keynote Address Presented at the Council on Hospitality Management Education, Glasgow, United Kingdom, May 12–15.
Pizam, A., and Y. Mansfield, eds.
  2000 Consumer Behaviour in Travel and Tourism. New York, NY: The Haworth Hospitality Press.
Plog, S.
  2004 Leisure Travel: A Marketing Handbook. Upper Saddle River, NJ: Pearson.
Popper, K.R.
  1994 Alles Leben ist Problemlösen, Über Erkenntnis, Geschichte und Politik. Munich: Piper.
Prentice, R.
  2004 Tourist Motivation and Typologies. In A Companion to Tourism, A. Lew, C. Hall, W. Michael, and M. Allan, eds., pp. 261–278. Oxford: Blackwell Publishing.
Reason, J.
  1974 Man in Motion. London: Weidenfeld & Nicolson.
Reisinger, Y., and J. Crotts
  2009 Applying Hofstede's National Culture Measures in Tourism Research: Illuminating Issues of Divergence and Convergence. Journal of Travel Research 48(4).
Reisinger, Y., and L. Turner
  2003 Cross Cultural Behaviour in Tourism. Oxford: Butterworth Heinemann.
Reisinger, Y., F. Mavondo, and J. Crotts
  2009 A Comparison of the Importance Attached to Tourism Destination Attributes: Western and Asian Groups. Anatolia 20(1):236–253.

Reynolds, T.J., and J. Gutman
1984 Advertising Is Image Management. Journal of Advertising Research 24(1):27–36.

Robinson, E.S.
1928 The Behaviour of the Museum Visitor. *Cited in* Environmental Psychology, P. Bell, J. Fisher, and R. Loomis (1978). Philadelphia, PA: W.B. Saunders.

Rosenow, J., and G. Pulsipher
1978 Tourism: The Good, the Bad and the Ugly. Lincoln, NE: Media Productions.

Rowan, J.
1998 Maslow Amended. Journal of Humanistic Psychology 38(1):81–93.

Rubenstein, C.
1980 Vacations. Psychology Today (May):62–76.

Rushton, P., H.G. Murray, and S.V. Paunonen
1983 Personality, Research Creativity, and Teaching Effectiveness in University Professors. Scientometrics 5(2):93–116.

Ryan, C.
1980 Introduction to Hotel and Catering Economics. Cheltenham: Stanley Thornes.
1991 Recreational Tourism: A Social Science Perspective. London: Routledge.
1995a Conversations in Majorca – The over 55s on Holiday. Tourism Management 16(3):207–217.
1995b Researching Tourist Satisfaction: Issues, Concepts, Problems. London: Routledge.
1997 The Tourist Experience: A New Introduction. New York, NY: Cassell.
1999 From the Psychometrics of SERVQUAL to Sex – Measurements of Tourist Satisfaction. *In* Consumer Behavior in Travel & Tourism, P. Abraham, and M. Yoel, eds., pp. 267–286. Binghamtom, NY: Haworth Press.
2002 Tourism and Cultural Proximity: Examples from New Zealand. Annals of Tourism Research 29(4):952–971.
2005 Ethics in Tourism Research: Objectivities and Personal Perspectives. *In* Tourism Research Methods: Integrating Theory with Practice, B.W. Ritchie, P. Burns, and C. Palmer, eds., pp. 9–20. Wallingford: CABI.

Ryan, C. ed.
2007 Battlefield Tourism: History, Place and Interpretation. Oxford: Pergamon.

Ryan, C., and B. Trauer
2005 Adventure Tourism and Sport – An Introduction. *In* Taking Tourism to the Limits, C. Ryan, S.J. Page, and M. Aicken, eds., pp. 143–148. Oxford: Pergamon.

Ryan, C., and H. Gu
2010 Constructionism and Culture in Research: Understandings of the Fourth Buddhist Festival, Wutaishan, China. Tourism Management 31(2):167–178.

Ryan, C., and I. Ninov
2009 Place Perceptions – The Relationship between Specific Sites and Overall Impression of Place: The Example of Dubai Creek and 'Greater' Dubai. Paper presented at EuroChrie, Helsinki, Finland.

Ryan, C., and X. Cui
  2009 Perceptions of the Impacts of Tourism – A Case Study of Ongoing Research in Ankang, China. *In* Proceedings of the International Conference on the Development Trends of Tourism and Hospitality Industry and Education, Jinwen University of Science and Technology, Taiwan, September 25–26, 2009.
Ryder, A., L. Alden, and D. Paulhus
  2000 Is Acculturation Unidimensional or Bidimensional? A Head to Head Comparison in the Prediction of Personality, Self Identity, and Adjustment. Journal of Personality Social Psychology 79(1):49–65.
Saaty, T.L.
  1977 A Scaling Method for Priorities in Hierarchical Structures. Journal of Mathematical Psychology 15(3):234–281.
Sagan, C.
  1996 The Demon-Haunted World: Science as a Candle in the Dark. New York, NY: Ballantine.
Salzberger, T.
  2009 Measurement in Marketing Research: An Alternative Framework. Cheltenham: Edward Elgar.
Sasidharan, V., F. Willits, and G. Godbey
  2005 Cultural Differences in Urban Recreation Patterns: An Examination of Park Usage and Activity Participation across Six Population Subgroups. Managing Leisure 10(1):19–38.
Schewe, C.D., and R.J. Calantone
  1978 Psychographic Segmentation of Tourists. Journal of Travel Research 16(3):14–20.
Schiebler, S., J. Crotts, and R. Hollinger
  1995 Florida Tourists Vulnerability to Crime. *In* Tourism, Crime and International Security, P. Abe, and Y. Mansfield, eds., pp. 37–50. London: Wiley.
Schmitt, B.H.
  2003 Customer Experience Management. Hoboken, NJ: Wiley.
Schreyer, R., and J.W. Roggenbuck
  1978 The Influence of Experience Expectations on Crowding Perceptions and Social-Psychological Carrying Capacities. Leisure Sciences 1:373–394.
Seligman, M.E.P.
  2002 Positive Psychology, Positive Prevention, and Positive Therapy. *In* Handbook of Positive Psychology, C.R. Snyder, and S.J. Lopez, eds., pp. 3–9. New York, NY: Oxford University Press.
  2008 Positive Health. Applied Psychology: An International Review 57:3–18.
Sharpe, G.
  1976 Interpreting the Environment. New York, NY: Wiley.

Shepherd, R.
In Press Historicity, Fieldwork, and the Allure of the Post-Modern: A Reply to Ryan and Gu. Tourism Management.

Simmel, G.
1950 The Sociology of Georg Simmel (translated by H. Woolf). New York, NY: Free Press of Glencoe.

Sirgy, M., and C. Su
2000 Destination Image, Self-Congruity, and Travel Behaviour: Toward an Integrative Model. Journal of Travel Research 38:340–352.

Smart, J.C., K.A. Feldman, and C.A. Etherington
2000 Academic Disciplines: Holland's Theory and the Study of College Students and Faculty. Nashville, TN: Vanderbilt University Press.

Smith, V.
1977 Hosts and Guests: The Anthropology of Tourism. Philadelphia, PA: University of Philadelphia Press.

Smithson, M., P. Amato, and P.L. Pearce
1983 Dimensions of Helping Behaviour. Oxford: Pergamon.

Sneed, J.D.
1971 The Logical Structure of Mathematical Physics. Dordrecht: Reidel.

Snepenger, D., J. King, E. Marshall, and M. Uysal
2006 Modeling Iso-Ahola's Motivation Theory in the Tourism Context. Journal of Travel Research 45:140–149.

Spiegel, B.
1961 Die Struktur der Meinungsverteilung im Sozialen Feld: Das Psychologische Marktmodell. Stuttgart: Huber.

Spirtes, P., C. Glymour, and R. Scheines
2000 Causation, Prediction, and Search (2nd edition). Cambridge: MIT Press.

Stankey, G.H., and J. Wood
1982 The Recreation Opportunity Spectrum: An Introduction. Australian Parks and Recreation (February):6–15.

Stebbins, R.A.
1982 Serious Leisure: A Conceptual Statement. Pacific Sociological Review 25:251–272.

Stegmüller, W.
1969 Probleme und Resultate der Wissenschaftstheorie und Analytischen Philosophie, Band I, Wissenschaftliche Erklärung und Begründung. Berlin: Springer.
1974 Probleme und Resultate der Wissenschaftstheorie und Analytischen Philosophie, Band II, Theorie und Erfahrung. Berlin: Springer.

Stringer, P.
1984 Studies in the Socio-Environmental Psychology of Tourism. Annals of Tourism Research 11:147–166.

Stringer, P., and P.L. Pearce
  1984 Toward a Symbiosis of Social Psychology and Tourism Studies. Annals of
    Tourism Research 11:5–17.
Tilden, F.
  1977 Interpreting Our Heritage (3rd edition). Chapel Hill, NC: University of
    North Carolina Press.
Tolman, E.C.
  1948 Cognitive Maps in Rats and Men. Psychological Review 55:189–208.
Tribe, J.
  1997 The Indiscipline of Tourism. Annals of Tourism Research 24(3):
    638–657.
  2009 Philosophical Issues in Tourism. *In* Philosophical Issues in Tourism,
    J. Tribe, ed., pp. 3–22. Bristol: Channel View.
Tse, P., and J. Crotts
  2005 Antecedents of Novelty Seeking among International Visitors: Hong
    Kong's Visitors' Propensity to Experiment with Culinary Traditions. Tourism
    Management 26:965–968.
Turner, L., and J. Ash
  1975 The Golden Hordes: International Tourism and the Pleasure Periphery.
    London: Constable.
Uriely, N.
  2005 The Tourist Experience: Conceptual Developments. Annals of Tourism
    Research 32(1):199–216.
Van Egmond, T.
  2007 Understanding Western Tourists in Developing Countries. Oxon:
    CABI.
Van Raaij, W.F.
  1986 Consumer Research on Tourism: Mental and Behavioral Constructs. Annals
    of Tourism Research 13:1–10.
Van Rekom, J.
  1994 Adding Psychological Value to Tourism Products. *In* The Economic
    Psychology of Travel and Tourism, J. Crotts, and W.F. von Raaij, eds.,
    pp. 21–36. Binghamton, NY: Haworth Press.
  1997 Deriving an Operational Measure of Corporate Identity. European Journal
    of Marketing 31(5–6):410–422.
Wang, N.
  2000 Tourism and Modernity: A Sociological Analysis. Oxford: Pergamon.
Waters, S.R.
  1966 The American Tourist. Annals of the Academy of Political and Social
    Science 368:109–118.
Weinberg, St.
  1994 Dreams of a Final Theory: The Scientist's Search for the Ultimate Laws of
    Nature. New York, NY: Vintage.

Wells, W.D. ed.
  1974 Life Style and Psychographics. Chicago, IL: American Marketing
    Association.
Wiseman, R.
  2007 Quirkology. London: MacMillan.
Woodside, A., G.I. Crouch, J.A. Mazanec, M. Oppermann, and M.Y. Sakai, eds.
  2000 Consumer Psychology of Tourism, Hospitality, and Leisure. Wallingford:
    CABI.
Yin, R.K.
  2009 Case Study Research. Los Angeles, CA: Sage.
Young, G.
  1973 Tourism – Blessing or Blight? Harmondsworth: Penguin.
Zimbardo, P., and J. Boyd
  2008 The Paradox of Time. London: Rider.
Zube, E., J. Crystal, and J. Palmer
  1978 National Parks Visitors Centres. *In* Environmental Design Evaluation,
    A. Friedmann, C. Zimring, and E. Zube, eds. New York, NY: Plenum.

Author Index

Subject Index